The Theory of Aggregate Investment in Closed Economic Systems

The Theory of Aggregate Investment in Closed Economic Systems

Kofi Kissi Dompere

Contributions in Economics and Economic History, Number 202

GREENWOOD PRESS
Westport, Connecticut • London

HB
843
.D66
1999

Library of Congress Cataloging-in-Publication Data

Dompere, K. K.
    The theory of aggregate investment in closed economic systems / by
Kofi Kissi Dompere.
        p.   cm.—(Contributions in economics and economic history,
    ISSN 0084–9235 ; no. 202)
    Includes bibliographical references and index.
    ISBN 0–313–30796–2 (alk. paper)
    1. Saving and investment.   I. Title.   II. Series.
HB843.D66   1999
339.4′3—dc21   98–15327

British Library Cataloguing in Publication Data is available.

Library of Congress Catalog Card Number: 98–15327
ISBN: 0–313–30796–2
ISSN: 0084–9235

First published in 1999

Greenwood Press, 88 Post Road West, Westport, CT 06881
An imprint of Greenwood Publishing Group, Inc.
www.greenwood.com

Printed in the United States of America

The paper used in this book complies with the
Permanent Paper Standard issued by the National
Information Standards Organization (Z39.48–1984).

10 9 8 7 6 5 4 3 2 1

TO MY
Mother, Adwoa Fosua;
Father, Kwasi Kissi;
Grandmother, Akua Somua;
Son, Kwaku Kissi Dompere;
AND
Special Friends and Admirers.

Contents

Preface

Practice without thought is blind; thought without practice is empty.
Kwame Nkrumah

Data without concepts are blind, concepts without data are empty.
Immanuel Kant

The ideas of economists, both when they are right and when they are wrong, are more powerful than is commonly understood. Indeed, the world is ruled by little else. Practical men, who believe themselves to be quite exempt from any intellectual influences, are usually the slaves of some defunct economist. Madmen in authority, who hear voices in the air, are distilling their frenzy from some academic scribbler of a few years back.
John Maynard Keynes

This book is a result of my continued search for a reasonable theoretical understanding of dynamics of economic evolution, viewed against the background of contemporary domestic and international politico-economic arrangements. As is argued in [123], economic evolution involves continual transformation of categories wherein an element in one category endogenously loses its previous properties and acquires a set of new ones that places it in a new category - such as from less developed (lower growth rate) to more developed (higher growth rate) - all these changes are due to the internal working mechanism of the economic system. The process is what I have called *categorial conversion* operating through a *dialectical moment* in transformation dynamics. The conversion processes are governed by a set of equations of motion that defines the transient paths as well as ensures successful transformation of the properties of one category to the properties of the other. The equations of motion are generated by the forces that produce the dialectical moment.

To be distinguishable, each category must be well defined as well as derivable from a primary category that is factually supported. Given the identifiable categories, the needed equations of motion involve time and descriptions of change in quantity and quality. Quantity involves distance, volume, size, etc., defining the qualitative disposition of the subject under transformation. Quality, on the other hand, defines the contents of the subject under the forces of categorial conversion; it is thus the internal expression of the external disposition of the quantitative aspects of the subject under general motion and self-transformation.

From this perspective, economic development and growth are quantity-quality transformation processes, locked in a dynamic unity. However, they have some important epistemic differences. Their study as I understand it requires the same methodological approach but different techniques of analysis. The important epistemic differences between the subject of economic development and growth rest on the nature and structure of their organicities, as they are related to society and its general social organization of production and consumption. The economic growth is a quantity-quality transformation of non-institutional variables such as output and factors of production and technology. Economic development includes economic growth. Additionally, it involves quantity-quality transformation of societal institutional arrangements (the outer structure) encapsulating the general social environment that gives legitimacy to socioeconomic decisions and actions. Economic growth is thus a transformation within a transformation of socioeconomic development, carried out in an interdependent and inseparable manner. The mechanism of the general transformation is produced by the evolving institutional arrangements, which are themselves products as well as determinants of development and growth.

In this respect, I came to think that any important and relevant theory of economic development must be composed of a theory of economic growth (output transformation) and a theory of institutional development and change based on the system's own internal forces that generate the mechanism of transformation. Here, four sub-aggregate equations of motion regarding quantity and quality changes must be abstracted from the internal forces of the socioeconomic system to explain the general dynamics of the development process. Two of these equations must specify the quantitative transformation of the set of institutions and aggregate output that represents the outcome of the internal decision dynamics of the members, operating through the socioeconomic institutions. The other two equations of motion must define the changes of the qualitative disposition of each quantitative state as we journey through time.

In Dompere and Ejaz [123] the primary concern was placed on the methodological problems of constructing a theory of the general economic transformation called "development." In the output transformation the primary concern is how the decision system utilizes its resources to generate a continual change in its output. Here we have a set of quantitative categories and a set of qualitative categories that must be linked together. For each quantitative element of the output there corresponds a potential set of qualitative dispositions, and vice versa. The understanding of the quantity-quality transformation dynamics requires us, I think, to indicate the endogenous mechanism that ensures transformations from one category to the other, based on the internal forces of the system itself. The manner in which the internal forces are generated must also be indicated.

The quantity changes of output depend broadly on changes in output quality, holding either input quantity constant or input quality constant, but not both, while others vary. The changes in quantity-of-factor input are called *factor widening*, while the changes in input quality are called *factor deepening*. With a given quality, factor widening is associated with constant factor productivity, while with a given quantity, factor deepening is associated with increasing factor productivity.

It stands to say that the usefulness of factors in production is not their physical existence and presence for the user but rather the flow of productive services they provide. The flows of productive services from factors depend on the quantity and quality of the factors and are conceptually measured in efficiency units that lend themselves to aggregation, at least in theory. Analytically, I have come to think of the problem of the input space as it relates to quantity-quality transformation in terms of how the flows of factor services, conceived in efficiency units, may be represented in theoretical constructs. The rationale for such a view is embedded in the idea that when the institutional framework of social production is given, the flow of output of the decision system depends on the flow of quantity of efficient–factor services used. There are two important inputs that are considered parts of the decision system. They are capital and labor, each of which has a flow of efficiency units per unit of time when used. The quality of capital is defined by its level of technological embodiment at a given degree of social knowledge, and production know-how, and institutional setup. Similarly, the quality of labor is defined by its level of knowledge embodiment, called "human-capital investment."

At any moment of time and for any economic system, the aggregate potential flow of factor services depends on the stocks of factors plus the average levels of technological embodiment (in the case of capital) and human-capital embodiment (in the case of labor). The concept is that the rates at which factor services flow, measure in efficiency units, depend on the time path of quality and quantity. In respect of this, the equation of motion governing output growth must be related to the equations of motion governing the flows of factor services, as measured in efficiency units. Each equation of motion of a factor-efficiency service flow is the sum of equations of motion on quality and quantity of factors.

The idea can be simply illustrated in a one-output and two-factor world of capital and labor. Let the path of quantity of physical capital be $M(t)$, with the corresponding average quality of $A(t)$. Similarly, let the path of the number of workers be $N(t)$, with a corresponding average human capital embodiment of $B(t)$. If the path of the flow of efficient capital services is $K(t)$ and that of labor is $L(t)$ for the production system, then I thought that a way must be found where we can write the levels of input flows at each time point as

$$K(t) = f_1(M(t), A(t)) \qquad ((0.1))$$

$$L(t) = f_2(N(t), B(t)) \qquad ((0.2))$$

The corresponding equations of motion that govern the dynamics of factors flows, under the assumption that all the variables are at least twice differentiable in the entire domain, are

$$\dot{K} = \frac{\partial f_1}{\partial M}\dot{M} + \frac{\partial f_1}{\partial A}\dot{A} \qquad ((0.3))$$

$$\dot{L} = \frac{\partial f_2}{\partial N}\dot{N} + \frac{\partial f_2}{\partial B}\dot{B} \qquad ((0.4))$$

Let the path of output flow, $Q(t)$, as a function of paths of factor service flows in efficiency units be specified as:

$$Q(t) = F(K, L) \qquad ((0.5))$$

The function $F(\cdot)$ is also assumed to be at least twice differentiable in its entire domain. The output dynamics are then governed by an interdependent equation of motion of the form

$$\dot{Q} = \frac{\partial F}{\partial K}\dot{K} + \frac{\partial F}{\partial L}\dot{L} \qquad ((0.6))$$

The general equation of motion that governs the dynamics of output flow in the production system with capital and labor as the productive input, given the dynamics of the input flows, is thus obtained by substituting eqn. (0.3) and (0.4) in equation (0.6) to obtain:

$$\dot{Q} = \frac{\partial F}{\partial K}\left(\frac{\partial f_1}{\partial M}\dot{M} + \frac{\partial f_1}{\partial A}\dot{A}\right) + \frac{\partial F}{\partial L}\left(\frac{\partial f_2}{\partial N}\dot{N} + \frac{\partial f_2}{\partial B}\dot{B}\right) \qquad ((0.7))$$

Equations (0.1) - (0.7) simply instruct us that the general output dynamics depend on the general factor dynamics. On this basis, I came to think that the theory of output growth, therefore, must be constructed on the basis of the theories of investment, employment and technical change for any given institutional arrangement. It thus follows, I was convinced, that when technical change and investment are assumed in the analytical construct to be zero, the theory of output growth coincides with the theory of employment, given the conditions of labor force growth. One the other hand, when net investment and new employment are assumed to be zero, the theory of output growth simply coincides with the theory of technological change. Finally, when new employment and technological change are taken to be zero, the theory of output growth coincides with the theory of investment, all at the aggregate level of the economy.

In this study, my main concern rests on the construction of a more or less general theory of aggregate investment and optimal capital accumulation The concern is driven by my understanding that capital dynamics have a profound influence on dynamics of development, output growth, labor employment, and income distribution. My interest in the theory of aggregate capital and investment was aroused at Temple University, during a macroeconomic seminar discussion on the Cambridge controversies in, and debate on, the theory of capital [257] [264] [548] [558] [609] [639] [675]. The seminar was conducted by Professor Eilen Applebaum. Another seminar, conducted by Professor W.L. Holmes, on the new microeconomics provided me with insights into the role of information in decision analysis and into the handling of information in theoretical constructs over the economic space. This seminar intensified my interest in the problems of aggregate capital, particularly in the aspects that dealt with uncertainties in the capital-decision space.

In these seminars, as well as others on history of economic thought given by Professors Karl Niebyl and Ingrid Rima, I learned to distinguish what is essential and what rests on accidents in attempting to understand the problems of capital against the background of concepts that have traditionally become characteristic in the construction of, and controversies in, theory of capital, from Marx to the present. Some of these concepts have become ingrained as logical necessities in economic discourse, they have sometimes been taken as a priori propositions–immutable data whose factual correctness is not verified. The result is that a critical understanding, without simply repeating established propositions, has become difficult, and also that the path of scientific progress in understanding the problems of the concept and measurement of capital, with implied data requirements, has become sometimes slippery, sometimes impassably muddy. Consequently, some important epistemic problems have become characteristic of the theory of capital dynamics.

These epistemic problems arise not from the errors of logic in the theoretical edifice that has been constructed but rather from the general confusion in data, experience, concepts, measurements, theoretical knowledge, empirical knowledge, and relationships that they epistemologically engender. The general confusion is the result of one seeking answers, during the theoretical construct of capital theory, as to whether data and experience are the same, whether concepts can arise without experience, what differences exist between theoretical propositions and empirical knowledge, and whether there can be empirical knowledge without experience.

In this respect, I came to a conclusion that some of the problems in capital theory are concept formation, concept measurements and establishment of a data construct. The concepts, measurements and data must be developed in a manner that allows one to distinguish among the role of experiential forms, the origins of the concept formation and the use of the concepts and subconcepts to prevent confusion in the experiential properties of capital and its role in growth dynamics, in order to abstract a general theory, which must be verified against the accumulated data.

In my search for the understanding of approaches to the construct of a general theory on aggregate capital and growth, I took a position, and kept it in mind, that every general theory is a logical attempt to give a rational account of, and universality to, the particular, which then deprives the general theory of any meaning or scientific utility unless it produces an explanation of the particulars as well as imposing some logical order on them. At the same time, I kept in mind that the greatest danger to the new truth lies in old delusions that are the result of established traditions. The task I face, and I suppose it applies to all of us, is how to emancipate myself from the tyranny of preconceived ideas, of old delusions in established theories of capital and growth.

On the side of capital, I accepted the idea that the basic concept of capital is experience-derived, thus affirming its empirical origins. In addition to the basic concept of capital is the conceptual superstructure, whose elements require measurement and development of the conceptual relations that will constitute the propositions of a theory of aggregate capital and investment. The development of the conceptual superstructure and theoretical propositions of capital, I thought, should not necessarily be driven by the available methods of measurement and collection of data. I have always held an epistemic position, right from graduate school at Temple University, that there cannot be data without measurement; there cannot be measurements without concepts; there cannot be concepts without experience; there cannot be theoretical propositions without conceptual relations; and there cannot be empirical propositions without data. There is, therefore, no logically unbridgeable gulf separating experience from concepts and the conceptual relations that may constitute the set of theoretical propositions. In other words, I came to reject the idea that there is free creation of thoughts that are not experience-derived. The methodological position wherein concepts are non-experientially derived will be incompatible with any construct of internally consistent logic-of-transformation dynamics of categories (i.e., categorial conversion).

The epistemic rejection of an experiential account of origin of concepts (e.g., capital) stems form the ontological condition and simple basic fact that in the abstract and super-abstract of theoretical constructs, concepts that have made themselves useful in organizing theoretical ideas in free logical permutations win such authority over us all that we completely forget not only their non-supernatural origins but also their experiential origins; some abstract thinkers in theory and practice take them to be free creations of thought, not experience-derived. This is true of the concept and measurement of capital, a situation which may have been an important source of the Cambridge controversies in the capital theory. While data on capital without capital concepts is impossible, the concept of capital without data is not empty. On the basis of the concept of capital and supporting conceptual superstructure, the intellectual measurement engine is called to action.

The concept and its measurement in general instruct us about the kind of data that must be constructed. In other words, concepts proceed data. They define the boundaries of the measurable and computable environment that is relevant to the concept and its conceptual relations. The conditions of measurement and computability acquire special importance when the concept, either in economics or elsewhere is given an operational significance. This is particularly true of the concept of capital in economic analysis, where aggregate capital, no matter how it is measured and computed, plays a role as an independent variable that influences other important variables, such as aggregate productivity of the economy, employment of labor, output and its distribution.

In all this I was influenced by the issue that if we do generally agree on the concept of capital but do not agree on the analytical procedures of its measure (in particular, on the list that contains heterogenous capital items), how do we construct the data requirements, how do we relate a possible constructed data to any empirical evidence, and how can we agree on the interpretation of the empirical evidence that may emerge? If scholars working in this important and difficult area of economics do not have a generally agreed interpretation of what capital data and its derived empirical evidence connote, how do we raise relevant questions and form conceptual relations that may constitute the theoretical propositions which can explain something?

These are troublesome question to which I thought I should seek reasonable answers while I was in graduate school. On the basis of this I was led to write my dissertation on an aspect of the neoclassical version of investment theory at the level of microeconomics. It was during my work on the dissertation that I started thinking critically about the conceptual and theoretical differences between the neoclassical and neo-Keynesian capital dynamics, how the types of knowledge they project affect our thinking and conception of growth and development, and how prices and thus the general price level are methodologically handled in both approaches. Substantial portions of my thought on capital could not fit into my dissertation for a number of reasons, including personal disagreements with accepted proposition in the established theories on capital and growth.

The study of dynamics of growth, development, capital, and general economic transformation continued as my major focus on economic analysis after my dissertation and when I joined Howard University as assistant professor. My interest in this area of economics was increased by my intensive probe into the structure of philosophy of science (motivated by my association with Professors Karl Niebyl of Temple University and L. Keita of Howard University, and by my appreciation for philosophical works of Kwame Nkrumah) and mathematics of fuzzy phenomena and decisions. My object was to convince myself of the logical and applied validity of established propositions, or, if I was not convinced, to seek new grounds of understanding.

These complementary studies on capital and fuzzy phenomena in economic analysis initially resulted in two unpublished monographs, "The Neo-Keynesian Theory of Optimal Aggregate Capital Accumulation and Investment" and "Cost-Benefit Analysis and the Theory of Fuzzy Decisions: A Contribution to Economic and Decision Analysis," two years after the completion of my dissertation. These monographs still remain as working documents in the practice of my craft. They are important personal reference sources for a number of my published works.

On the basis of the monography on the neo-Keynesian theory of aggregate capital accumulation and the understanding that I gained form the work on my dissertation, I diverted my attention to the microeconomic aspects of the theory of capital accumulation. Here, because of the manner in which information is handled in the analysis of capital decisions, the neoclassical theoretical framework with its flexprice method, became accessibly useful. In the process I developed the opinion that the neoclassical theory of investment decisions must incorporate into its analytical structure technological change. The manner in which technological change is modeled alongside the investment decisions must be such that we can analyze its effects on dynamics of technique, employment, productivity, and inventory management through the effects of technological change on the dynamics of absolute and relative shadow prices of factors and output.

As viewed, the development of the theory of investment is thus placed in a conflict space, where tension is produced by changes in the relative factor prices that affect income distribution and economic agents, response to the changes in the economic decision space. The resolution of the conflict propels the level of accumulated capital either forward or backward. I came to think that while this technological progress and the mechanism of change of capital level are internal to the economy, they are not necessarily internal to the firm. The research on the subject resulted in such publications as [117], [118], [119], [124] and [546].

At the point when the foundations of the neoclassical theory of economic growth was under question, it became clear to me that I should return to my monograph on the neo-Keynesian theory of aggregate capital and investment. The objective was to revise it and incorporate analysis of certain questions and answers that the theory of aggregate capital and growth can bring to our understanding of the nature of aggregate dynamics of transitional economies. Here again, the manner in which we handle the dynamics of technology (the central analytical objection by an endogenous growth theorist to the neoclassical analysis) and price is crucial to the development of the analytical structure of the dynamics of capital and how capital dynamics influence the economic growth process.

It turned out that two approaches are available to us. The preference of one over the other depends on the problems and questions that require solutions and answers. The neo-Keynesian framework adopts the method of fixprice and maximum-profit technique from a given set of blueprints. I like to refer to this approach as the *fixprice-fixtechnique method*. The neoclassical framework, on the other had, adopts flexprice and flexible technique approach. I refer to it as the *flexprice-flextechnique method*. These two approaches, I believe, tend to produce difference in the theoretical structure and the results that are the consequences of the analysis.

From the point of view of aggregate dynamics of real capital and real output growth and how they relate to the economic development process, I think the neo-Keynesian framework with its fixprice and fixtechnique method has some important analytical superiority over the neoclassical framework, with its flexprice and flextechnique method. The fixprice technique allows reasonable construction of a price-stable aggregate measure of output (volume index) even if we are unable to obtain the "true" measure of output. With the method of maximumprofit and fixtechnique we are able to relate the acceleration principle and capacity-creating effects of capital to employment and output growth with a given productivity level. Additionally, I have always had a methodological objection to the manner in which the acceleration principle is grafted onto the neoclassical capital (aggregate) dynamics and how it is related to the capacity-creating effect of capital.

A problem always arises, I think, when one attempts to find a logical continuity between the neoclassical growth theory and the neoclassical theory of optimal capital accumulation and investment. Within the neo-Keynesian analytical framework, however, with prices fixed on the aggregate and maximumprofit techniques always selected, changes in aggregate productivity are explainable by labor's learning by doing, improvements in the efficient operations of the existing institutional arrangements and their changes from within, and by socioeconomic forces that are internal to the economic system.

With all these in mind, this monograph, *Theory of Aggregate Investment in Closed Economic Systems* is the result of the project of revision of my working monograph on neo-Keynesian optimal aggregate capital. The book presents a theory of aggregate capital dynamics wherein the aggregate investment process and capital accumulation are propelled by forces from within the economy and hence are endogenous to the system. The object is to isolate theoretically the key aggregate variables that the internal forces affect in the process of accumulation, and how such process relates to real output growth. In an essential way the book is also about the *theory of output growth* in a closed economy.

Central to the development of the theory are such concepts as laws of motion, key aggregate variables, inventory, mechanisms of change, and endogenous growth, and how they relate to one another in the aggregate capital accumulation process. A set of questions is important to the study. For example, what should the rate of accumulation be if the economic system is to maintain full employment of the labor force, whatever its growth rate, given fixed price and maximum profit technique?

The study is organized in eight parts. Chapter 1 introduces the problem and the subject. Chapter 2 presents the essential elements of the neo-Keynesian framework, while Chapter 3 develops the neo-Keynesian optimal capital theory. In Chapter 4 the theory of aggregate investment behavior in a closed economy is advanced. The role played by fiscal policy in optimal capital accumulation is modeled in Chapter 5, while Chapter 5 examines the logical relationship between the theory of aggregate investment and the neoclassical one-sector growth in a closed economy. Chapter 7 presents a methodological critique and appraisal of the neoclassical theory of investment. The book ends with Chapter 8, which presents conclusions, general comments and suggestions.

Acknowledgments

I wish to express my thanks to all members of the Temple University faculty who have influenced my thought process even remotely, particularly the departments of economics, mathematics, philosophy, statistics and operations research, during my student years. Special thanks go to Professors Eilen Appelbaum, L.W. Holmes, Ingrid H. Rima, Karl Niebyl and Ben P. Klotz, all of Temple University. May I also express my gratitude to the following people at Howard University: Ms. Kahlil M. Kuykendall for her excellent research support, and Ms. Mary McCalop for her initial secretarial assistance and Ms. Alicia Powers for technical support, without which the typing of this monograph would have been difficult. I would also like to express my special thanks to Professor Kofi O. Nti, of Penn State University at College Park, for criticisms and suggestions and also for having the patience to listen to my discontent with some aspects of economic theory, particularly those related to aggregate dynamics and the development process. Thanks also to Mr. Kofi Yamoa for his spiritual support and encouragement throughout the work, especially during periods of intense workload, and to my students in advanced graduate macroeconomic theory for their discussions on the alternative views of the neoclassical tradition.

All errors are my responsibility. All controversial ideas are deliberate and well intended, even though my escape from intellectual prejudice and methodological preconceptions may not have been successful.

Chapter 1

Introduction

1.1 THE PROBLEM

Economic theory has increased our understanding of certain economic problems. It has also made it perhaps more difficult to understand others. Among the problems that are more difficult to understand in this context are those of capital accumulation, growth and development. The problem of investment activities invariably appears with those of capital accumulation and growth. The level of an economy's accumulated capital reflects realized investment decisions that have been taken in the past. Future changes in this level reflect current and subsequent investment decisions that are to be actualized. In some sense, it may be argued that the level of real accumulated capital determines the productive potential for the economy, given the labor force. The volume of investment decisions, on the other hand, determines the growth in this productive potential under the same conditions. The speed of this growth, however, is determined by the rate of realized investment in the capital-goods sector. All these combine to set the direction of economic development.

The analysis of capital accumulation, growth and investment of an economy must therefore be viewed as the analysis of conscious human decisions that are taken to improve productive potential. Such analysis has always been a troublesome venture, irrespective of the type of social organization of production under examination. The analytical difficulties acquire different and important dimensions if the system is such that the locus of power in investment decisions is not only decentralized but individualized. This is the case in capitalist economic systems. Analysis of investment decisions in this system will be our main concern in this study. We shall focus our interest on aggregate investment and its determinants over time. Given such an interest, there is always the question of where the entry point should be.

In choosing the starting point for the investigation, one may resort to data analysis. From this starting point one may adopt an empirical investigation to ascertain information regarding the past trend of investment activities. Within

1

the empirical investigation one may also examine the data for regular structures and patterns of associations. The results that emerge are purely historical, and they are very useful insofar as they provide us a summary of the facts and show how these facts fit into experience, which may form the groundwork for theoretical exposition. Alternatively, one may proceed from a theoretical construct and then subject the theory to empirical analysis to see how the theory explains the observed behavior. This alternative approach is also useful to the extent that it provides us with an understanding of the underlying causal relationships and of how such understanding can be used to shape the future and improve the economy.

One fact stands out clearly from the available empirical literature: the volume of capital per worker has been increasing for all advancing economies. This means that the stock of productive capital, properly measured, has been growing in these economies. Such a growth in the stock of productive capital reflects growth in demand for future services of capital input. It also reflects growth in the average positive trend in the volume of aggregate investment activity, as the economy moves through time and accumulates productive assets. While the growth in the stock of productive capital is consequence on actualized plans for investment activities in new capital goods, the volume of planned investment is the consequence of anticipated needs for capital services, either now or in the future. In this respect we are called upon not only to ascertain the underlying structure of the data but to explain it. The explanation must involve the factors that affect the evolution of aggregate capital and investment.

To explain the behavior of aggregate investment in any economy, it is necessary to identify the essential determinants of the aggregate demand decision for capital services and their increases, and how these determinants are translated into demand for actual aggregate volume of investment. Such determinants cannot be convincingly abstracted from pure data analysis or direct empirical generalizations. They must be abstracted from a judicious use of theory construction that allows critical investigation of underlying assumptions and expeditious comparison of the assumptions of similar theoretical constructs. The use of data analysis of all forms and empirical examinations will, however, help in isolating the important factors that may enter into the construction of the theory, since the possible list of such investment-influenced factors may be many and extensive.

Given that a construction of a theory is chosen as a starting point of an investigation, we observe that a theory of aggregate investment behavior in a capitalist economic system may logically proceed from either of two starting points. The theory may proceed by logically abstracting possible relationships among essential microeconomic variables so as to obtain a set of microeconomic behavioral equations relevant to investment analysis. From such a set a macroeconomic behavioral equation is derived through some acceptable aggregation process. The result is taken to explain aggregate investment behavior. Alternatively, aggregate variables may be constructed from the underlying microeconomic variables; one may then abstract from them a macroeconomic, structurally functional relationship that may be taken to explain the aggregate investment behavior of the economy.

The explanation obtained from the former approach may or may not be at disparity with the latter. In fact, one would hope and wish that they lead to the same explanatory understanding. Each of these two alternative paths of developing a theory of aggregate investment may in turn be approached from two different perspectives on the technology of factor usage: the *substitution* and *non-substitution* conditions of factor combinations. The theories that may emerge out of these perspectives may be referred to as substitution and non-substitution theories of investment. Input ratios are fixed in the latter, while they are allowed to change in the former, as one traces the aggregate investment behavior of the macroeconomic system over time. Both the fixed and variable proportions of factor inputs relate directly to assumptions that are made about factor prices in terms of their fixity and variability, respectively. Fixed input ratios relate to fixed factor prices, whose technique of analysis is that of fixprice. Similarly, variable factor proportions relate to flexible prices, whose method of analysis is that of flexprice. Implicitly, therefore, substitution theory finds its logical framework in the flexprice method, while the non-substitution theory finds its analytical foundation in the fixprice method, as we seek an explanatory basis for the behavior of aggregate investment.

Factor substitution as an explanatory basis of investment activities is an important characteristic of the neoclassical theory of investment, where the starting point is an individual investor and the method of analysis is that of flexprice. The theory seems to be appropriate in explaining long-run trends in sectorial investment behavior in the economy, since factor substitution as the basis of the theory may be convincingly justified. There is a real danger, however, in its particular-to-general analysis, where the individual investor's behavior is the center of explanation. This danger lies in the fact that in a closed economy there is a possibility that a transfer of ownership of existing productive capital will occur. For a single individual or a firm, such an ownership transfer would be considered an investment that increases its stock of productive capital; from the viewpoint of the whole economy, such a capital transfare cannot be considered an investment. Thus care must always be taken when the economy's aggregate investment is sought from the neoclassical approach. The problem must be formulated in such a way as to avoid aggregation duplication and overvaluation of transferred productive assets that occur in buyouts.

In the short and medium runs, factor ratios are either fixed or rigid. Under such conditions of rigid factor combination, a theory built on the basis of smooth factor substitution may not be able to explain investment in new productive plants and equipments. One important assumption in the factor-substitution approach is that factor proportions are sensitive to changes in factor-cost ratios. The corresponding changes in factor, proportions require time. Furthermore, successful research and development and the construction of plants and equipments that embody such changes take time. As such, the theory of investment built on the basis of factor-substitution characterization has little explanation to offer if the factor-proportion sensitivity assumption is not met in practice. This may precisely be the case in short-run economic fluctuations and instabilities.

Even if factor proportions are sensitive to changes in factor-cost ratio, firms may be prevented from investing in new plants and equipments with different factor ratios due to costs of retooling, training and coordination. Thus it seems inappropriate, or at least questionable, to use the neoclassical theory of investment to study the effects of certain fiscal policies if such policies are meant to promote short-run economic stability and smooth out aggregate capital-investment decisions.

For one thing, it may be argued that factor proportions are economically sensitive only at certain critical cost ratios. Hence substitution of factors may not occur between critical points of factor-cost ratios, given that factor prices do change. The reason may be that cost may be prohibitive as valued against gains. In other words, net economic gain does not justify a change of factor proportion as induced by available technology. Between these critical points the economy may be said to be on short-run courses. When the questions that we need to answer about investment are therefore of short-run nature, when the factor price ratio is fixed, then the appropriate basis of the theory of investment is that of non-substitution, and the method of analysis is fixprice but not flexprice, it seems. Aggregate investment, by increasing the level of aggregate capital, increases the output potential and hence potential growth. In this respect, the flexprice method presents some important difficulties in studying such aggregate investment, capital accumulation and growth. It is thus not by accident but a logical necessity that neoclassical theory of growth is constructed without prices. A general theory of investment on the aggregate must, we think, seek to combine the conditions of substitution and non-substitution in factors as one traces the time path of behavior of aggregate capital accumulation and investment. In this case, changes in technology that render some productive capital obsolete may constitute an important factor in investment decisions.

It is therefore fitting to recognize that the choice of the starting point of an abstraction and explanatory path of a theory of investment will depend on the general and specific questions to which answers are required of the theory. Thus the first problem is to identify the relevant questions that require answers and then to select an appropriate starting point and explanatory basis for the theory. Because of shortcomings of the neoclassical investment theory, it may be useful to seek a different starting point and explanatory basis for a theory of aggregate investment. Ideally, the alternative theories of aggregate investment should be derived from a common set of assumptions about firms' objectives, national economic goals, general organization of production and conditions of finance.

It may be pointed out that the statement that in the short and perhaps medium runs factor ratios are either fixed or rigid and that factor proportions may be sensitive to factor-cost ratios only at critical points does not imply discontinuities in the production set. It implies, of course, the presence of finite discontinuties in the technological surface. As such the suggested theoretical difficulties and criticism of the neoclassical investment theory may not be construed as motivated by the conditions of discontinuities in the production surface. Neither are they based on the presence of discontinuties in the technological set. A detailed analysis of these theoretical difficulties and criticisms is fully explored in Chapter 7.

It will be required in this essay that the theory of aggregate investment be able to answer some relevant questions about short and medium-run investment activities, in addition to many other questions, including long-run behavior. Our interest is in a theory of aggregate investment behavior. Accordingly, the starting point will be the general-to-particular, while the explanatory path will follow the path of non-substitution with fixprice method. The non-substitution basis for the theory of aggregate investment, on the other hand, may be viewed from two alternative but interdependent viewpoints, growths of profit and/or output as engines of aggregate investment changes. The theory that is sought here will be based on the neo-Keynesian framework of aggregate income determination. The analytical framework, however, will be drawn from the works of such Cambridge economists such as Robinson [589] [590] [596], Kaldor [346] [347] [352] [355] and Pasinetti [560] [561] [562], and many others who have presented seemingly different analyses of the role problems of capital accumulation following the Keynesian tradition. The objective here is to present an integrated logic of capital dynamics and how such logic can assist us in understanding the role of capital accumulation in Growth and development dynamics of closed and open macroeconomic systems. The contribution of Harrod will be examined [269] [272]. Before presenting the theory of aggregate investment behavior from the viewpoint of the neo-Keynesian persuasion, it would be a useful thrust point to examine the contents and forms of the key questions that have been raised by those concerned with the structure and form of investment behavior. This thrust point, is essential since the answers provided by the theory would only be meaningful in relation to the questions raised.

1.2 THE INVESTMENT QUESTIONS

There are many important questions that one may ask about investment and the role of investment in advancing economies. Some of the questions are general to all social systems; others are social-system specific. It is always useful and important to identify which questions are general and which are social-system specific. Such an identification helps to sharpen the focus on the relevant questions under consideration and the theory that may be required.

In the Keynesian theory of aggregate income determination and employment analysis, the real sector is said to be in an equilibrium when the volume of planned investment decisions is equal to the volume of planned saving decisions. Thus given the economy's aggregate propensity to consume, as determined by the socio-personal psychology, the question is: What aggregate investment-decision process would induce such an equality, and under what set of conditions can such an equilibrium be maintained over time when it is attained? The skeleton of the investment problem of the Keynesian school, therefore, is to seek the time path of an aggregate investment process (policy) that would bring about the Keynesian equilibrium.

The Keynesian statement of equilibrium has more than one meaning when one considers the full production surface and the complete technological set.

The proposition may be taken to mean that the level and distribution of aggregate income are such that they induce the firms and households to wish to undertake a volume of aggregate savings that would equal the volume of aggregate investment, no matter what it is. This interpretation of the Keynesian equilibrium condition in aggregate production dynamics is appropriate when either a theory of optimal aggregate savings or income distribution, or both, are sought. In fact, this is one way of looking at the relevance of Professor Ramsey's optimal-savings problem [582]. This interpretation has nothing to offer if the problem of analysis is that of investment and capital accumulation, since it takes investment as given.

There is an alternative interpretation of the Keynesian equilibrium condition that is appropriate and important for the study of dynamics of aggregate capital accumulation. This interpretation simply asks, given that income distribution and hence prices are institutionally determined, what path of aggregate investment would bring about an aggregate savings-investment equality no matter what the volume of aggregate savings, as jointly carried out by firms, household and government? In this case, income distribution and the volume of aggregate savings are given. When the equilibrium condition is of the latter interpretation, the problem is to isolate and analyze the determinants of the path of aggregate investment behavior.

But these problems and questions, understood in themselves, are barren; they are uninteresting unless they are considered in the general framework of the Keynesian characterization of the capitalist economy and of how aggregate employment, income, money and prices are determined. Insofar as one views the question and problem from the perspective of the General Theory, the question translates into: (a) What are the determinants of the level of aggregate capital stock, and how are these determinants translated into aggregate investment demand and its variations over time? and (b) What are the effects of aggregate investment and its variations on general economic activities such as employment and output? Finally, what set of conditions would maintain a macroeconomic system on the dynamic equilibrium path, when attained? While the analysis is on an aggregate investment, the theoretical foundation is drawn from the microeconomic nature of decision making. The questions are raised on an aggregate level, however.

In contrast with the problems and questions of Keynesian concern, are the investment questions and problems of the neoclassical concerns. The investment problems of the neoclassical school may be viewed from two perspectives as one examines the literature on capital accumulation: there are the questions raised by the Wicksellian school, and there are the questions raised by the Fisherian school. In the Wicksellian school the investment problems translate into a search for an optimal investment policy of individual investors and into an answer to the question of how their accumulation decisions affect the level of the *rate of interest*. In other words, what are the determinants of individual investment decisions, and what effect do increases in the volume of capital stock have on the level of interest rate [756] [757]? A similar interpretation of the problem of the Wicksellian school is offered by Lutz [467]. The question may be extended to encompass the effect of capital accumulation on the structure of relative price.

The investment problems, however, are different for the Fisherian school. In the Fisherian school the problem is not only to find the optimal investment policy at the level of the enterprise but also to look for an answer to the question of how changes in the level of the interest rate affect such an optimal policy. Here, the determinants of investment decisions are sought; given these determinants, a question arises as to how changes in the information set, including the rate of interest considered as a price, affect the optimal investment decision [193] [329].

In the analysis of these problems, the concept of optimality is used in a specific sense; and also is the concept of equilibrium that may be associated with optimality. The Wicksellian problem is raised in a static environment. Both the Keynesian and Fisherian problems are posed in dynamic environments, in the sense that the main analytical interests do not center around only the equilibrium levels of capital stock but also on the adjustment process between capital-stock equilibria.

The investment problems of the Wicksellian school may be seen as embedded in the logic of the "classical" idea of a stationary economy. To clarify and sharpen the focus on how they differ from those of the Fisherian school, let us consider a set of stationary states. Let us also consider sets of interest rates and levels of capital stock (all of these concepts defined in a way that we can agree upon). Suppose that each stationary state has a unique volume of capital stock and corresponding to it a unique value of the interest rate. Assume that the set of stationary states is ordered by the level of capital stock. Suppose we observe that stationary states with higher levels of capital stock correspond to those with lower values of interest rates. In order to maintain each stationary state the volume of replacement investment must be commensurate with the size of the capital stock. Greater volume of replacement investment will be needed for higher levels of capital stock, given a constant rate of depreciation. This will imply that lower interest rates will correspond to higher volumes of replacement investment when various stationary states are compared. Two questions immediately come to mind. What are the determinants of the optimal levels of capital stock for stationary states? Does accumulation of capital affect the level of interest rate, or do variations in the level of interest rate affect the levels of capital stock at stationary (equilibrium) states? A side question may be raised as to whether levels of interest rate affect replacement investment. The body of explanation leading to answers to the above questions may be seen as the classical theory of optimal capital accumulation for a stationary economy in the sense of Bohm-Bawerk and Wicksell [47] [757] [759]. It is purely static in the sense that the analysis does not deal with the determinants of acquisition of new capital or the transitional process between stationary states of capital levels.

The statement "greater values of replacement investment will be needed for higher levels of capital stock," must be carefully interpreted. First, one must observe that the stock of capital is a composite index, so also the proportionality of replacement value for the aggregate process. Secondly, the stock of capital in one state is said to be greater than that of any given state if its capital service flow per unit time is greater. When the stock of capital is viewed in this way, it takes account of size and technique. Furthermore, higher level of technique is associated with a greater flow of capital services per unit of time, while it may be associated with a higher or lower volume of depreciation depending on the conditions of durability. Thus for each state, knowledge of depreciation proportion and capital stock leads to knowing the depreciation investment that corresponds to the rate of interest in that state.

In an advancing economy, we are not interested in isolating only the important determinants of optimal levels of capital stock but also the determinants of the optimal speed with which one level of capital stock is moved to the other as the equilibrium conditions alter. The environment, in this case, is dynamic. We must therefore determine the optimal level of capital stock for each state and the speed of adjustment from one state to another when new conditions present themselves. One may also examine whether variations in the levels of interest rate have any effect on the speed of capital adjustment. The system of explanation for dealing with these dynamic problems of capital accumulation is the neoclassical characterization, in the sense of Fisher. In analyzing the speed of capital adjustment, two investment components are considered. We consider the rate at which the existing capital stock can be maintained and the rate at which new capital stock (positive or negative) can be acquired. The system of explanations providing the answers to the questions raised by the Wicksellian and Fisherian schools constitutes the modern neoclassical theories of optimal capital accumulation and investment and their extentions to output-growth dynamics.

Investment problems in the neoclassical framework are microeconomic in their orientation. The problem of optimal capital stock must have a similar orientation. However, within the neoclassical framework problems and confusions are often encountered as to whether capital is being used in a microeconomic or aggregate sense. We shall return to this point in later discussions (Chapter 8). It is important to remark at this juncture that the differential theoretical positions taken by some neoclassicists, the conclusions arrived at by such scholars as Haavelmo [236] and Jorgenson [329], and many other disagreements stem from whether one is dealing with the neoclassical conditions in the sense of Wicksell [758] or in the sense of Fisher [193].

While each set of problems of the neoclassical and Keynesian schools, and the corresponding questions raised, are both conceptually interesting and analytically important to the study of an advancing economy, we observe that much of the emphasis in the literature on capital accumulation and investment has been concentrated on answers to the neoclassical questions and problems. Except in the Cambridge school (England), little attention, if any, has been given to the investment problems and questions of Keynesian concern. This situation is completely reversed when the questions to which we seek answers concern output growth.

A number of factors have contributed to this unparalleled development. Among them is the relative ease with which classical optimization theory can be utilized in the neoclassical framework in developing a theory of capital and investment. Another (and perhaps the most important) factor is the individualistic analysis offered by the neoclassical framework, which allows the firm's accumulation problem to be analyzed in a market setting. The neoclassical approach seems more appealing, since it makes explicit the ideology of democratic individualism in the marketplace. There are also some objections to the development of investment theory in the framework of Keynesian aggregate income determination. One of such has been voiced by Haavelmo, who argues that there is a difficulty in deriving the demand for investment as a function of profitability of employing capital in production. He suggests that "the existence of profitability for increased earnings by using more capital does not by itself determine the speed at which capital will actually be increased" [236]. A further objection is raised concerning the use of expectations in the theory of investment, since such expectations render predictions impossible. There are still other objections. One such objection is suggested by Hamberg, who argues that there is nothing in the neoclassical theory of the firm that would support any theory derived from the profit principle as an explanation of aggregate investment demand. It is a change in output and interest rate, not the levels, that influences investment demand, according to the theory of the firm. It seems therefore that there is a contradiction between the neoclassical theory of investment and the Keynesian postulate that aggregate investment depends on the rate of interest, and current level of economic activity as measured by real income, given the existing level of capital stock [446a]. Another objection is voiced by Jorgenson, who in response to Haavelmo's criticism of the demand for investment derived from the classical scheme of producer behavior suggests that the Keynesian construct of marginal efficiency of the investment schedule must be dismissed as naive [329].

There is also a general bias in favor of the neoclassical economic research program, where the individual is made the focus of analysis. As a result of this bias other economic research programs are received with ideological skepticism at best, and at worst they are not received with kindness. In particular, the Keynesian methods and techniques of aggregate thinking have been ideologically suspect since the publication of the General Theory [374]. This bias has been carried over to the development of capital theory and investment analysis of the aggregate economic behavior. The results obtained in Keynesian framework are suspect to the extent that they cannot be substantiated by neoclassical economic logic. Such a bias has also produced a number of confusions, whereby attempts are often made to reconcile certain Keynesian results with the neoclassical results. An example is the reconciliation of marginal productivity determination of optimal capital stock and the marginal efficiency determination of optimal investment [254] [445] [446a] [700]. Objections are encountered if such reconciliation and justifications cannot be found within the neoclassical logic. There is also an implied objection to the fixprice method used in Keynesian framework, where income distribution and prices are external to the system as opposed to the flexprice method, where prices and hence income distribution are determined in equilibrium states (in a specific sense) in the neoclassical framework.

As far as research on capital theory is concerned, these objections depend on particular interpretations of investment and the role of investment in an advancing economy. Furthermore, they depend on the types of capital investment

9

questions to which answers are sought. They also depend on whether the theory is flexible enough to account for the differences arising from the different institutional organizations of production. When questions and problems for a theory are defined, the class of methods for the construction of the required theory and the analysis of its results is also defined. Sometimes there is not enough room for flexibility.

Let us now turn our attention to the general task of the book. But before doing so it may be pointed out that when the questions to which we seek answers concern output growth, there is an important analytical shift by the neoclassicals from their framework to that of the Keynesian. How this shift allows capital formation to be connected to output growth in the neoclassical framework is a mystery, which the reader is left to unravel.

The rest of the book is so organized that in Chapter 2 we present the neo-Keynesian framework for the analysis of aggregate investment. We explore the theoretical difficulties and advantages of this framework. We then state the basic assumptions required to develop a theory of optimal aggregate capital accumulation and investment. In Chapter 3 we present the complete development of the neo-Keynesian optimal capital theory. We then explore the links among income distribution, savings and capital accumulation. Conditions for equilibrium and its stability are stated and analyzed, and the relationships and differences between the marginal efficiencies of investment and capital are explored. The theory of aggregate investment behavior in a closed economy is developed in Chapter 4. The theories of both optimal capital and investment are extended in Chapter 5 to incorporate the effects of taxation and government budgetary behavior. In Chapter 6 we explore the logical link between the theory of aggregate investment and neoclassical one-sector growth. Chapter 7 presents a methodological critique and appraisal of the neoclassical theory of investment. Conclusions and reflections are the subject of Chapter 8.

Chapter 2

The Neo-Keynesian Framework

The concept of aggregate investment is central to all analysis of macroeconomic systems. One cannot analyze in a basic way the growth and employment situations without statements about the nature of aggregate investment. Aggregate investment plays two roles: it plays a role as a growth factor, by increasing the levels of capital and output potential; it is also an important determinant of the economy's capacity to offer jobs for the currently unemployed and to create new jobs for the future generation. Despite these important roles played by investment in the aggregate behavior of the economy, its study is very difficult and most controversial. Even though great effort has gone into the study of investment and capital accumulation, these areas are perhaps the least understood and most confusing in economic analysis. Furthermore, substantial portions of the study has been within the neoclassical framework, where the focus is on microeconomic behavior. The critical contributions made by neo-Keynesian aggregate thinking is epistemically neglected. From the viewpoint of macroeconomic policy which affects growth and development, it is aggregate thinking that is most incisive and instructive. It is from this understanding that a study of an aggregate investment in the neo-Keynesian framework is conceived and proposed; it is a study that does not rely on the microeconomic details of the economy. Its analytical process is based on the fixprice method.

2.1 OBJECTIVE

The objectives in this study are twofold. The first objective is to develop two complementary theories of optimal aggregate capital accumulation and aggregate investment that would allow us to answer the questions raised in the Keynesian framework of aggregate thinking, in order to emphasize some of the major contributions to capital, investment and growth. The second objective is to develop a framework that would allow an empirical analysis of the theoretical results. The theory therefore must not only justify the Keynesian postulate, whereby investment demand depends on income, rate of interest and capital stock in existence, but be viable and econometrically testable. The logical thread of the theory sought will be drawn from the Cambridge school, where the basis of evaluating evidence on the determinants of aggregate investment and capital behavior is made explicit within the Keynesian framework.

Once the theory is placed in its proper perspective, it is hoped, the objections and skepticisms that have been raised will lessen at worst and evaporate at best. It may be pointed out that the analysis of the Cambridge school extends beyond the problem of capital accumulation. Nevertheless, our main concern in this study centers around those abstractions that are directly or indirectly applicable to the analysis of the aggregate investment behavior of the economy. The logical system of explanation, consisting of assumptions, maintained hypothesis and conclusions that would be developed for the optimal aggregate investment in the sense of Keynesian and Cambridge schools will be referred to as the *Neo-Keynesian Theory of Aggregate Capital and Investment Behavior*. Its analytical foundation is anchored in the logic of Keynesian saving-investment equality at the equilibrium, where given the aggregate saving habits of the society, an optimal aggregate investment program is sought in such a way that it not only leads to such an equality but maintains it over time under a specified set of conditions.

The neo-Keynesian theory of investment as presented here combines the profit, output and capacity principles of a given technique, which constitute the basic core of the non-substitution theory of explanation of aggregate investment behavior in a capitalist economy. It thus accounts for the effects of existing and potential unutilized capital capacity on both current and future investment activities. We shall derive from the neo-Keynesian framework the set of conditions under which these statements may be validated. It would then be demonstrated from the set of derived conditions that the neo-Keynesian theory of aggregate investment behavior lends support to the Keynesian aggregate investment function, where the economy's volume of investment is negatively related to the interest rate and positively related to the aggregate income. We shall also derive the conditions that would allow us to analyze the relationship among the volume of aggregate investment, level of capital stock and capacity utilization.

The neo-Keynesian theory of aggregate investment advanced in this study requires simply that accumulation of aggregate capital be based on the general objective of optimizing aggregate factor employment and hence output, given the profit motives of producers, social institutions and the consumption-saving psychology of the population. Thus full employment of all factors is taken as the optimal benchmark around which the system of capital accumulation evolves. It is a positive statement in the sense that under-capacity utilization is not allowed, while we trace the path of new investments that will bring about growth in productive capacity and potential output. Among the full employment paths

12

we seek one whose potential output is maximum, with aggregate savings equal to aggregate investment. The profit motive in the capital accumulation process is taken to mean that the best available technique is always selected by the producers.

The optimal real income is reached when the aggregate investment is equal to aggregate saving and all the relevant factors are fully employed at the optimal technique. This optimal income is what is generally known in macroeconomics as the "full-employment equilibrium level of income." A less-than-full-employment equilibrium is said to exist when the planned aggregate investment is equal to a given planned aggregate saving along with factor unemployment. The problem of the neo-Keynesian theory of investment and capital accumulation is to explain the aggregate investment behavior between equilibria for any given savings behavior.

A theoretical difficulty naturally arises when the neo-Keynesian capital-investment problems are posed in this light wherein two different states of equilibrium are distinguished, unused existing investment opportunities and new investment opportunities that go to update accumulated capital overtime. The former is usually associated with the existence of under-capacity utilization and a correspondingly possible unplanned aggregate inventory investment. The latter is associated with the growth of capital stock in place, whether in use or not, and a link with the growth of potential aggregate output and new employment opportunities.

While it is impossible to discount increased activities in new investment opportunities between less-than-full-employment disequilibria in practice, it is theoretically useful to identify the investment activities among such equilibria with inventories. The new investment opportunities that may occur in the economic system between less-than-full-employment equilibria may be attributed to either changes in the structural composition or technological obsolescence, but not necessarily to an increased level of potential economic activities. The possible changes in inventory investment and utilization of unused existing investment opportunities between less-than-full-employment disequilibria may be associated with changes in the levels of economic activities at the existing accumulated capital. The theory of inventory investment seems apt for the explanation of investment activities among less-than-full-employment disequilibria. This position may be sustained on the grounds that the relative magnitude of new investment opportunities between less-than-full-employment equilibria can be neglected because of size. This is the position taken here, in the sense that new investments are assumed to be negligible between less-than-full employment equilibria.

Increased economic activities in investment opportunities are associated with full-employment disequilibria and are linked to the expansion of potential output and new employment opportunities. To each new set of resource conditions there will correspond a full-employment equilibrium output in the sense of Keynes, and corresponding to it an optimal capital, given the choice of technique. The path of such full-employment outputs where the saving-investment equalities are maintained is the path of dynamic equilibrium. The development of a theory that will explain the determinants of the paths of aggregate investment behavior that would sustain the path of full-employment equilibria is the task of this present study.

Ideally, the theory would account for the effects of unused existing investment opportunities on the path of optimal capital accumulation. In addition, it would account for investment in new plants and equipments which would not only increase the level of stock of productive capital but also extend the domain of output potential. The extension of the domain of such output potential will in turn be reflected in the growth of important economic indicators used to assess the health of the economy.

Some clarification of the nature of the aggregate capital and investment with which we are concerned is required. The economy's aggregate investment and capital may be said to consist of two components, private and public. From the viewpoint of the economy's capital and growth, this distinction may not be important. Furthermore, in some economies the volume of aggregate public investment relative to the growth of potential output is just as important as, or even more important than, the volume of private aggregate, productive capital formation. This may be the case for most developing mixed economies. In some advanced mixed economies such a distinction may be ambiguous and messy when one examines the nature of productive capital. Such a distinction cannot be easily made for some advanced economies like that of the United States of America.

The most important thing is not whether one is dealing with a private or public productive aggregate capital but whether one is generally concerned with the whole aggregate capital accumulation of the economy. The need for the distinction would be very important if one were interested in analyzing the relative contribution of the two components to the whole capital accumulation process of the economy. The distinction is unnecessary for the analysis of aggregate capital accumulation process if it is maintained that both private and public investment decisions are guided by the same efficiency criterion. We may assume that all producing agents are profit maximizers in the Robinsonian sense [589] that is, they select the maximum-profit technique or the minimum-cost technique available. In the current work we shall not make such a distinction. We shall be concerned only with the analysis of the whole process of aggregate capital accumulation. We shall assume that private and public investment decisions are guided by the same aggregate criterion. One may take issue with this assumption, but this issue is unnecessary, since the theory is first developed without the government. The role of the government is then introduced to examine the effects of its policy behavior on the aggregate capital accumulation process.

2.2 A REFLECTION ON SOME THEORETICAL DIFFICULTIES AND ADVANTAGES

The neo-Keynesian framework for the study of aggregate investment has a number of advantages and disadvantages. It also has a number of theoretical difficulties, which must be clarified from the onset. In moving through texts on macroeconomics one encounters a conceptual difficulty as to the sense in which investment is used and the role that aggregate investment plays in the analysis. This conceptual difficulty may be attributed to a confusion on the part of the authors who fail to distinguish and make clear the conditions that define the static macroeconomic system as compared to those that define the dynamic macroeconomic system. The conceptual difficulty involves the defining terms of investments in inventories on one hand, and plants and equipments on the other, as they relate to macroeconomic system in static and dynamic states.

The conditions defining static and dynamic macroeconomic systems are specified in terms of key aggregate variables of stocks of capital, labor and technology. A static macroeconomic system is implied when all key aggregate variables are invariant with time. The macroeconomic system is defined as be dynamic if any of the key aggregate variables change with time. Given these definitions, the conceptual difficulty vanishes when two types of Keynesian investment function are identified. One type specifies inventory investment, and it is analyzed in a static macroeconomic system. The other type involves the specification of investment in terms of plants and equipments, and analyzed in a dynamic macroeconomic system. The increase in inventory investment relates to factor utilization and an increase in actual output for any given fixed stocks of aggregate factors within the static system. An increased investment in plants and equipments goes to increase capacity, potential output and employment. Static and dynamic macroeconomic systems are thus defined in the sense of the classical economists, in that the key aggregate variables defining potential output and its growth are fixed and variable, respectively. New capital creation is associated with macroeconomic dynamics. The two types of investments can be used in the study of macroeconomic dynamics, while investment in plants and equipments is not allowed in macroeconomic statics.

In macrostatics, where capital creation, in the sense of new plants and equipments, is out of the picture, the question is what optimal inventory investment would support full-employment output and utilization of existing factors, whatever the savings habits of the society. Thus, during periods of recession and depression, fiscal policy, in the sense of increases in government expenditures, must be seen as affecting the level of aggregate inventory investment as a component of aggregate demand. In this way, an increase in government expenditure, is investment-creating, in the sense of inventory, for example stockpiling and use. In inflationary periods of macrostatic systems, fiscal policy in terms of reduction in government expenditures, must be seen as disinvestment in terms of inventory decumulation. The implicit assumption of such an interpretation of a macrostatic system is that the time period is too short for capital to depreciate. There is no depreciation investment. The macrostatic system will be the classical stationary state, if the time is extended is long enough. In this case we may either assume an automatic replacement investment or analyze the determinants of replacement investment.

In macroeconomic dynamics, where new plants and equipments must be created, the question is, what optimal investment in plants and equipment would support the *"desired growth"* of output potential? This implies that in addition to replacement investment, new investment opportunities must be created to increase the level of aggregate capital stock. Fiscal policy, in the sense of government expenditures and capital-tax changes, must be seen as creating or destroying new investment opportunities when the rate of private investment is either oversupporting or incapable of supporting the desired rate of growth of output potential, whatever the savings habits of the community may be. In the neo-Keynesian framework, this interpretation of capital dynamics requires us to find an optimal aggregate investment and its determinants that would support the desired growth rate of potential aggregate output needed to support full-capacity utilization of a growing stocks of factors, and at the same time maintain a continual equality between aggregate investment and saving.

This interpretation, for the development of the neo-Keynesian theory of aggregate investment, raises a number of theoretical and practical difficulties. There is the practical problem of separating inventories of consumer goods from those of plants and equipments and synchronizing them with savings possibilities at equilibrium, in the sense of Keynes. If consumer demand is well synchronized with the supply of consumer goods, saving must be viewed as capital-formation potential; otherwise at the dynamic equilibrium the unsold consumer goods must be interpreted as capital formation with capacity-creating effect. There is another difficulty, which stems from the observation that productive capital can result in two important ways. Productive capacity can increase as a result of changes in technology embodied in the plants and equipments, while the physical quantity of capital remains the same. This includes the problems of factor substitutions as new plants and equipments are built and producing units shift from low-technology equipments to higher ones. Productive capacity can also grow because of increases in the physical units, while the technology of production remains the same. This includes the case of non-substitutability in factors as new plants and equipments are created. The epistemic role of these interpretations in economic evolution is provided in [123], where the analytical process is made explicit.

The aggregate investment problem, as posed implicitly, assumes that the economic system has savings-creating capacity; hence the problem is to analyze the determinants of investment that would support the desired rate of growth of output potential. There is an alternative problem, which may be characteristic of developing countries. In this case, there are "unlimited" investment possibilities, and the problem is to find the appropriate rate of growth of savings and its determinants that would support the desired rate of growth of output potential, no matter what the rate of investment. The analysis of this problem belongs to the theory of optimal saving. There is another important problem within the analytical structure of macroeconomic thinking. This problem is peculiar but not limited to developing and newly industrialized economies, where there is an excess of real aggregate savings. The economies are, however, constrained by available technological know-how from transforming the accumulated real savings into investments in plants and equipments that would increase the output and job-creating potentials of these economies.

The advantages of the neo-Keynesian framework in developing a theory of optimal aggregate capital accumulation and investment in a unified setting are many. The framework allows us to construct directly a theory of aggregate optimal capital and investment without direct appeal to the structure of microeconomic decisions. By the method of fixprice with its supporting assumptions the theory may be developed under the conditions of no government; the role that governments can play in aggregate capital formation can be examined when the assumption of no government is relaxed. The framework also offers us a rare possibility for examining the macroeconomic system as either closed or opened for aggregate capital formation. Accordingly, we have an opportunity to examine the effects of international borrowing, indebtedness and commercial policy on a country's capacity to create new investment in plants and equipments that would support the desired rate of growth of output potential when the economy is technologically limited in its tool-making capacity and innovation. Furthermore, the neo-Keynesian framework of direct aggregate thinking allows us to link the theory of aggregate capital formation to the theory of aggregate economic planning. It must be pointed out that the paths of optimal capital and investment obtained in this framework do not depend explicitly on prices, as will become clear in the chapters that follow.

We shall now turn our attention to the analysis of required assumptions needed to develop a theory of aggregate investment in a neo-Keynesian setting. The theory will be presented for closed macroeconomic systems, without and with a government sector.

2.3 BASIC ASSUMPTIONS

The basic assumptions of the neo-Keynesian theory of aggregate capital accumulation and investment range from propositions about the characteristics of social institutions to propositions about technical properties of production. They may be stated in the following form.

2.3.1   The organization of production is capitalistic, with no government participation except otherwise stated. The system is a closed one.

2.3.2   The economy is scarce-free of natural resources, technical know-how is always available to convert real savings into investment in plants and equipments.

2.3.3   The total population, Ω, of the economy may be divided into income (or social) classes, X; $\bigcup_i X_i = \Omega$. The classes need not be pairwise disjoint subsets of the population.

2.3.4   Each member of the social classes supplies one or more of factor services of labor and capital, which may or may not be in demand. The motive to supply the factor service is compensation by income that may be received. Such income is in the form of one or more of the following: wages, profit or rent. The distribution of total social income among income types is institutionally determined.

2.3.5   Saving is the sole activity of income earners. Each income class has a different propensity to save out of earned income. Such a propensity to save is a constant that lies between zero and one, inclusively.

2.3.6 Production-employment-investment decisions are the sole responsibility of firms. The driving force of such decisions is the profit motive (defined in a specific sense).

2.3.7 The technology of production is known at each point of time. The input-output relation is a fixed coefficient type for each new capital goods and choice of technique.

2.3.8 Expectations about future variables are "static" in the sense that they are always realized. The market structure and its information are given and known to the economic units and may be influenced by their output-employment-investment decisions. Prices are the summary of the relevant market information; they are fixed and cover cost when profits are normal.

2.3.9 The initial conditions are such that the economic system can reach its final destination as planned by firms in terms of output, employment and investment on the aggregate.

Some of these basic assumptions need explanation. Assumption (2.3.1) is an institutional one that makes explicit the ideological and normative foundation for the analysis. The no-government assumption will be relaxed in order to examine the degree to which a government can directly or indirectly influence aggregate capital formation in a closed system. The system will then be opened in order to examine the effects of some important international factors on aggregate capital formation. Assumption (2.3.2) allows us to escape the problem of resource constraint on domestic capital formation. The division of the population into classes in (2.3.3) is by type of income received. Since there is no reason to rule out the possibility that some individuals may receive different types of income, the classes are assumed not to be pairwise disjoint.

Assumption (2.3.4) requires that each member of the population be endowed with one or more of the relevant factor services. It complements assumption (2.3.3). Assumption (2.3.5), on the other hand, must be interpreted, as income recipients have different propensities to save out of different income types, if they receive more than one income type. Firms in assumption (2.3.6) may be viewed as institutional organizations designed to administer the interest of the capital-owning class. The interest is profit, which is obtained by combining capital and labor services to produce an aggregate surplus. The size of such a surplus will depend on the structure of income distribution, which is institutionally determined. The assumption (2.3.7) of expectations concerns the nature of future variables that cannot be fully controlled. These variables may be viewed as parameters for decision. Static expectation as used in the assumption includes the cases where future variables change in accord with known structure. A perfect forecast or rational expectations will fit in this class of expectations.

Given these assumptions, the development of the neo-Keynesian theory of aggregate capital accumulation and investment starts with the Keynesian social accounting identity and then adds the conditions of equilibrium, in the sense of Keynes. As such, we shall start with Keynesian social accounting identity for a closed macroeconomic system. It is useful to bear in mind that prices are given, known and fixed; hence, the analysis can be undertaken in terms of real variables or in constant monetary units. The flow conditions of the

18

variables may be represented as in figure 2.3.1, in terms of supply and demand
interactions. In terms of aggregate accounts we have

$$Q = C_1 + \mathbb{S} \tag{2.3.1}$$

$$Q = C_2 + \dot{K} \tag{2.3.2}$$

Figure 2.3.1
Flow Conditions on Consumption-Investment Production Synchronization

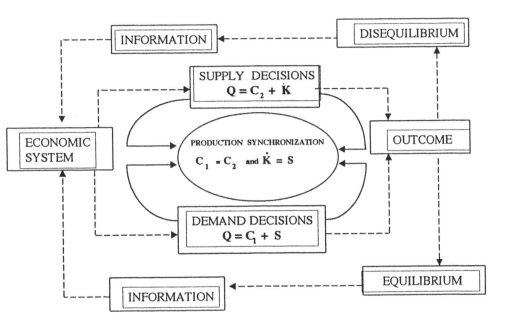

where $K, \dot{K}, Q, C$ and $\mathbb{S}$ are real capital stock, net investment (change in the
level of capital stock), output, consumption and savings respectively. These are
aggregate variables that may be constructed from the underlying microeconomic
variables according to some acceptable logic [224] [646]. We shall see that with
the given, known and fixed prices the aggregation can be undertaken in some
real units. The variables are assumed to be either time or vintage continuous.
Equation (2.3.1) is taken to express use and demand composition, while (2.3.2)
is taken to express production and supply composition.

The variable C_1 is the planned consumption of goods and services, while
C_2 is the planned production of consumption goods and services in terms of

aggregate economic decisions. Since the factors affecting consumption-demand decisions are different from those affecting the decisions to produce consumer goods and services, it is not necessarily the case that $\dot{K} = \mathbb{S}$; that is, savings as planned should be equal to investment as planned on the aggregate. At the very best one can only deduce from equations (2.3.1) and (2.3.2) that

$$\left. \begin{array}{l} C_1 + \mathbb{S} = C_2 + \dot{K} \qquad ^{a)} \\[2ex] C_2 - C_1 = \mathbb{S} - \dot{K} \end{array} \right\}_{b)} \qquad (2.3.3)$$

In order for the production of planned units of consumption goods to be equal to the planned units of consumer goods and services demanded on the aggregate, it is necessary and sufficient that $\mathbb{S} = \dot{K}$, which is precisely the Keynesian equilibrium condition. Thus we seek an aggregate decision process of investment that would lead to such an equilibrium condition in a one-commodity economy by abstraction on aggregation. Since our main concern is on investment in plants and equipments, we shall initially assume that inventory investment does not exist or that it is always optimal in the sense of producer's plans. This assumption is one of convenience that allows us to concentrate on investment in productive capital. We shall relax it when the problem of capital accumulation is linked to the adjustment process and economic planning. The existence of inventories due to lack of perfect synchronization between consumption composition and production composition will be examined as a constraint on the accumulation path. In a static economic system, $\dot{K}$ will be associated with inventory investment, while $\mathbb{S}$ will be associated with unconsumed goods and services when a one-commodity world is the focus of analysis. Here, real inventories constitute real savings that establish equality between investment and savings. In macroeconomic dynamics the real savings as excess of consumption over income is transformed into investment in plants and equipments, when technical capacity is available to convert savings into capital creation in such a way that the inventories of consumer goods are sufficient to support the creation of new capital goods. Thus $C_1 = C_2$ and $\dot{K} = \mathbb{S}$ as a required condition for equilibrium.

Finally, we would like to say something about the conditions of aggregate finance. We are interested in the total real finance, defined in the sense of aggregate saving of the economic system. As such, explicit mention of supply of, and demand for, money will play no essential role in our analysis. This is a necessary abstraction, since prices are fixed, expectations are static, and our main concern is on supply of real aggregate saving. In a closed economy, the total real finance available for investment will always be equal to the total domestic real savings. This total finance is distributed through organized financial institutions, in a case where savers and investors happen to be different economic units. In capitalist economic systems, such financial institutions will be considered as firms among the producing units.

The organized monetary system is viewed as a technology of exchange, whose increased efficiency increases the synchronizations between savings and investments. Thus its effects on the accumulation path is through improvement in efficiency. The complexities of the whole monetary and financial system will depend on further assumptions that we make regarding the nature and source of available domestic finance, which in a closed economy cannot exceed the total available real savings. We thus exclude artificial creation of savings (credit) as a source of finance except where otherwise stated. This may create a limitation in the analysis. Such a limitation may be taken care of by introducing bank credit. Such assumptions will be made explicit in each state of the analysis.

Money plays very little role in the theory that we are constructing; it is not the availability of money but that of real finance that defines the limitations on investment, given the production and technological possibilities. The role that the interest rate plays will be introduced at an appropriate point. We shall then examine its effect on real aggregate capital accumulation. The presence of money, we should add, provides us with the possibility of an aggregation process, since money appears in the consumption of the baskets of goods and services for all economic participants.

One may, and rightly so, question the meaningfulness of a one-commodity economy and the aggregate variables that come with it. This question will be taken up in a later chapter, where microeconomic implications of the Keynesian macroeconomic equilibrium will be drawn.

2.4 THE FIXPRICE METHOD

A major assumption in the neo-Keynesian framework for the development of the theory of aggregate investment is fixed prices. This assumption of fixed prices is part of assumption (2.3.4). Implied in the assumption is the notion that prices and hence the aggregate price are exogenously determined and linked to income distribution, which in turn is assumed to be institutionally determined (Assumption (2.3.4)) and hence exogenous to the internal dynamics of the theory. This fixity of prices in the development of Keynesian and neo-Keynsian economic theorizing has been called the "fixprice method" by Professor Hicks [303] [304].

In theorizing about aggregate economic behavior, the fixprice method provides a way out of a number of theoretical difficulties. It allows the quantity of goods and services to be aggregated by their monetary values or in cost units which then constitute at any moment of time the index of the economic state. Different economic states can then be compared when an appropriate assumption about expectations is imposed. Since prices are exogenously fixed, the adjustment mechanism in this framework takes place through changes in the levels of stocks. The second advantage of the fixprice method requires that the production system and the corresponding inventories be partitioned into consumption goods and investment goods. We thus have two sectors in the production and inventory analysis, in terms of their interaction and composition. At any moment of time there is either an excess of effective demand or excess supply in the consumer goods sector. To maintain fixed prices, excess demand is either satisfied from inventories or substitutes, or it becomes unplanned savings. On the other hand excess supply becomes unplanned additions to inventories.

Thus there is a flow disequilibrium at current demand and stock disequilibrium at current supply at the fixed prices.

The stock-flow disequilibrium process that maintains fixed prices does not imply nonexistence of equilibrium (in a specific sense) in the economy. What it implies is that in a dynamic macroeconomic system, the equilibrium path, when it is constructed, provides a reference on the basis of which the stock and flow conditions can be analyzed for the adjustments and capacity building that are responsible for establishing the actual path of the economy. Such an adjustment process depends on expectations. Since prices are fixed and exogenously determined, the expectation are formed around demand on the part of producers, while consumers form expectations around supply. In this sense, the equilibrium stock at any point of time is viewed as the level of accumulated inventories that must satisfy the demand as expected. On the part of consumers the equilibrium savings is that which must satisfy the expected supply. As such, quantity adjustment is an explicit character of the neo-Keynesian framework, given the nature of expectation formation. The assumption of static expectation in this framework guarantees that time-point stock and inventory levels can be compared in a consistent manner and that the dynamic equilibrium, if attained, implies stock and flow equilibria. Our main concern in this framework is to examine the forces that determine aggregate investment. Such forces must be related to the dynamics of the disequilibrium adjustments in terms of inventories and savings. With prices fixed, the volume of aggregate investment will be financed from real aggregate savings that flow from the dynamics of stock and flow disequilibria.

The volume of real aggregate saving given fixed prices and static expectations must be related to levels of inventories. It depends on production composition, attitudes toward saving, and the structure of income distribution, which is institutionally determined. The income distribution is exogenous to the model but essential to the internal dynamic of the model and its logic. The volume of investment that is taking place, on the other hand, at normal prices (fixed prices) depends on whether producers are making profits. Such profits depend on the structural relationship between investment and production composition, on one hand, and savings and inventories, on the other.

The relationship between expectations and equilibrium is essential in understanding the logic of the neo-Keynesian framework. But this is not the complete story; the relationship between fixed aggregate price and the structure of income distribution is just as essential and important. Income distribution is said to be in "expectational equilibrium" when expectations about class income shares are realized and such proportions sum up to unity, even when the aggregate income is on a growth path. This condition of income distribution must hold at all times in order to have prices fixed, irrespective of whether labor market follows "wage leadership" (cost-push price changes) or the commodity market follows price leadership (demand-push price changes). The dynamics of the system are thus governed by flow, stock and income distribution conditions. Price distortions of the aggregate index brought about by price overvaluations and undervaluations at a given quality are eliminated over the dynamic path. We thus have the opportunity to analyze the growth, accumulation and distribution processess in real goods and services by eliminating the price effect on the aggregate index. Since prices are fixed, changes in distribution of productive activities over commodities are signaled by demand expectations and actual supply-demand disparities, as effective demand is out of line with supply. Non-quality-induced price changes are completely discounted from the process, while possible quality-induced price changes are handled in terms of greater flow of services from commodities and hence an increase in real aggregate income.

Chapter 3

The Neo-Keynesian
Optimal Capital Theory

To present a version of the neo-Keynesian theory of aggregate investment, it
is necessary to identify within the Keynesian logical framework the important
determinants of demand for aggregate capital and its optimal level for the economy and how the optimal level changes over time. This requires the analysis of
stock and flow conditions relevant to capital optimality. The theory of aggregate
investment that is sought to explain the changes in optimal level of aggregate
capital requires us to develop and present a theory of optimal aggregate capital accumulation under Keynesian conditions. The theory of optimal capital
accumulation should lead us to identify and explain the determinants of the
optimal level of aggregate capital under a given set of conditions. The theory
of investment that follows should allow us to explain the changes in the optimal
level of aggregate capital. We shall now develop and present the essentials of
the neo-Keynesian theory of optimal aggregate capital accumulation.

3.1 THE ESSENTIAL OF THE THEORY

The central force behind firms' aggregate investment decisions and thus decisions to accumulate productive capital is the expected rate of profit over the
accumulated capital. The firms in the aggregate economy seek to maximize
their rates of profit subject to socio-technical limitations of production possibilities and market information. Since expectations about the behavior of future
parameters are realized, the net revenue flow is known. Furthermore, the consideration of discounted net revenue stream is unnecessary if firms' optimizing
behavior is myopic. The long-run behavior in this respect is similar, since expectations are static and prices are fixed. Increases in revenue is due to increases
in real output.

Even though firms are interested in the profit rate but not simply profit size, one would expect that the level of aggregate capital accumulation would influence both the profit level that it generates and the profit rate over the accumulated capital. On the other hand, given the level of accumulated capital, the expected profits at each time point would depend on the volume of expected investment decisions that would maintain them on the basis of accumulated information. The rate of capital accumulation decision at each time point is facilitated by the expected profit size and restricted by the level of accumulated capital that is generating such a profit size at the same point of time. The logical structure that emerges is an interdependent feedback system whose dynamic behavior may or may not be stable.

Furthermore, in such a closed macro-system the expected real aggregate finance of the expected aggregate investment projects, given adequate financing of previous investments and investment-creation technology, would depend on the expected real aggregate saving, which would, in turn, depend on the structure of income distribution and the savings habits of the society with respect to incomes of various sources. On the aggregate, the expected actual volume of investment that would take place given its profitability at each point would, therefore, depend on the aggregate real savings that would be generated in the economy to maintain such volume of investment, conditional on availability of know-how.

However, given the social distribution of income and the consumption habits of the society, the volume of aggregate real saving is determined by the volume of aggregate real income being generated by the accumulated real capital and maintained by the current investment. The behavior of income flow over time, on the other hand, may be seen as capturing the expectations about the future behavior of these essential aggregate real variables. As outlined, there are two important sectors of saving and investing that constitute the essential structures of the aggregate accumulation process. The system is said to be in a desired state if the expected real aggregate investment is just right for the expected aggregate real savings needed to support it, and the technical know-how in the economy is just right to allow the real aggregate savings to be transformed into productive investment. Such a desired state of the economy will occur where aggregate real investment is just equal to the aggregate real savings needed to maintain it. This is the Keynesian equilibrium for the economy.

The essential features of the neo-Keynesian theory of optimal aggregate capital accumulation, therefore, lead to a postulate that the central functional relationship among the key aggregate variables, on the basis of which the theory attempts an explanation of how the rules and motives of human behavior are translated into aggregate investment activities and hence capital accumulation, is the dual and interdependent relationship between rates of profit and net capital accumulation. The motives of capital accumulation is profit, while the force behind increasing profit is capital accumulation, both of which are constrained by the available aggregate savings and its process, given the available technical know-how. The mechanism of the decision process is succinctly described by Professor Joan Robinson [589, p. 121] [590].

26

Furthermore, the essentials of the theory lead one to expect that the optimal current investment will depend on the current profit, as an estimate of productivity of aggregate capital; on the output level, which indicates general expectations in the economy; and on the level of current capital stock, which determines the current output and profit potential as well as restricts the rate of investment that is taking place. All these aggregate variables are estimated on the basis of current prices and are normalized by appropriate base-year index. The existing capital stock, however, is evaluated either on the basis of expected current profit or its current replacement price, with a proper base-year norm. Alternatively, all the aggregate variables may be valued in terms of current commodities, where such commodities may be reduced to a common denominator by an appropriate index that allows intertemporal comparison. All these are consistent with price fixity and static expectations.

3.2 CAPITAL ACCUMULATION, INCOME DISTRIBUTION AND AGGREGATE SAVINGS

The macroeconomic system that we have described so far postulates a close connection between capital accumulation on the aggregate and income distribution, to the extent that the structure of distribution of real social income among social classes affects the accumulation of aggregate real social savings that is needed to finance the aggregate capital accumulation, conditional on available or potential technology. Whether the structure of distribution of social income directly or indirectly affects the societal capacity to accumulate productive capital in the economy may be viewed as a statistical question and problem. This question and problem may be resolved through a development of a theoretical structure that permits income-distributional factors to be incorporated in a manner that allows empirical examination. Given the theoretical construct, the methods of sensitivity analysis and theoretical simulation make it possible to analyze the effects of income distribution on the accumulation paths.

In this way, we can analyze the effects of structural changes in the distribution of social income on accumulation, given the social attitude toward saving. Such an analysis presents a new opportunity to examine the criteria for an optimal income distribution conditional on the desired rate of capital accumulation and growth of output, if such output growth is meaningfully linked to the rate of aggregate accumulation.

From a casual observation of economic events and their history, one is likely to suspect, like the classical economists, that the path of distribution of social income affects the path of accumulation of social capital that would emerge from the historical process. But this is only a suspicion, which can be put forward as a conjecture. The conjecture seems appealing. It has to be justified in theory and transformed into either an empirically verifiable proposition or a scientifically testable hypothesis in order to convince a sceptic. In order to establish such a hypothesis we need to establish a link between income distribution, on one hand, and both the saving that is taking place and surplus of savings that have accumulated, on the average. In this connection, two possible concepts of

27

distribution of social income would have to be considered: (1) *scale-distribution* of income; and (2) *type-distribution* of income. Scale-distribution addresses only the magnitude of income received, not the source of income. Type-distribution addresses only the source of income received, not the magnitude. In this analysis, two income types of wages and profits are considered. The source of wages is work, while that of profits is ownership of productive capital. Wages and salaries belong to the same source and the same income type. The same thing applies to "rent" and profits.

Some interesting questions emerge if one accepts the hypothesis of a link between the structure of income distribution and accumulation. Given that saving is an increasing function of income, can one make any definitive statement about the rate of growth of aggregate saving if it is known that aggregate income has been growing? In answering this question we need to know the structure of income distribution and the savings habits of the income recipients regarding income types and sizes as the economy moves through time. Upper-skewed income distribution, given the income type, would suggest to lead to higher savings if it is believed that high-income recipients are not ostentatious consumers and hence save a greater proportion of their incomes as their incomes increase. On the average this may not be generally the case in economies of developing countries, where ostentation is the characteristic of the ruling and business elites. Alternatively, a lower-skewed income distribution would be postulated to lead to higher savings if it is believed that lower-income recipients are thrifty in the sense that they believe in the future. Whether lower-income recipients save proportionately more of their income than higher-income recipients as income increases is left to be resolved statistically. Furthermore, even if higher-income recipients are more thrifty than the lower-income recipients, there is no reason to believe that the available aggregate saving for financing investment will increase if the income pie at each point of time is redistributed in favor of higher-income groups and vice versa. The possible increase in savings would depend on the relative size of the income groups and the relative intensity of the psychological propensity to save, out of income size and type.

The analysis of possible effects of the structure of income distribution on the volume of aggregate savings and thus aggregate investment, if any, is complicated by the problem of income types. The complication is immediately made simple if one assumes that the social attitude toward saving is the same irrespective of the type of income received. In other words, the proportion of income saved is independent of the source of income; the volume of savings is thus determined solely by the magnitude of total income. In this case, the most important element of the income-distribution effect is the income scale. Alternatively, one may assume that the scale-distribution of income is not important to the propensity to save; it is rather the source of income that affects attitudes to saving, when the path of aggregate saving is examined.

To analyze the possible effects of the structure of income distribution, we shall assume that earnings up to a certain defined level are purely wages when it is earned by workers; over and above that we shall consider it as a rent to workers. The rent and profit incomes will be placed in the same cohort. The effect of savings on capital accumulation will be analyzed under these conditions.

Aggregate saving is directly linked to investment through inventories in the consumer-goods sector. With prices fixed, the system's feedback process is through quantity adjustments. The quantity adjustments are the results of excess supply or excess demand. The excess supply at any point in time goes to increase the accumulated level of aggregate inventory, while excess demand produces the opposite effect in a closed economy. For a closed economy, the accumulated inventory is total available savings, valued in consumption or cost units. It is the excess of real consumption over real income at any time point. The total saving may or may not be in equilibrium, in the sense of expectations. The driving force that alters the levels of aggregate saving is the disparity between demand decisions in the consumption sector and supply decisions in the production sector, as they relate to expectations. The system is said to be in equilibrium when expectations are fulfilled in all sectors regarding stock and flow conditions.

The conditions of stock-flow equilibria are necessary but not sufficient for the economy as a whole in terms of its capital formation. The sufficient conditions for a dynamic equilibrium relate to income distribution and production synchronization between consumption goods and investment goods and to how they synchronize with the distribution of consumer goods between consumption and saving. Let us recall from equations (2.3.1)-(2.3.3) the basic decision relation

$$
\begin{array}{llll}
Q & = & C_1 + \mathbb{S} & \text{a)} \\
Q & = & C_2 + \dot{K} & \text{b)} \\
C_2 & - & C_1 = \mathbb{S} - \dot{K} & \text{c)}
\end{array}
\tag{3.2.1}
$$

In this theoretical system, inventories accumulate in the consumption-goods sector. The accumulated inventories plus current additions become the available total saving for financing the creation of current investment goods. Investment goods are immediately integrated into production, and hence no inventories accumulate in the investment goods sector. Any unused investment goods are valued in consumption units as part of inventories.

Just as accumulated inventories can serve as additions to current savings for financing the creation of current investment goods, so also can it serve as addition to current supply. Thus if $\mathbb{V}(t)$ is the accumulated inventory, the current potential supply, $\mathbb{Z}(t)$, is the sum of existing inventory and current output, $Q(t)$, which may be expressed as

$$
\mathbb{Z}(t) = Q(t) + \mathbb{V}(t)
\tag{3.2.2}
$$

Similarly, the current potential demand, $\mathbb{D}(t)$, is the sum of current factor earnings, $W(t)$, and accumulated saving, $\mathbb{U}(t)$, less current saving, $\mathbb{S}(t)$. Thus

$$
\mathbb{D}(t) = W(t) - \mathbb{S}(t) + \mathbb{U}(t)
\tag{3.2.3}
$$

The total factor earnings is the factor cost and is taken as the wage bill. It is the sum of factor costs in the consumer-goods sector and investment-goods sector. The total profit, $\prod(t)$, of the system is the sum of profits from the consumer goods sector, $\prod_c$ and the investment goods sector, $\prod_I$. Thus

$$\prod(t) = \prod{}_c(t) + \prod{}_I(t) \tag{3.2.4}$$

which is also specified as the excess over factor cost

$$\prod(t) = Q(t) - W(t) \tag{3.2.5}$$

The current supply, $\mathbb{Z}(t)$, may be written in terms of income distribution by substituting the value of $Q(t)$ from equation (3.2.4) in (3.2.2) to obtain

$$\mathbb{Z}(t) = W(t) + \prod(t) + \mathbb{V}(t) \tag{3.2.6}$$

For the system as a whole the total current supply must be equal to total potential sup ply. Thus by equating equations (3.2.2) and (3.2.5) we obtain

$$\mathbb{S}(t) = \mathbb{U}(t) - \prod(t) - \mathbb{V}(t) \tag{3.2.7}$$

The total available savings at each time point in equal to total inventories, which is composed of current savings, profit and beginning inventories, all of which are valued in cost units and stored in consumer goods.
Thus

$$\mathbb{U}(t) = \mathbb{S}(t) + \prod(t) + \mathbb{V}(t) \tag{3.2.8}$$

The path of production state is said to be perfectly synchronized if the volume of consumption goods produced is equal to the volume of consumption goods demanded. In this case the accumulated inventories at any time point is zero. The implication is that for all t's

$$\mathbb{V}(t) = \int_0^t [C_2(\tau \,|t) - C_1(\tau \,|t)] d\tau = 0 \tag{3.2.9}$$

Under perfect synchronization, the available finance in terms of total saving is the sum of current saving from factor income and current profit, under the assumption to no portion of profit is spent. Thus

$$\mathbb{U}(t) = \mathbb{S}(t) + \prod(t) \tag{3.2.10}$$

Equations (3.2.9) and (3.2.10) imply that total profit goes to finance all or part of the creation of new investment goods, depending on further assumptions that we make about $\mathbb{S}(t)$ Given that we start from a path of stock equilibrium, the path of flow equilibrium requires that total savings equal total current inventories, which is equal to the total net investment valued in cost units. Additionally, total currently produced consumption goods equals the total current consumer goods demanded, all of which are valued in cost units.

The analytical edifice that is being set up has as its core concepts aggregate saving, inventory and investment. Current saving, inventory and investment are identified with flow conditions. Accumulated saving, inventory and investment (capital) are identified with stock conditions. Under the flow conditions, current total inventory becomes current total saving, which is thus used to finance the creation of new investment goods valued in cost units. Under the stock conditions, accumulated aggregate inventory becomes accumulated total savings, which relates to the total potential capital stock. In addition to flow and stock conditions there must be the conditions of production synchronization at each point of time. Thus the conditions of stock and flow equilibria are necessary but not sufficient in specifying and analyzing the economy's capital accumulation equilibrium. Such equilibrium requires a perfect synchronization of production between flows of investment and consumption goods. The two fundamental equations that govern the stock-flow process are equations (3.2.8) and (3.2.9). They connect aggregate saving to aggregate investment, where savings-investment process governs the dynamics of the system's capital accumulation. Let us now specify the optimal capital accumulation process.

3.3 THE CAPITAL ACCUMULATION PROCESS

The decision process of aggregate capital accumulation may be specified under the postulate that given the conditions of business riskiness, the expected current profit, $\prod(t)$, depends on the planned net accumulation, $\dot{K}(t)$, and the level of accumulated capital, $K(t)$, up to that time point, t. The implication here is that higher levels of accumulation expands production possibilities and the flow of revenue. Given that prices are fixed, expectations are static and distribution are exogeneous, higher revenue flow implies higher levels of aggregate profit. The aggregate profit generated under these conditions is higher, the higher the level of accumulated capital and the planned accumulation taking place. As stated, aggregate profit is the result of the aggregate capital accumulation process that widens the production possibilities. The capital stock in existence defines the productive capacity, the aggregate employment that can be offered, and hence aggregate profit that is obtainable given the income distribution. The investment that is taking place is an affirmation of profit possibilities and its realizations. The aggregate profit is of a dual character; it is the result of capital accumulation as well as the driving force of the accumulation.

The aggregate profit therefore acquires a dynamic decision role, in that it is not simply a product of the accumulation process but assumes a driving force to accumulate further. Higher profits provide greater incentive to accumulate. Thus the rate at which firms, on the aggregate, plan to accumulate depends on the expected aggregate profit and the level of aggregate capital stock available at that time point. The accumulation process and the creation of new investment goods are financed from total real domestic saving, $\mathbb{S}(t)$, at each point of time. The total real domestic savings is connected to the distribution of real aggregate income, $Q(t)$, which is composed of different income types. In this essay, two income types of aggregate wage, $W(t)$, and profit, $\prod(t)$, are assumed. The propensities to save from these income types are taken to be different and stable proportions of the income types. They are S_w and S_c respectively, where S_w is the proportion of total wages saved and S_c is that of total profit saved. The system's evolution may be specified as

$$\text{Current Profit: } \prod(t) = F(K, \dot{K}) \qquad (3.3.1)$$

$$\text{Net Accumulation: } \dot{K} = G(K, \prod) \qquad (3.3.2)$$

$$\text{Technical Possibilities: } Q(t) = \min[\frac{K(t)}{\gamma_1}, \frac{L(t)}{\gamma_2}] \qquad (3.3.3)$$

where $L(t)$ is the time path of labor input and γ_1, γ_2 are the inverse of factor efficiency norms.

$$\text{Income Distribution: } Q(t) = W(t) + \prod(t) \qquad (3.3.4)$$

$$\text{Savings Distribution: } \mathbb{S}(t) = S_w W(t) + S_c \prod(t) \qquad (3.3.5)$$

where $0 \leq S_w, S_c \leq 1$ and $S_w < S_c$.

The specification of the aggregate capital accumulation process requires some explanation. The specification assumes full-capacity utilization of existing capital. Even though fixed proportion has been assumed for each time point, nothing has been said about the technological progress or the innovation that is taking place. The technique of production is assumed to be known. Income is completely distributed between wages and profits, which are all valued in cost units and stored in the units of consumer goods. We have not advanced, in this framework, a sub-theory to explain the factors that affect the structure and form of income distribution. One may choose to subscribe to Kalecki's principles of degree of monopoly and thus the market structure [357] [358]; or to Kaldor's approach, wherein income distribution depends on investment and saving propensities [346] [355]; or consider that income distribution is institutionally determined, as is argued by Joan Robinson [590], as long as the distribution of income is exogenous to the system.

The basic problem of the capital accumulation process as specified above may be stated as: If we take the distribution of income type as given, determined either by the mode of production (the social organization of production, exchange and consumption) or the market structure, and consider the flow of savings is to be determined by the consumption habits of the people, the logical process is to find an expected rate of profit that would induce an equality between the expected rates of accumulation and savings, whatever may be the rate of aggregate social savings, and at the same time satisfies the conditions of harmonization between demand and supply of consumer goods, on one hand, and demand and supply of investment goods, on the other. This is the principle of "production harmonization," which implies that there is always effective demand. Since the distribution of income and savings have been exogenized, technical possibilities are given to us and production synchronization is assumed, the problem of aggregate capital accumulation may be analyzed by considering the interactive effects of equations (3.3.1) and (3.3.2).

We assume that the functions defined by equations (3.3.1) and (3.3.2) are linearly homongeneous. Thus the two functions may be written in their intensity forms as:

$$\rho(t = F(\xi, 1) = \psi(\xi) \tag{3.3.6}$$

$$\xi(t) = G(\rho, 1) = \phi(\rho) \tag{3.3.7}$$

where $\rho = \prod/K$ and $\xi = \dot{K}/K$. Other properties of the functions are expressed in their slope behaviors as $\psi' > 0$, $\psi'' < 0$, $\phi' > 0$, $\phi'' < 0$, and hence the slope of the inverse function of ϕ is increasing. In other words, both the functions, ψ and ϕ, are convex in the $(\rho - \xi)$ plane. The functional restrictions may be justified on economic grounds.

The expected rate of profit increases at a decreasing rate as more capital is accumulated. This is because an increasing rate of capital accumulation, for any given technique of production and set of market conditions, leads to a reduction in the "marginal efficiency of capital" and the rate of profit on accumulated capital. The function for the expected rate of capital accumulation, on the other hand, increases at a decreasing rate with the expected profit rate. The justification can be abstracted from the behavior of the marginal efficiency norm of capital. As capital accumulates, the profit rate does not rise as fast as the capital-accumulation rate, due to decreasing marginal efficiency of capital. The restriction-of-profit rate that would support an increasing accumulation restricts the rate of net capital accumulation. Since the ϕ-function is assumed to be well behaved, we can write its inverse function as:

$$\rho = \rho(\xi), \ \rho' > 0, \ \rho'' > 0 \tag{3.3.8}$$

and $\psi(0) > 0$, $\phi(0) > 0$, $\rho(0) > 0$ for all $K(0) > 0$.

In this neo-Keynesian framework investment decisions on the aggregate, are independent of consumption-saving decisions on the aggregate. Thus, we can construct theories of consumption and savings independently of theories of aggregate capital accumulation and technological progress. This may be viewed as the counterpart of problem separation in the neoclassical framework, in the sense of Fisher [193] [329], where the present-value maximization of the firms is considered as an independent problem from the problem of utility maximization by the owners of the firms. The aggregate capital accumulation problem as outlined in this neo-Keynesian framework is to seek the highest expected rate of accumulation that simultaneously satisfies the profit constraint and the equation of motion that governs the system's dynamics, while simultaneously finding the highest expected rate of profit that would maintain and support the rate of accumulation that is taking place. Thus there is an interdependent relationship between the rate of profit that is taking pace on the aggregate, and the aggregate rate of accumulation.

Given fixed prices, static expectations and production harmonization, the maximum rates of aggregate accumulation and profit may be obtained by maximizing either the rate-of-accumulation function, subject to the rate of profit, or the rate-of-profit function, subject to the rate of accumulation at all points of time, with properly defined constraints. Thus we seek the highest expected aggregate rate of capital accumulation that simultaneously satisfies the implied profit constraint and the equation of motion that governs the dynamics of the macroeconomic system. The problem may be mathematically stated by combining equations (3.3.6) and (3.3.8). Thus the firms, on the aggregate, maximize the rate of profit by selecting the rate of accumulation

$$\max_{\xi \in \mathbb{A}} \rho(\xi)$$

(3.3.9)

$$ST. \ \mathbb{A} \ = \ \{\xi \in \Omega \mid \psi(\xi) - \rho(\xi) \geq 0\}$$

where Ω is a set of all possible rates of capital accumulation. The optimization where Ω is a set of all possible rates of capital accumulation. The optimization problem stated in (3.9a) is equivalent to $\rho(\xi) \cap \psi(\xi)$, which defines the intersection of the two functions. The optimal accumulation rate, ξ^*, is that rate $\xi^* \in \Omega$ such that

$$E(\xi^*) = \psi(\xi^*) - \rho(\xi^*) = 0 \qquad (3.3.10)$$

where the E-function is the excess investment possibility function relative to the rate of profit. The value ξ^* depends on the initial conditions on stocks, flows and production synchronization. We shall assume that the initial conditions of the system are right for the appropriate solution. Furthermore, since it is assumed that expectations are always realized and that both profit and net-accumulation functions are well behaved in the proper space, the solution is anticipated to be stable. Before characterizing the solution, let us examine the behavior and properties of the excess-investment-possibility function. The geometry of the problem is given in figure 3.6.1(a). This optimization problem and its solution will be shown to correspond to a particular dynamic equilibrium that is consistent with conditions of Keynesian equilibrium, where investment is equal to savings.

3.4 PROPERTIES OF THE EXCESS INVESTMENT POSSIBILITY

From the properties of equations (3.3.1) and (3.3.2), it may easily be inferred that $E(\xi) = 0$ for at most two points. Let such points be A and B [Figure 3.6.1 a and b]. At these two points the functions for the rates of profit and accumulation are equal; however, the rate of accumulation and the rate of profit are not necessarily equalized. The point A and all other such points constitute a set of short-run equilibria, while the point B and all other such points also form a set of long-run equilibria. This implies that when the functions $\psi(\cdot)$ and $\phi^{-1}(\cdot) = \rho(\cdot)$ are evaluated at points A and B with the values $\psi_A < \psi_B$ and $\phi_A^{-1} < \phi_B^{-1}$. If this economic system finds itself in a position such as A, firms, on the aggregate, would soon realize that the rate of profit on investable capital far exceeds the rate of accumulation that tends to generate it. Even though at this situation of accumulation the marginal efficiency of investment (meI) is equal to the rate of profit as viewed in cost units, it far exceeds the shadow price, the cost of finance that would support such an investment. The situation is such that the demand for consumer goods exceeds the supply and the conditions of production synchronization between consumer and investment goods have not been met. In such a situation, firms' expectations on the aggregate about future profit yields would be high and rising. Such high expectations would induce an increased rate of aggregate investment plans.

It may be abstracted from the system that the meI is very high and increasing (at a decreasing rate) between A and B. As such, the expected rate of profit over capital far exceeds the rate of expected accumulation that would maintain it. Thus, one would expect both the rates of profit and capital accumulation to be rising. Between A and B, $E(\xi) \geq 0$ and less than zero otherwise. Furthermore,

$$E(\xi) \gtreqless 0 \Rightarrow \rho \gtreqless \xi, \forall \xi \in \Omega \tag{3.4.1}$$

The inverse of the excess investment possibility function will be referred to as the "excess profit possibility function". Both the excess-possibility functions are bounded from below and above. From the initial point, A, to the point B we have

$$a \leq E(\xi) \leq b, \forall \xi \in \mathbb{A} \tag{3.4.2}$$

The upper bound implies that investment and profit opportunities are limited at any relevant period to the society. The lower bound implies that minimum investment opportunities exist if the system is to advance in its capital accumulation.

In general there are many points for which $E(\xi) = 0$ as expectations and other parameters change. We shall refer to these points simply as "functional equilibrium points". Not all these points, however, will satisfy the savings-investment equality constraint required by the Keynesian equilibrium process. In other words some of these points may not be Keynesian equilibrium points. The aggregate savings that is taking place may be less or more than adequate to support the aggregate investment that is induced by profit that is being generated. Furthermore, by the logic of fixed-point theorems it may be shown that there exist within a unit square at least one of ξ and ρ such that

$$\left.\begin{array}{l} \hat{\rho} = \phi_1(\hat{\rho}) \\[2mm] \hat{\xi} = \phi_2(\hat{\xi}) \end{array}\right\} \tag{3.4.3}$$

Not all these fixed points will simultaneously satisfy both the conditions $\hat{\rho} = \hat{\xi}$ and $E(\hat{\xi}) = E^{-1}(\hat{\rho}) = 0$. We shall, thus, examine the set of conditions that will specify the neo-Keynesian equilibrium for capital accumulation where enough savings is being generated to support the accumulation that is taking place.

The capital accumulation presented so far and specified by equations (3.3.6) and (3.3.7) is consistent with Professor Joan Robinson's analytical framework that "the central mechanism is the desire of firms [on the aggregate] to accumulate, and we have assumed that it is influenced by the expected rate of profit. The rate of investment that they are planning for the future is, therefore, higher the greater the rate of profit on investment (estimated on the basis of current prices). Valuing the existing stock of capital on the basis of the same rate of profit, we can then express their plans in terms of a rate of accumulation" [589, p. 47]. Keynes puts it as "profits (or losses) are an effect of the rest of the situation rather that a cause of it. But profits (or losses) having once come into existence become a cause of what subsequently ensues; indeed the mainspring of change in the existing economic system" [375, p. 140].

3.5 THE NEO-KEYNESIAN EQUILIBRIUM FOR CAPITAL ACCUMULATION

Let us now link the excess investment (of profit) possibility function to the Keynesian equilibrium. Two sets may be defined as:

$$\mathbb{R} = \{\xi \mid \xi = \psi(\xi)\} \tag{3.5.1}$$

$$\mathbb{P} = \{\rho \mid \rho = \phi(\rho)\} \tag{3.5.2}$$

Definition 3.5.1
The neo-Keynesian equilibrium for a capital accumulation is attained if there are $\rho^*, \xi^* \in \mathbb{R} \cap \mathbb{P}$, and ρ^* is a maximal element which is equal to ξ^*.

Proposition 3.5.1
If the economic system is in a neo-Keynesian capital equilibrium, the volume of aggregate profit is exactly equal to the volume of aggregate investment, and hence the equilibrium exists.

Proof

At neo-Keynesian equilibrium

$$\rho \quad = \quad \phi(\rho) = \xi = \phi(\xi)$$

$$\Rightarrow \quad \frac{\Pi}{K} = \frac{\dot{K}}{K} \Rightarrow \dot{K} = \Pi \square$$

Definition 3.5.2

The level of capital accumulation is said to be optimal if the economic system is in neo-Keynesian equilibrium, where the profit rate is exactly equal to the rate of accumulation as normalized by the level of accumulated capital, and ξ^* is a maximal element.

The optimal level of accumulated aggregate capital is given as

$$K^*(t) = \Pi(t)/\phi(\xi^*)$$

where $\xi^* = \rho^*$. Thus the value of optimal capital is defined in terms of the rate of profit in such a capital equilibrium.

3.6 STATE-SPACE REPRESENTATION

The capital accumulation process and the properties of its solution leading to the optimal level of capital is represented in a state-space diagram in Figure 3.6.1.

In Figure 3.6.1, we observe that at point B not only are the behavioral functions of aggregate profit and accumulation rates simultaneously satisfied by expected flows of profit and accumulation, but that the expected profit and accumulation rates are equalized. The planned rate of accumulation is thus generating the desired expectations about profits for any given technique of production. The rate of profit in this situation is just that which is required to maintain the rate of accumulation that is taking place and the profit expectations that it tends to induce in that state. In such a state the economy is in an equilibrium with respect to the rate at which capital accumulation takes place. The level of aggregate capital stock is precisely optimal with respect to the profitability conditions in the economy for any given set of available techniques.

The rate of profit induced by accumulation taking place in such a state is not only equal to the *meI* but it is also just equal to the real aggregate rate of interest (cost) chargeable on that finance needed to maintain the accumulation and induced profit. At this equilibrium state, where not only are the functions of rates of accumulation and profit equal but the rates of profit and accumulation are realized, the level of aggregate capital stock is optimal. See panels (c) and (d) of figure 3.6.1, where $K(\dot{K}/K)$ specifies the level of capital to depend on the capital accumulation rate, and $\rho(K)$ is the rate of profit as a function of capital stock, or alternatively, $\rho = \rho(K(\dot{K}/K))$. The optimal capital stock is that which equates the rates of accumulation and profit $(\rho^* = \xi^*)$.

3.7 EXISTENCE AND STABILITY OF EQUILIBRIUM AGGREGATE CAPITAL

In the analysis of optimal aggregate capital accumulation, we are usually faced with two problems: first, the existence of optimality defined in a specific sense; secondly, analysis of how stable the system is if the initial conditions are such that the system can actually attain this optimal level of capital stock. The first problem is existence, and the second is that of stability. In section 3.6 we presented the conditions of existence that the set $\mathbb{R} \cap \mathbb{P} \neq \phi$ such that $\xi^* = \rho^* \in \mathbb{R} \cap \mathbb{P}$ We shall now argue that the system is stable if the equilibrium is achieved for the underlying data.

Figure 3.6.1

Geometry of the General Aggregate Capital Accumulation Equilibrium

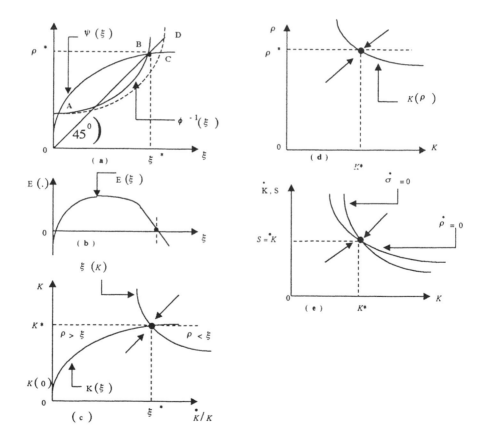

Let us make reference to Figure 3.6.1 panels, (a), (b), (c) and (d). Point B is an equilibrium point. If the system is stable for any given underlying data, then any departure from point B must set in motion forces that will cause the system to move toward B on the condition that the functions of the rates of accumulation and profit are true expressions of investors' expectations regarding profit and investment possibilities, on the aggregate. The forces are summed up and expressed by the differences between the expected rates of profit and accumulation that are mutually induced and determined. The system as specified exhibits an asymptotic and limiting behavior that may characterize a property of effective learning, in addition to the convexity and concavity properties of the functions.

It may be observed that there is no natural reason why the rate of accumulation and profit functions must intersect on the 45-degree line such that the rate of accumulation is equal to the rate of profit. The equality between the rate of accumulation and profit functions may occur either to the right or left of the 45-degree line, such as point C. The collection of all such points for which $\psi(\xi) = \phi^{-1}(\xi)$ but $\rho \neq \xi$ will constitute temporary situations, and some of them may be Keynesian aggregate short-run equilibrium (savings equals investment) states, where either $\dot{K} > \prod$ or $\dot{K} < \prod$. These temporary states and/or short-run equilibrium states are unstable; they cannot be maintained, because firms, on the aggregate, would soon find out that their expectations about the rates of accumulation and profit as expressed by the functional relations are equalized but out of line with current experience, conditional on the underlying data. They will then revise their expected accumulation decisions either downward or upward, given that the expected path of profit rate is fixed. This will cause the ϕ^{-1} function to rotate upward or downward to intersect point B.

Alternatively, given the path of the rate of accumulation, firms on the aggregate would make an either downward or upward revision of their profit expectations, thus causing another downward or upward rotation of the rate of profit function to intersect the rate of accumulation function at point D. It is only when expectations about profit and accumulation are correctly calculated, and hence realized and in line with current experience, that the economy is in a stable equilibrium state. Such equilibrium states are on the long-run equilibrium path, where not only is the stock of capital optimal but the rate of profit is equal to the rate of accumulation. We speak of the long-run equilibrium path but not the long-run equilibrium state.

The stability condition that we have outlined may be stated in a compact way. It may be stated from the position of the excess investment possibility function.

Definition 3.7.1

The capital accumulation equilibrium of the macroeconomic system $\mathbb{S}$ is said to be investment stable locally, if

$$\lim_{\substack{\xi \to \xi^* \\ t \to \infty}} E(\xi) = 0, \text{ given } \mid E(\xi_0) - 0 \mid < \delta$$

where δ is a positive constant.

Definition 3.7.2

The capital accumulation equilibrium of macroeconomic system, $\mathbb{S}$, is said to be stable at large if

$$\lim_{t \to \infty} \xi(t) \quad = \quad \xi^* \text{ given } \mid \xi(t_0) - \xi^* \mid < \delta_1,$$

$$\lim_{t \to \infty} \rho(t) \quad = \quad \rho^* \text{ given } \mid \rho(t_0) - \rho^* \mid < \delta_2,$$

and $\xi^* = \rho^*$ where δ_1 and δ_2 are positive constants.

The adjustment process to the equilibrium path as we have outlined is motivated through the divergence between the rates of accumulation and profits relative to expectations, on the aggregate. The equilibrium path of aggregate capital accumulation, as we have stated, is specified by equality between aggregate profit and aggregate investment. Nothing has been said about the role of savings when the system is on or off the capital equilibrium path. Let us turn our attention to the role of aggregate savings as it relates to aggregate profit and investment.

3.8 THE SAVINGS-INVESTMENT-EQUALITY CONSTRAINT

The theory of optimal aggregate capital accumulation outlined above arrives at a conclusion that the optimal capital is that which has the highest rate of profit, where such a rate of profit is equal to the rate of capital accumulation. This is a stock equilibrium, and the flow equilibrium support for the capital stock equilibrium path is such that the aggregate profit which the accumulated capital is generating must be equal to the aggregate net investment which is maintaining the capital stock equilibrium at each time point. Given the conditions of stability and equilibrium of the capital accumulation path, a question arises as to whether the macroeconomic system is generating enough real finance to support the investment that is taking place on the aggregate. Is the saving over-financing or under-financing the accumulation that is being generated by expectation of profit on the aggregate? Is the capital equilibrium path a Keynesian one, where the savings-investment equality constraint is met? If it is not, what then are the set of conditions for which the savings-investment-equality constraint may be met? What should be the flow of aggregate savings to maintain the stock-flow equilibrium path and at the same time ensure production synchronization?

The answers to these questions may be obtained by finding the necessary and sufficient conditions for equality between aggregate savings and investment. Such necessary and sufficient conditions may be abstracted by combining the conditions of optimal capital equilibrium path, total real savings (equation 3.3.5), income distribution (equation 3.3.4) and production synchronization (equation 3.2.1). These conditions must then be examined against the two fundamental equations that govern the stock-flow process, defined by equations (3.2.7) and (3.2.8).

The required necessary and sufficient condition for the macroeconomic system to generate sufficient finance to support the equilibrium investment is that aggregate savings from income earned from all income types must be equal to aggregate profit at every point of time. This will be called the "profit-savings-equality condition." The condition translates into equality between the rate of profit and the rate of savings over capital, on the aggregate. To see how the profit-savings-equality condition emerges, recall from equations (3.2.1) and (3.2.3) that total profit from the consumer and investment goods sectors is valued in cost units and stored in consumer goods. From the conditions of income distribution, savings and production synchronization we have:

$$
\begin{aligned}
Q(\cdot) &= W + \Pi &\quad (a) \\
Q(\cdot) &= C_1 + \mathbb{S} &\quad (b) \\
Q(\cdot) &= C_2 + \dot{K} &\quad (c)
\end{aligned}
\qquad (3.8.1a)
$$

If all wages are computed at cost and paid in consumer goods, then $C_2 = W$, and if production is well synchronized then $C_1 = C_2 = W$ and hence $\Pi = \mathbb{S}$, given that equation (3.2.9) holds for each t.

The profit-savings-equality condition only requires that real aggregate savings generated in the macroeconomic system be equal to the profit that the accumulated capital is producing in each state over the entire spectrum of the path of capital equilibrium. There are three behavioral situations in which this condition of equality between profit and savings on the aggregate may be satisfied. The situations require placing analytical limitations on the average propensity to save out of income types, in terms of savings behavior. One condition that satisfies this savings-profit equality is a postulate that all profits are saved and all wages are spent. Thus $S_w = 0$ and $S_c = 1$ in equation (3.3.5). Thus

$$
\left.
\begin{aligned}
\dot{K} &= \Pi = \mathbb{S} \\
\rho^* &= \xi^* = \sigma^*
\end{aligned}
\right\}
\qquad (3.8.1b)
$$

where $\sigma = \mathbb{S}/K$ is the rate of aggregate savings over capital, K^*.

Alternatively, we may consider a case where it is only required that the aggregate profit be equal to the aggregate real social savings, irrespective of the source of income. Suppose income recipients can consume from profit and that they can save from wage income. The problem is to find the conditions, given the distribution of saving, such that $S = \Pi = \dot{K}$. To find a solution to this problem we define the rate of profit over total wages as:

$$\prod /W \;=\; \tilde{\mu},\; 0 < \tilde{\mu} \le 1 \tag{3.8.2}$$

$$W \;=\; \alpha \prod,\; \alpha \ge 1$$

where $\alpha = 1/\tilde{\mu}$. Substituting equation (3.8.2) in (3.3.5) we can write the savings function as

$$\mathbb{S} = (\alpha S_w + S_c) \prod,\; \alpha > 1 \tag{3.8.3}$$

The α is an income distribution parameter which varies in accord with structural changes in income distribution. The conditions for savings-investment equality then requires that

$$\mathbb{S} = \prod,\; \text{if } (\alpha S_w + S_c) = 1 \tag{3.8.4}$$

Suppose that at stable equilibrium of an optimal level of capital the structure of distribution of income is a stable and hence α is a stable income distributional parameter. Then, given the social attitude toward saving from different income types we have:

$$\alpha = \frac{1 - S_c}{S_w},\; S_w \ne 0 \tag{3.8.5}$$

$$\mathbb{S} = \prod = \dot{K} \text{ if } S_w = (1 - S_c)\tilde{\mu} \tag{3.8.6}$$

or

$$\mathbb{S} = \prod = \dot{K},\; \text{if } \prod = \frac{S_w}{1 - S_c} W \tag{3.8.7a)}$$

and

$$\frac{S_w}{1 - S_c} = \frac{\prod}{W} \tag{3.8.7b}$$

In other words, the satisfaction of conditions of savings-investment equality depends on the relative income shares of profit to aggregate wage, and propensity to save out of these income types.

A third case where the value of aggregate savings is equal to aggregate profit may be specified: where all profits are spent and the required finance to support investment comes from wages. In this case, the total savings out of wage income must be equal to total profit if the stock-flow equilibrium path as well as effective demand are to be maintained, and equivalence of the value of profit is to be ploughed back as productive investment. Thus

$$\mathbb{S} = S_w W = \prod \tag{3.8.8}$$

and

$$(\frac{S_w}{1 + S_w})Q = \prod \qquad (3.8.9)$$

and hence

$$\frac{S_w}{1 + S_w} = \frac{\prod}{Q}. \qquad (3.8.10)$$

where the profit share is computed with the knowledge of propensity to save from wage income.

In this neo-Keynesian framework, the method of fixprice is analytically central. On the optimal path of capital equilibrium, the rate of profit is maximum, and aggregate profit is equal to aggregate investment, which is equal to aggregate savings. In such an equilibrium path effective demand is ensured. It is by this capital equilibrium that distribution of income is computed, when we know social savings psychology over different income types. Given the conditions that savings and investment on the aggregate are equal on the path of capital equilibrium, we may now strengthen the logic of the stability of the equilibrium and the adjustment needed when the system is out of it.

A need for adjustment mechanism arises on three logical grounds of disparity between (1) investment and profit; (2) profit and savings; and (3) investment and savings, on the aggregate. We have analyzed the situation when investment-profit disparity occurs. This may be connected to conditions of inventory accumulation, real savings and production synchronization required to maintain the system on the capital equilibrium path. Suppose that aggregate savings is different from aggregate profit. In this respect, we may examine alternative capital equilibrium paths for conditions that are responsible for making the rate of savings diverge from the rate of profit and hence the rate of capital accumulation. We may thus use these conditions to specify the adjustment dynamics.

When aggregate savings is greater (less) than aggregate profit $[\mathbb{S} > \prod (\mathbb{S} < \prod)]$, we have two situations to examine. One situation involves the condition of production synchronization, and the other involves conditions of income distribution, both of which may lead to the lack of effective demand. From equation (3.8.1a) two inequalities involving disparities in production synchronization and income distribution may be derived as:

$$C_2 - C_1 \begin{cases} > 0 & \text{if } \mathbb{S} > \prod \\ < 0 & \text{if } \mathbb{S} < \prod \end{cases} \qquad (3.8.11)$$

and

$$\frac{\prod}{W} \begin{cases} < \dfrac{S_w}{1 - S_c} & \text{if } \mathbb{S} > \prod \\ > \dfrac{S_w}{1 - S_c} & \text{if } \mathbb{S} < \prod \end{cases} \qquad (3.8.12)$$

43

Equation (3.8.11) defines a situation where the production of consumer goods exceeds (falls short of) the effective demand. Alternatively, we may view the macroeconomic system in terms of investment goods production relative to production expectation under current savings possibilities, where less (more) investment goods are produced.

Inventories of consumer goods accumulate (drop) due to the failure of producers to synchronize correctly production between consumer goods and investment goods relative to effective demand and the given income distribution. The failure of production synchronization is due to a situation where profit expectations are too high (low) in the consumer goods sector and too low (high) in investment goods sector, given the path of income distribution. In other words, profit expectations are incompatible with the realization of profit in equation (3.2.3) given the income distribution of equation (3.2.4). Profit expectations at the fixprice will be adjusted to realization, such that production of consumer goods will match effective demand, where inventories are eliminated with $C_2 = C_1$ and $\prod = \mathbb{S}$. The implication is such that adjustments of inventories motivated by expectational disequilibria will lead to a reduction (increase) in the production of consumer (investment) goods when aggregate savings exceeds aggregate profit. Similarly, an increase (reduction) in consumer (investment) goods production will take place when aggregate savings is less (greater) than aggregate profit, given the path of income distribution.

An alternative analysis may be conducted by examining conditions of the income distribution path that fail to produce a savings path that will support the path of capital equilibrium on the aggregate, given that production is well synchronized. It is observed from equations (3.8.11) and (3.8.12) that the fulfillment of conditions of production synchronization also implies that the income distribution path is generating a savings path that is supporting the path of equilibrium capital, at the given data. Since the propensities to save of income types (S_w and S_c) are given constants and the path of profit is consistent with net investment, the mechanism of adjustment to bring the aggregate savings into line with profit and investment is through changes in the aggregate wage bill. Changes in production synchronization imply changes in the value of aggregate wage, as production and inventories are adjusted between sectors of consumer and investment goods and profit expectations are aligned with the actual. The following working definitions are essential to the equalibrium capital accumulation process.

Definition 3.8.1

The economic system $\mathbb{S}^*$ is said to be in a Keynesian equilibrium if aggregate investment is equal to aggregate savings, that is, $\mathbb{S} = \dot{K}$.

Definition 3.8.2

The economic system, $\mathbb{S}^*$, is said to be in a neo-Keynesian equilibrium in the long run if aggregate saving equals aggregate investment and the rate of investment is equal to the rate of profit on the accumulated capital.

Proposition 3.8.1

Among all neo-Keynesian equilibrium paths of capital accumulation in a closed economy, the highest rate of accumulation, on the aggregate, is attained and sustained by aggregate savings when the rate of profit is maximum and is equal to the rate of savings, all of which are normalized by the accumulated capital. It is the optimal equilibrium path of capital accumulation.

Proposition 3.8.2

The neo-Keynesian optimal equilibrium path is on the path of Robinsonian golden age if full employment of labor is supported.

In this neo-Keynesian framework, with fixprice, the relative shares of income distribution are computed at the equilibrium. From equation (3.8.7.b) we have the ration of net profit to wages. Profit is computed in equilibrium, where wages emerge as residual in the short run, in addition to the condition that in the long run the aggregate profit being generated on the optimal accumulation path is such that consumption out of profit is exactly equal to savings that flow from wages, where $S_w W = (1 - S_c) \prod$ (see also [75] [346] [554] [561]).

3.9 SUMMING UP

To sum up, the neo-Keynesian theory of optimal aggregate capital accumulation may be developed by considering an interdependent relationship among profit, the level of capital stock and the rate at which this level is changing for the given level of labor force. The system is closed. Firms are myopic in "maximizing profit" at each point of time. The driving force of accumulation is the profit motive, in the sense that firms will always use the most profitable technique available. The optimal aggregate capital accumulation is reached when the rate of profit is maximum and equal to the rate of aggregate capital accumulation, and savings are completely invested. Furthermore, the volume of aggregate saving is equal to the volume of aggregate profit, irrespective of societal savings behavior towards different income types. Both the volume of aggregate savings and profit are equal to the volume of aggregate investment that generates them, in a manner that maintains effective demand.

By considering such an interdependent relationship within the neo-Keynesian framework, output at each point of time is defined in a value-added, and measured in cost-unit, sense. Given the aggregate value added in the economy, its distribution between wages and profits is taken to be institutionally determined at each time point. The system is such that the initial conditions will allow the optimal aggregate capital to be reached. The complete model may be represented as:

$$\rho(t) = F(\frac{\dot{K}}{K}, 1) = \psi(\xi), \ \psi' > 0, \ \psi'' < 0 \qquad (3.9.1)$$

$$\xi(t) = G(\frac{\prod}{K}, 1) = \phi(\rho), \ \phi' > 0, \ \phi'' < 0 \qquad (3.9.2)$$

$$E(\xi) = [\psi(\xi) - \phi^{-1}(\xi)] = 0 \qquad (3.9.3)$$

$$\rho^* = \xi^* \qquad (3.9.4)$$

Side conditions are:

$$\dot{K} = \prod = \mathbb{S}, \ \text{if} \ \left(\frac{S_w}{1 - S_c}\right) W \qquad (3.9.5)$$

$$Q(t) = \min[\frac{K(t)}{\gamma_1}, \frac{L(t)}{\gamma_2}] \qquad (3.9.6)$$

$$Q(t) = W(t) + \prod(t) \qquad (3.9.7)$$

$$\mathbb{S}(t) = S_w W + \mathbb{S}_c \prod \qquad (3.9.8)$$

$$\rho^* = \xi^* = \sigma^* \qquad (3.9.9)$$

Taken together, these conditions will determine the levels of optimal aggregate capital, output potential, employment, corresponding optimal profit rate, optimal rate of capital accumulation that generates and maintains such an optimal profit rate for a given set of market data, labor force, social conditions of income distribution and the consumption habits of the population. The nature of the savings function (3.9.8) will be altered if we assume two social classes of workers and capitalists, in such a way that workers and capitalists receive both wage and profit incomes as groups that their propensities vary according to income type. We shall deal with this case later on.

3.10 EFFICIENCY NORMS AND OPTIMAL CAPITAL-INVESTMENT POLICIES

We have examined the role of optimal rate of profit in the capital accumulation process and how such an optimal rate relates to the rates of optimal investment and savings that will support the optimal path of accumulation. We shall now examine the relationship between the optimal profit rate at the equilibrium path and the efficiency norms of aggregate investment and capital, on the basis of which the system of capital accumulation moves toward the preferred destination at the margin. To do so, we shall connect the Keynesian concepts of marginal efficiencies of investment and capital to the optimal capital accumulation process. Two important questions arise in this process of theoretical examination. Do the marginal efficiency of investment (meI) and marginal efficiency of capital (meK) relate to one other? A second question arises as to whether both concepts relate to the determination of the level of optimal aggregate capital stock and to the speed with which it is updated through aggregate investment when the first question has been answered.

These questions bring into focus a number of theoretical difficulties when the marginal concepts are related to the capital accumulation process in a manner that demands defining the role and measurements of these concepts [56], [230] [254] [329] [254] [445] [446].

To examine the theoretical and operational difficulties of these marginal concepts, let $\tilde{C}(t)$ be the replacement cost of accumulated capital; and $q(t)$ the replacement cost of the current aggregate investment. In a continuous analysis the meK and meI may be specified as:

$$\tilde{C}(t) = \int_0^\infty R(K,t)e^{-Mt}dt \qquad (3.10.1)$$

$$q(t) = \int_0^\infty \hat{R}(\dot{K},t)e^{-mt}dt \qquad (3.10.2)$$

where $M = meK$, $meI = m$, $t = time$, $R(K,t)$ is the profit that is being generated by the accumulated capital and $\hat{R}(\dot{K},t)$ is the profit that is being generated and maintained by new aggregate investment

A number of interesting things are observable about the specification of equation (3.10.1) and (3.10.2). For each K there is at least one M such that the condition (3.10.1) holds. Similarly, for each $\dot{K}$ we can find at least one m such that there is at least one M such that the condition (3.10.1) holds. We can, therefore, define two different sets whose elements appear in pairs as:

$$\mathbb{M} = \{(K,M) \,|\tilde{C}(t) = \int_0^\infty R(K,t)e^{-Mt}\,dt\} \qquad (3.10.3)$$

$$\mathbb{D} = \{(\dot{K},m) \,|q(t) = \int_0^\infty R(\dot{K},t)e^{-mt}\,dt\} \qquad (3.10.4)$$

Equation (3.10.3) defines a schedule of meK, while equation (3.10.4) defines a schedule of meI. Equations (3.10.3) and (3.10.4) may both be used to specify either the dynamic or static processes regarding capital accumulation decisions. When the specification is used for dynamic process, the change is interpreted as taking place over time according to the previous decisions to accumulate, as the underlying data alters over-time. When, on the other hand, the specification is used for a static process, a thought experiment is involved as to the behavior of current capital accumulation decisions as the current underlying data alters in the existing state, or alternative production plans are compared with each other in the same state.

Within Keynes' logical framework, [374], a difficulty arises as to whether the demand for investment schedule is interpreted in the sense of equation (3.10.3) or (3.10.4). This difficulty is seen in Keynes' statement:

> We can then aggregate the schedules for all the different types of capital, so as to provide a schedule relating the rate of *aggregate investment* to the corresponding marginal efficiency of *capital* in general which that rate of investment will establish. We shall call this the investment demand-schedule, or, alternatively, the schedule of the marginal efficiency of capital. [374, p. 136]

In the Keynes framework no distinction is made between equations (3.10.1) and (3.10.2). In fact, the concept of marginal efficiency of investment was not introduced, it was implicitly assumed to be the same as marginal efficiency of capital. There are no *a priori* reasons for the sets M and D to be equal. There might, however, be a set of conditions for which marginal efficiency of capital may just be equal to the marginal efficiency of investment, and hence the demand for capital stands in some strict relation to the demand for investment. These conditions will be examined within the neo-Keynesian framework.

Furthermore, if $M[m]$, corresponding to $K(t)[\dot{K}]$, is to change to a new level that corresponds to a new level of capital (net investment), $K(t+\tau)[\dot{K}(t+\theta)]$, then it must be the case that a signal for change is provided in the logic of decision making and analysis. Similarly, if the net revenue flows and replacement costs are given for each state of $K(t)$ and $\dot{K}(t)$, there are M and m such that equations (3.10.3) and (3.10.4) are defined. The M and m can be obtained by solving the respective equation. A theoretical difficulty arises: how do we know that M and m from the solutions are attainable through a decision process? In order for these M and m to be attainable, some process of search implied in a change must be established regarding the whole accumulation process. This explicit establishment of a signal for capital-decision adjustment when the underlying data changes is required. Some implied adjustment is suggested by Keynes: "the rate of investment will be pushed to the point on the investment demand-schedule where the marginal efficiency of capital in general is equal to the market rate of interest," [374, p. 136]. This implied adjustment must originate from the basic structure of the capital accumulation process.

To resolve these theoretical and empirical difficulties, establish an automatic signal for adjustment, and make the meK and meI measurably useful and relevant to the dynamics of accumulation within the neo-Keynesian framework, it is useful to specify the following definitions.

Definition 3.10.1

The marginal efficiency of capital, meK, is that rate of profit over accumulated capital which would make the present value of net revenue flow just equal the replacement cost of the accumulated aggregate capital. That is,

$$meK = M = \prod(t)/K(t) = \rho(t)$$

and hence

$$\tilde{C}(t) = \int\limits_0^\infty R(K,\tau)e^{-(\prod /K)t}dt$$

It may also be called the "capital efficiency norm."

Definition 3.10.2

The marginal efficiency of investment meI is that rate of increased profit over new investment which will make the present value of the flow of net-revenue increased just equal to the replacement cost of such aggregate net investment. That is,

$$meI = m = \dot{\prod}/\dot{K}$$

and hence

$$q(t) = \int\limits_t^\infty R(K,\tau)e^{-(\dot{\prod} /\dot{K})\tau}d\tau$$

It may also be called the "investment efficiency norm."

From the above definitions, the meK is identified with the profit rate induced and maintained by the accumulated capital per unit of time. The meI is identified with the increase in profit per unit of investment that generates it and is maintained by it. These two efficiency norms are not necessarily equal in the various states of the system. We may ask whether there are conditions under which the two may be equal.

To answer this question, let us suppose that capital-investment decisions are myopic over the range of decision time. Profit is maximized at each point of time, in neo-Keynesian sense in that the most profitable technique is always chosen. In such a myopic decision process, the decision to invest and accumulate at each point of time is revised against the set of currently underlying data, which contains the preceding ones, and as the current profit rate is weighed against the previous rate and compared to the expected, and previously held expectations are checked against current and expected future experiences. If every producer is following a path of profit-optimizing behavior, subject to technology of production and structure of income distribution, it is not absurd to assume that the system as a whole follows such a behavior.

Under such a social condition, we shall interpret the profit-maximizing behavior to mean not the maximization of the volume of profit but the maximization of the profit rate over the accumulated capital. The optimal level of aggregate capital is that level which corresponds to the maximum profit rate. The maximum profit rate is reached when

$$\dot{\rho} = \frac{\Pi}{K} \left(\frac{\dot{\Pi}}{\Pi} - \frac{\dot{K}}{K} \right) = 0 \tag{3.10.5}$$

Since $\Pi / K \neq 0$, we obtain:

$$\frac{\dot{\Pi}}{\Pi} = \frac{\dot{K}}{K} \tag{3.10.6}$$

and

$$\frac{\dot{\Pi}}{\dot{K}} = \frac{\Pi}{K} \tag{3.10.7}$$

The aggregate capital-investment policies are optimal when the meK is equal to meI. Within this neo-Keynesian framework, Professor Lerner's specification of meK as equal to meI when $\dot{K} = 0$ in the long run [446b] for a growing economy is inconsistent. For a growing economy, the meK is equal to the meI when the profit rate is maximum (i.e., $\dot{\rho} = 0$).

A theoretical problem arises in Professor Lerner's case. In an arbitrary stationary state, net investment is zero; however, it is not necessarily the case that $meK = meI$. The current system of the neo-Keynesian logic suggests that the sufficient condition for the meK to be equal to the meI in a growing economy is that the rate of profit on aggregate capital is optimal, not that the capital stock has stopped growing. The structure may be viewed in terms of steady states. From equation (3.10.7) and definitions (3.10.1) and (3.10.2) we may specify the following set:

$$\mathbb{D} \cap \mathbb{M} = \left\{ (K, \dot{K}, \hat{\rho}, t) \, \middle| \, \begin{array}{c} \tilde{C}(t) = \int_t^\infty R(K, \tau) e^{-\hat{\rho}\tau} \, d\tau \\ \text{and} \\ q(t) = \int_t^\infty \hat{R}(\dot{K}, \tau) e^{-\hat{\rho}\tau} \, d\tau \end{array} \right\} \tag{3.10.8}$$

and that $\mathbb{D} \cap \mathbb{M} \neq \phi$. Furthermore, it may be observed that an economic system may be stagnating with respect to its level of capital stock, where $\dot{K} = 0$, while the level of aggregate capital stock is suboptimal. These difficulties are resolved within the neo-Keynesian framework.

In the Keynesian framework, the economy is said to be optimal with respect to its investment policy when the meI is equal to the rate of interest, r, chargeable on loanable real funds that may be used to finance the investment that maintains the growing capital stock. Such an aggregate rate of interest may be defined as the ratio of total interest cost, H, over the total volume of borrowed funds, B. That is

$$r = \frac{H}{B} \tag{3.10.9}$$

The interest expense is viewed in this analysis as the cost of distributing real finance from surplus spenders to deficit spenders, as capital accumulates and the rate of profit is checked against its cost of finance in the closed system. In the neo-Keynesian framework that we have presented here, the economy is said to be optimal with respect to its growing capital stock if the rate at which capital accumulates $(\dot{K}/K)$ is just equal to the rate of profit $(\prod/K)$, meK, that is being induced and maintained by it. It is said to be optimal with respect to its aggregate investment policy when the meK is just equal to the meI which is induced and maintained by additional new investments. All these optimalities may be both short-run and partial.

The economy is said to be in a "complete" equilibrium with respect to its capital-investment policies and savings decisions, given the underlying data, if not only the rate of accumulation $(\dot{K}/K)$ is equal to the rate of profit on the accumulated capital $(\prod/K = meK)$ but both are equal to the increased profit per unit of investment $(\prod/\dot{K} = meI)$ and the rate of saving $(S/K = \sigma)$ which the economy can generate to support such a rate of capital accumulation. In other words,

$$\frac{\prod}{K} = \frac{\dot{K}}{K} = \frac{\dot{\prod}}{\dot{K}} = \frac{S}{K} \tag{3.10.10}$$

and $\dot{\omega} = 0$ where $\omega = \frac{W}{K}$. At the optimal rate of profit not only is the aggregate capital and investment policies optimal but the rate of savings that the economy is generating to support and maintain the attained path is just right. The following side conditions are derivable:

$$\frac{\dot{S}}{\dot{K}} = \frac{S}{K} = \frac{\dot{S}}{S} = \frac{\dot{\prod}}{\prod} = \frac{\dot{K}}{K} \tag{3.10.11}$$

A number of things are observable about equations (3.10.10) and (3.10.11). The condition $S/K = \dot{K}/K = \prod/K$ suggests that the optimal level of accumulated capital must generate enough profit and savings to support and maintain it in its optimal state. The statement $\dot{S}/\dot{K} = \prod/\dot{K}$ implied in equations (3.10.10) and (3.10.11) suggests that the optimal investment must bring in enough increased savings and profit to support it. In this optimal state, capital accumulation is taking place at the same rate as the rates of profit and savings. These conditions may be illustrated by a system of phase diagrams in Figure 3.10.1, where $\omega = W/Q$.

So far we have presented the picture of accumulation as if there were a process that allows the unused aggregate social income to accumulate as savings, and furthermore, an established process that allows such aggregate savings to be transformed into investment. In fact, we shall assume that these processes exist and work through a configuration of social "institutions." Such a configuration of social institutions that allows savings to be generated to support aggregate investment activities will be referred to as the "financial sector." The accumulated savings in the financial sector are thus equal to the total social savings. In order to acquire the right to use part or all of the social savings for financing investment, a rate of interest, r, is chargeable. If H is the total interest cost for a borrowed amount, B, then the rate of interest is just as defined in equation (3.10.9). At any optimal state of the system we observe that

$$B \leq S \equiv \prod \tag{3.10.12}$$

If the optimal investment is completely financed from the total social saving it must be the case that $B = S$ and hence

$$r = \frac{H}{S} \tag{3.10.13}$$

If the economic system is functioning at its optimal level of capital accumulation, it must also be the case that investment is generating enough increased profit $(\dot{\prod})$ to just cover the interest cost. Hence

$$r = \frac{H}{S} = \frac{\dot{\prod}}{\dot{K}} \tag{3.10.14}$$

At complete equilibrium in the neo-Keynesian sense, $S = \dot{K}$ and $\prod = \dot{S}$. Hence

$$r = \frac{\dot{\prod}}{\dot{K}} = \frac{\dot{S}}{S} = \frac{\prod}{K} = \frac{\dot{K}}{K} \tag{3.10.15}$$

and

$$r = \rho^* = \xi^* = meK = meI \tag{3.10.16}$$

In other words, at the optimal capital-investment policies, the meK is not only equal to the meI but is equal to the rate of interest, r, at which the economy can borrow from within to support such accumulation, if the finance must be acquired. The rate of interest may be taken to be established by a market system or other system of intertemporal preferences. The relationships between the neoclassical marginal product of capital and the Keynesian marginal efficiencies will be explored in details in Chapter 7.

Figure 3.10.1
Phase Diagram of *meI, meK*, Rates of Accumulation, Savings and Profit

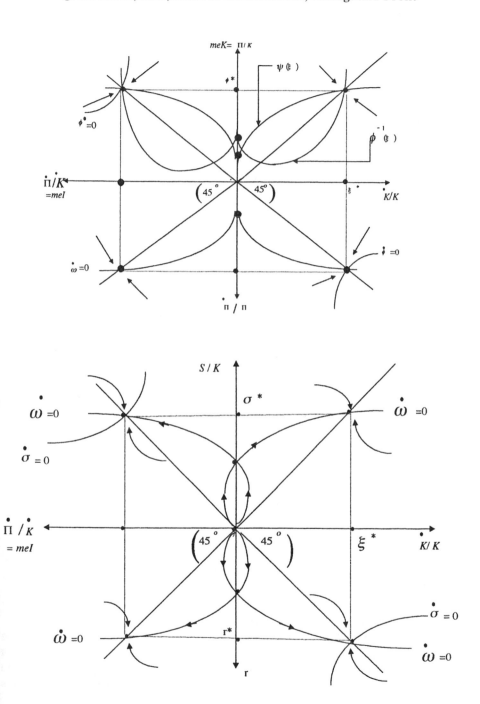

53

Chapter 4

The Theory of Aggregate Investment Behavior in a Closed Economy

From the model of the neo-Keynesian aggregate optimal capital accumulation, we obtain quantities that are related to each other in specific ways that are consistent with the optimal level of aggregate capital and corresponding potential aggregate output at each relevant time point. Thus the economic system is on its optimal path when the savings-investment-equality constraint is satisfied on the transient process and the rate of profit is optimal. Whether the optimal path can be maintained or not when it is reached will depend on the subsequent aggregate investment policy. Such an aggregate investment policy, given the initial conditions, also determines whether the optimal trajectory can be reached or not. It also determines the speed to which the system moves to the optimal path when it starts from a suboptimal position.

The problem of the neo-Keynesian theory of aggregate investment is to construct a function of an aggregate investment demand that will define the transient process among optimal positions; to examine the conditions that will allow the maintenance of the system on the optimal path through an optimal investment policy when it is reached; and to examine the effects of parameter variations on the optimal investment policy due to changes in the underlying data.

The construction of an aggregate investment demand functions is a delicate one, since a number of them can be constructed, depending on the description of the economic system and the conditions imposed. Some of these aggregate investment demand functions may not directly relate to the rate of interest, depending on the concept of the interest rate and its measurement used. We shall thus impose from the onset the condition that the level of aggregate capital of the previous state is always maintained. In this situation, even if new investments are not undertaken, we must have total aggregate investment, $I(t)$, in that state to be just equal to replacement. For a straight-line depreciation with constant δ we can then write

$$I(t) = \delta K(t) \tag{4.1}$$

4.1 A GENERAL OPTIMAL AGGREGATE INVESTMENT POLICY

In general, the theory of aggregate investment may proceed from the hypothesis that the optimal path of aggregate capital accumulation, given the initial conditions, can be reached. At each stage of the accumulation process we may write

$$\dot{K} = (\xi/\rho) \prod \tag{4.1.1}$$

Thus the expected net aggregate investment is some multiple of the expected profit being generated by the current level of accumulated capital. The proportion is specified by the ratio of actual rate of accumulation to profit, where such ratio is computed at each time point. If the actual rates of profit and accumulation tend to be equal, firms will find themselves in a state where the value of aggregate investment is just equal to the profit being generated by the accumulated capital. It does not imply that all profits are being reinvested. If the system is such that the rate of accumulation is equal to the rate of savings over capital and all profits are saved while all wages are spent, not only is the expected net investment equal to the aggregate real profit but both are equal to the total real social savings is being generated in the system. This is the steady-state path, where all relevant accumulation variables are growing at a constant rate. It may also be viewed as a long-run dynamic equilibrium path, but that is not necessarily the case.

In the short run, we may algebraically combine equations (3.3.6) and (3.3.7) to obtain

$$\xi = \phi(\rho) - \psi(\xi) + \rho \tag{4.1.2}$$

The investment path defined in equation (4.1.1) may then be described by substitution of equation (4.1.2) in (4.1.1) as:

$$\dot{K} = \frac{[\phi(\rho) + \rho - \psi(\xi)]}{\rho} \prod(t) \tag{4.1.3a}$$

Let

$$D(\rho, \xi) = \frac{\phi(\rho) + \rho - \psi(\xi)}{\rho} \tag{4.1.3b}$$

We may then write equation (4.1.3b) compactly as

$$\dot{K} = D(\rho, \xi) \prod(t) \tag{4.1.4}$$

where

$$D(\rho, \xi) \begin{cases} = 1, & \text{on the equilibrium path} \\ \gtrless 1, & \text{for all other states} \end{cases} \tag{4.1.5}$$

The D-function has an interesting economic interpretation. As an economic calculus to an economic decision problem, it is a response function that allows new investment to be adjusted to the profit that the accumulated capital is generating. It states that the response of aggregate investment to the current profit in terms of "plowing back" depends on the realized and expected rates of accumulation and profits. Furthermore, it states that in the long run the economic system is in a dynamic equilibrium not only when the expected rates of accumulation and profit are equalized and realized but when both are equal to the rate of profit over net investment, in such a way that expected saving is equal to the expected new investment being generated and maintained by the accumulation process. The response function and the corresponding adjustment process work through signals provided by the disparities among expected and actual profit rates, leading to responses of new investment activity, which then affects the expected rate of capital accumulation and the current level of capital.

In this accumulation process, the aggregate savings as a constraint on the system takes effect, given the distribution of income, which is assumed to be institutionally determined. The accumulation process may thus be linked to the savings condition as specified by equations (3.8.3), (4.1.3) and (4.1.5) to obtain a net investment function as

$$\dot{K} = [\frac{\phi(\rho) + \rho - \psi(\xi)}{(\alpha S_w + S_c)\rho}] \mathbb{S}(t) \tag{4.1.6}$$

or

$$\dot{K} = [\frac{D(\rho, \xi)}{\alpha S_w + S_c}] \mathbb{S}(t) \tag{4.1.7}$$

On the assumption of a constant δ—depreciation of the level of capital due to use, and that such depreciation is always replaced to maintain the level of capital stock, the path of aggregate investment may be obtained from the identity

$$I(t) = \dot{K} + \delta K(t) \tag{4.1.8}$$

and hence

$$I(t) = D(\xi, \rho) \prod(t) + \delta K(t) \tag{4.1.9}$$

or

$$I(t) + \frac{D(\xi, \rho)}{\alpha S_w + S_c} \mathbb{S}(t) + \delta K(t) \tag{4.1.10}$$

Some interesting observations can be made about the D-function. The function is polynomial in ξ and ρ. It is homogeneous to the degree zero in its augments. In other words, the response function is illusion-free in the meaningful sense that if the inputs are changed by the same constant the response of aggregate investment will not alter. The function is continuous and differential in its entire domain.

Let us suppose that $K(t)$ is a piecewise differentiable function of time and that new aggregate investment plans are being considered at the current time, t. Then for all $\tau < t$ we may write the accumulated aggregate capital as

$$K(t) = \int_0^t \dot{K}(\tau; t) d\tau \qquad (4.1.11)$$

By combining equations (4.1.11), (4.1.9) and (4.1.10) we obtain the time path of gross investment as either

$$I(t) = D(\rho, \xi)[\prod(t) + \delta \int_0^t \prod(\tau; t) d\tau] \qquad (4.1.12)$$

or

$$I(t) = \frac{D(\rho, \xi)}{S_w + S_c} [\mathbb{S}(t) + \delta \int_0^t \mathbb{S}(\tau; t) d\tau] \qquad (4.1.13)$$

Equation (4.1.12) suggests that gross investment plans depend on expected current profit, the time path of past history of realized profit expectations and the stimulus response provided by the differences between actual and expected profit rates. Alternatively, equation (4.1.13) suggests that the time path of aggregate investment depends on expected current savings being generated by current accumulation, the time path of past history of realized savings, and normalized response defined by the income distribution parameters, savings propensities and the differences between actual and expected profits. All the relevant variables and parameters are computed on the basis of current data.

It may easily be observed that in the dynamic equilibrium $D(\rho, \xi) = 1$, and hence a value equals to profits must be completely reinvested if the system is to stay on the optimal course. The income distribution must be such that given the social attitude toward saving, aggregate savings generated in the system are just equal to profits. If all profits are saved and all wage income is spent, the savings-equality constraint will be met irrespective of the social distribution of income, to the extent that all profits are reinvested. If, on the other hand, not all profits are saved and not all wages are spent, the income distribution must be such that the total savings must be equal to the total profit. Given the profit flow, changes in differential propensity to save must be compensated for by changes in the structure of income distribution, if the system is to stay on the equilibrium path. We shall now examine the contributions made by Robinson, Kaldor, Pasinetti and others within the general framework outlined here.

4.2 JOAN ROBINSON AND OPTIMAL INVESTMENT POLICY

Let us now examine the essentials of Robinsonian system of investment and capital accumulation within the general neo-Keynsian framework. In the Robinsonian system, firms calculate the expected rate of profit on investment on the basis of current data. The central mechanism of the process is the desire of firms to accumulate. The decision to accumulate is assumed to be influenced by the expected rate of profit. Thus the greater the rate of profit that firms, on the aggregate, expect on investment, the higher the rate of investment. When the existing stock of accumulated capital is valued on the basis of the same rate of profit, the firms' plans may be expressed as depending aggregatively on the rate of accumulation. The mechanism is such that the accumulated capital determines the level of profit, which then determines the expected profit rate on investment at a given expectation. The rate of profit expected, on the other hand, determines the rate of accumulation. The mechanism is such that an interdependent relation is induced. In this respect, disparities among actual and expected values generate the law of motion that propels the accumulation process forward. The mechanism of accumulation process in the Robinsonian system is such that the profit function may be written as [589] [590] [596]:

$$\prod = a_0 + a_1 \dot{K} \qquad (4.2.1)$$

The intensity form may be written as

$$\rho(t) = \alpha_0 + \alpha_1\,\xi(t) \qquad (4.2.2)$$

where $\alpha_0 = a_0/K$ and $\alpha_0, \alpha_1 > 0$. The simultaneous system for optimal capital may thus be written as

$$\rho(t) = \alpha_0 + \alpha_1\xi(t) \qquad (4.2.3a)$$

$$\xi(t) = G(\rho, 1) = \phi(\rho) \qquad (4.2.3b)$$

We may solve the system of equations (4.2.3a) and (4.2.3b) to obtain the optimal capital stock. First we observe that α_0 is the autonomously expected minimum rate of profit without investment. The α_1 is expectational adjustment of the rate of profit to increases in the rate of accumulation. Secondly, the solution may be illustrated graphically as in Figure 4.2.1.

The equilibrium at B in Figure 4.2.1 is similar, in terms of structure and economic interpretation, to that in Figure 3.6.1. At point B, aggregate level of capital is at its optimal level. Both the rates of profit and accumulation are optimal at state B. Things are slightly different at state E in Figure 4.2.1, where the rate at which profit changes with increasing new investment is just equal to the rate of accumulation induced by the expected current rate of profit. In this state, expectations about the rate of profit relative to those about the current rate of accumulation are not in line with the current experience at the given data. In fact, $\prod/\dot{K} = d\prod/d\dot{K} = \alpha_1 < 1$. In other words, the current level of capital is not generating enough profit to support the current new investment decision in this state. The indication is that the new aggregate investment decisions taking place in this state cannot be maintained by the profit flow that is being generated by the accumulated capital.

Figure 4.2.1
A Phase Geometry of Robinsonian System of Aggregate Capital Accumulation

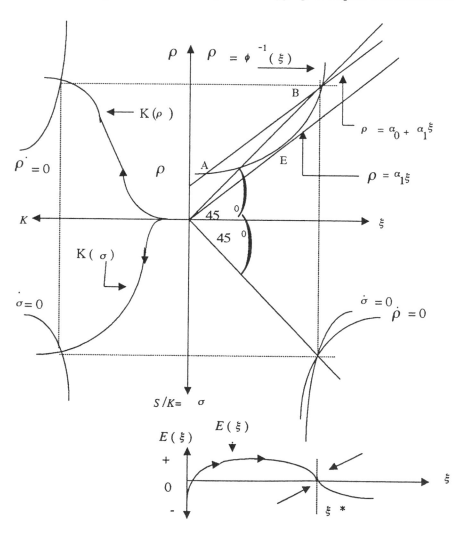

There will then be a tendency toward a revision in the calculations of expectations. This may result in either a continual rotation or a continual upward shift of $\rho(t) = \alpha_1\xi(t)$. This will induce the expected accumulation to be in line with the expected profit, conditional on the underlying data. The process will continue until the optimal aggregate level of capital is reached for the given underlying data. The optimal investment process may be described by combining equations (4.2.3a and b) (4.2.3), (4.1.9) and (4.1.11), to obtain

$$I(t) = [\frac{\rho + \phi(\rho) - \alpha_0}{(\alpha_1 + 1)\rho}][\prod(t) + \delta\int_0^t\prod(\tau;t)d\tau] \qquad (4.2.4)$$

The response function is thus specified as:

$$D(\rho,\xi) = \frac{\rho + \psi(\rho) - \alpha_0}{(\alpha_1 + 1)\rho} \qquad (4.2.5)$$

In the dynamic equilibrium, when expectations are always realized, $\alpha_0 = 0$, $\rho = \phi(\rho)$ and $\alpha_1 = 1 = D(\rho,\xi)$. In this state we have an instantaneous adjustment. In the Robinsonian system, where all wages are consumed and all profits are saved, the complete neo-Keynesian equilibrium is ensured. The rates of profit, savings and investment are equalized. The meK and meI are also equal. In this Robinsonian system the analysis of effects of changes in social propensity to save is not necessary, since all profits are always saved. The most important parameter is the structure of income distribution. Thus changing the structure of income distribution will alter the optimal path of aggregate accumulation.

4.3 NICHOLAS KALDOR AND
THE OPTIMAL INVESTMENT POLICY

Kaldor's entry into the neo-Keynsian theory of optimal capital accumulation and investment policy may be abstracted from his essays [346] [347] [352] [353]. It is basically an extension of the Robinsonian system, where the Keynesian apparatus of reason is extended to deal with the problem of income distribution on the accumulation process. Here the principle of the multiplier is viewed in terms of determination of the relation between prices and wages, where the level of output and employment are assumed as given instead of being viewed in terms of determination of level of employment at a given distribution. Thus a dynamic theory is implied where the path of capital accumulation and optimal investment policy is sought and related to the process of income distribution.

When output and employment are given and propensities to save from different income types are known, the distribution of income is determined in the Keynesian equilibrium path, where the profit share in output depends on the proportion of output devoted to investment. The inverse process suggests that the rate of investment depends on the income distribution, given the propensities to save from different income types. These statements are based on Keynesian hypothesis that investment can be treated as independent variable that does not depend on savings propensities. When full employment is assumed, as we have, the Keynesian hypothesis implies that income distribution, viewed in terms of the level of prices and nominal wages, is demand determined.

In the Kaldorian system of accumulation as an extension of the Robinsonian system, the community saves from both work and profit incomes, where work income is distributed to workers and profit income is distributed to capitalists. The savings of the workers can be used in investment financing but do not entitle them either to interest income or a share in capital ownership. The workers' savings also do not entitle them to a share in the profit earnings. The aggregate savings is thus specified as:

$$\mathbb{S}(t) = (S_c - S_w) \prod(t) + S_w Q(t); S_c > S_w, 0 \le S_c, S_w \le 1 \qquad (4.3.1)$$

where $Q = W + \prod$. The condition $S_c > S_w$ relates to the stability of the equilibrium process. The Keynesian equilibrium requires that aggregate savings is just equal to aggregate new investment at the given data. Thus

$$\dot{K} = (S_c - S_w) \prod(t) + S_w Q(t), S_c > S_w, 0 \le S_c, S_w \le 1 \qquad (4.3.2)$$

From equation (4.3.2) we may write the intensity form of accumulation as:

$$\xi(t) = (S_w - S_c)\rho + S_w \nu \qquad (4.3.3)$$

where $\nu = Q/K$ is the output capital ratio, which may be viewed as an overall efficiency norm of productive capital.

The neo-Keynesian optimal capital accumulation process may thus be represented in its intensity form by the following system

$$\left.\begin{array}{rcl} \rho(t) & = & \psi(\xi), \psi(0) > 0 \\[2mm] \xi(t) & = & S_w \nu + (S_c - S_w)\rho(t) \end{array}\right\} \qquad (4.3.4)$$

The equilibrium process for capital states may be specified from (4.3.4) as

$$\rho(t) = \frac{\xi + \psi(\xi) - S_w \nu}{1 + S_c - S_w} \qquad (4.3.5)$$

The rate of profit depends not only on the rate of accumulation that generates and maintains it but also on the overall average capital efficiency at the given data. In the Kaldor's original formulation, investment is given [346]. In this formulation, aggregate investment is simultaneously determined in the system, as an endogenous variable. The solution path defined by equation (4.3.5) may be represented geometrically as in Figure 4.3.1. It is useful to note that when Kaldor's system is compared with that of Robinson, $\alpha_0 = S_w \nu$ and $\alpha_1 = (S_c - S_w)$.

By combining the optimal process, optimal relative to technique, of equation (4.3.5) with equations (4.1.9) and (4.1.11) we may write the optimal investment process as:

$$I(t) = \frac{(1 + S_c - S_w)\xi}{\xi + \psi(\xi) - S_w \nu} [\prod(t) + \delta \int_0^t \prod(\tau; t) d\tau] \qquad (4.3.6)$$

Equation (4.3.6) defines interequilibrium adjustments, and since in the Keynesian equilibrium aggregate savings equals aggregate investment, we can also write

$$I(t) = \frac{(1 + S_c - S_w)\xi}{\xi + \psi(\xi) - S_w\nu}[\mathbb{S}(t) + \delta \int_0^t \mathbb{S}(\tau; t)d\tau] \tag{4.3.7}$$

where aggregate savings is equal to aggregate profit.

Figure 4.3.1
A Phase Geometry of Kaldorian System of Aggregate Capital Accumulation

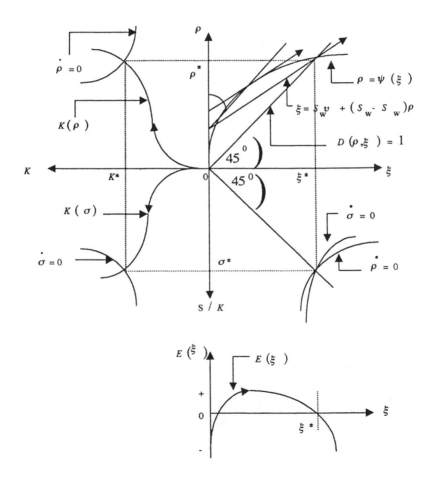

The response function for capital adjustment between equilibria may thus be written as:

$$D(\rho, \xi) = \frac{(1 + S_c - S_w)\xi}{\xi + \psi(\xi) - S_w \nu} \tag{4.3.8}$$

At the state when the level of optimal capital is reached $\rho = \xi = \rho^*$, and hence the response function of equation (4.3.8) becomes

$$D(\rho^*, \xi^*) = \frac{(1 + S_c - S_w)\rho^*}{2\rho^* - S_w \nu} \tag{4.3.9a}$$

or

$$D(\rho^*, \xi^*) = \frac{(1 + S_c - S_w)\xi^*}{2\xi^* - S_w \nu} \tag{4.3.9b}$$

On the equilibrium path, $D(\rho^*, \xi^*) = 1$, and hence

$$\nu^* = \frac{(1 + S_w - S_c)\rho^*}{S_w}, S_w \neq 0 \tag{4.3.10}$$

The optimal aggregate investment policy over the capital equilibrium path, if it is attained, may be written as

$$I(t) = \frac{(1 + S_c - S_w)\rho^*}{2\rho^* - S_w \nu} [\prod(t) + \delta \int_0^t \prod(\tau; t)d\tau] \tag{4.3.11a}$$

An important observation in the optimal investment process is that the capital adjustment process and expectations about profit are affected by the capital efficiency norm, ν. Notice from equation (4.3.11) that there is an instantaneous adjustment if workers do not save and capitalists save all profit. In this case, the overall output capital norm is not response influencing. The optimal investment in this case is

$$I^*(t) = \prod(t) + \delta \int_0^t \prod(\tau; t)d\tau \tag{4.3.11b}$$

where all current profits and accumulated depreciation are reinvested and hence $D(\rho^*, \xi^*) = 1$. In this case, ν^* of equation (4.3.10) is indeterminate.

The Kaldorian system may be viewed as an extension of the Robinsonian system of optimal capital accumulation, as we have pointed out. The difference as presented here lies in the structure of social propensity to save. Furthermore, from the Kaldorian system we can compute the optimal rates of accumulation and profit at the equilibrium. On the path of dynamic equilibrium, $D(\rho^*, \xi^*) = 1$, and hence from equation (4.3.10)

$$
\begin{aligned}
(1 + S_c - S_w)\rho^* &= 2\rho^* - S_w \nu \\
S_w \nu &= (1 + S_w - S_c)\rho^* \\
\Rightarrow \rho^* &= \frac{S_w \nu}{1 + S_w - S_c}, S_w \neq 0 \text{ and } S_c \neq 1
\end{aligned} \tag{4.3.12}
$$

By substituting equation (4.3.12) in (4.3.5) we can immediately can write

$$\frac{S_w \nu}{1 + S_w - S_c} = \frac{2\xi - S_w \nu}{1 + S_c - S_w}$$

$$\Rightarrow \xi^* = \frac{S_w \nu}{1 + S_w - S_c}, \quad S_w \neq 0$$

(4.3.13)

From equations (4.3.12) and (4.3.13) we can readily compute the optimal rates of accumulation and profit, if we know the output-capital ratio. In the equilibrium states, where aggregate investment instantaneously responds to profit, the rates of profit and accumulation depend on the overall capital efficiency, given the social distribution of income and societal attitude toward saving. Indirectly, therefore, profit and accumulation rates depend on effective demand. The degree of stability of equilibrium is determined by the difference between the marginal propensities to save from different income types $(S_w - S_c)$. Implied in equation (4.3.13) is the acceleration principle, where

$$\dot{K} = (\frac{S_w}{1 + S_w - S_c})Q$$

(4.3.14)

Proposition 4.3.1

In Kaldorian system of optimal capital accumulation, the optimal equilibrium implies an equality between the value of consumption out of profit and that of savings out of wages given differential marginal propensities to save out of work income and profit such that $0 < S_w < S_c < 1$ and hence $(1 - S_c) \prod^* = S_w W^*$.

Proof

From equation (4.3.13) we have

$$\prod^* = (\frac{S_w}{1 + S_w - S_c})Q$$

and hence

$$W^* = (\frac{1 - S_c}{1 + S_w - S_c})Q$$

and

$$\frac{\prod^*}{W^*} = \frac{S_w}{1 - S_c}$$

which implies that

$$(1 - S_c) \prod^* = S_w W^* \square$$

Proposition 4.3.2

If the optimal path of capital equilibrium in the Kaldor's system is attained and maintained by a savings-investment process then for any given set of propensities to consume out of income types, total savings is equal to the total profit $(\prod^* = \mathbb{S}^*)$.

Proof

By definition, savings, $\mathbb{S}$, is

$$\mathbb{S}^* = S_w W^* + S_c \prod^*$$

but from proposition (4.3.2) we have

$$S_w W^* = (1 - S_c) \prod^*$$

and by substitution we have

$$\mathbb{S}^* = \prod^* . \square$$

See also the results of Professor Champernowne [73] [74].

4.4 LUIGI PASINETTI AND THE OPTIMAL INVESTMENT POLICY

Let us consider the contribution of Pasinetti [554] [561] [562]. The Pasinettian system is an extension of Kaldorian system, which is also an extension of the Robinsonian system. In It, social income is considered as made up of profit and wage incomes. Workers receive work income, while capitalists receive profit income, according to the structure of distribution of social income. Alternatively, the structure of income distribution is such that some people receive both profit and wage incomes. In the case of the former, the Pasinettian system is such that workers not only save from their work income but receive interest payments at a rate,r, on such savings. Capitalists, on the other hand, consume from their profit income. In the case of the latter, the income recipients consume and save from both income types, with differential propensities to save from income types.

Under the Pasinettian system, the aggregate saving-investment equality constraint that combines accumulation, income distribution and Keynesian equilibrium may be written as:

$$\dot{K} = S_w[rK + (1 - S_c r\mu)Q + (S_c - S_w) \prod] \tag{4.4.1}$$

where $\mu = K/\dot{K}$. The intensity form may be written as

$$\xi = S_w[r + (1 - rS_c\mu)\nu] + (S_c - S_w)\rho \tag{4.4.2}$$

The system of optimal capital accumulation process satisfying the Keynesian savings-investment constraint may thus be written as

$$\left.\begin{array}{rcl} \xi & = & S_w[r + (1 - rS_c\mu)\nu] + (S_c - S_w)\rho \\[2mm] \rho & = & \psi(\xi), \psi(0) > 0 \end{array}\right\} \qquad (4.4.3)$$

The equilibrium process may be induced by solving equations (4.4.3) to obtain:

$$\rho = \frac{\xi + \psi(\xi) - S_w[r + (1 - rS_c\mu)\nu]}{1 + S_c - S_w} \qquad (4.4.4)$$

The geometry of the solution is similar to the one provided in Figure 4.4.1. By combining equation (4.4.4) with equations (4.1.9) and (4.1.11) we may write the corresponding optimal investment process as

$$I(t) = \frac{(1 + S_c - S_w)\xi}{\xi + \psi(\xi) - S_w[r + (1 - rS_c\mu)\nu]}[\textstyle\prod(t)$$

$$+\delta \int_0^t \textstyle\prod(\tau; t)d\tau] \qquad (4.4.5)$$

A number of observations can be made. The response function $D(\rho, \xi)$ may be written as:

$$D(\rho, \xi) = \frac{(1 + S_c - S_w)\xi}{\xi + \psi(\xi) - S_w[r + (1 - rS_c\mu)\nu]} \qquad (4.4.6)$$

The response function in Pasinettian system depends on the signals provided by the share of investment in aggregate output, the differences between the expected and actual rates of accumulation and profit for, given conditions on attitude to save, and the rate of interest paid to workers for the use of their savings.

When the optimal level of aggregate capital is reached, $\xi = \rho = \psi(\xi) = \rho^*$. The response function becomes

$$D(\rho^*, \xi^*) = \frac{(1 + S_c - S_w)\xi^*}{2\xi^* - S_w[r + (1 - rS_c\mu)\nu]} \qquad (4.4.7a)$$

or

$$D(\rho^*, \xi^*) = \frac{(1 + S_c - S_w)\rho^*}{2\rho^* - S_w[r + (1 - rS_c\mu)\nu]} \qquad (4.4.7b)$$

On the dynamic equilibrium path for the advancing economy, $D(\rho^*, \xi^*) = 1$. Hence the optimal output-capital ratio, or the overall norm of production efficiency, is

$$\nu^* = \frac{(1 + S_w - S_c)\xi^* - rS_w}{S_w(1 - rS_c\mu)}, S_w \neq 0 \qquad (4.4.8a)$$

The corresponding rate of interest in the equilibrium states given capital efficiency may be written as:

$$r = \frac{(1 + S_w - S_c)\xi - \nu^* S_w}{S_w - \nu^* \mu S_c} \qquad (4.4.8b)$$

A positive interest rate requires that

$$\frac{\dot{K}}{Q} > \frac{S_w}{1 + S_w - S_c} \qquad (4.4.8c)$$

The rate of profit at this equilibrium state is thus

$$\rho = \frac{S_w r}{1 + S_w - S_c} + \frac{S_w(1 - rS_c\mu)\nu}{1 + S_w - S_c} \qquad (4.4.8d)$$

The optimal investment over the equilibrium path is given as:

$$I(t) = \frac{(1 + S_c - S_w)\xi^*}{2\xi^* - S_w r + (1 - rS_c\mu\nu}[\textstyle\prod(t)$$

$$+ \delta \int_0^t \textstyle\prod(\tau; t)d\tau] \qquad (4.4.9a)$$

A difficulty is encountered in the Pasinettian system. In order to determine the response function, we must have a way of determining interest rate paid on the workers' savings, or the distribution of profit between the share of workers' capital and that owned by the capitalists. This requires a theory of interest-rate determination. We shall not deal with such a theory here. However, in the previous sections we argued that over the optimal path of capital accumulation the rate of interest is equal to the rate of profit: in other words, the rate of profit is the same for all capital, irrespective of the ownership. The optimal output-capital ratio of equation (4.4.8a) therefore becomes

$$\nu^* = \frac{(1 - S_c)\rho^*}{S_w(1 - S_c\mu\rho^*)} \qquad (4.4.9b)$$

or

$$\nu^* = \frac{(1 - S_c)\xi^*}{S_w(1 - S_c\mu\xi^*)} \qquad (4.4.9c)$$

where $\rho^* = \xi^*$ when the rate of interest is assumed to be equal to the rate of profit.

In this case, the optimal capital ratio will depend on either the equilibrium rate of accumulation or the equilibrium rate of profit. Observing that $\mu = K/\dot{K}$ and that at equilibrium $\prod = \dot{K}$, we obtain

$$\nu^* = \frac{\rho^*}{S_w} = \xi^*/S_w \qquad (4.4.10)$$

Thus in equilibrium, with the rate of interest just equal to the rate of profit and the Keynesian savings-investment equality constraint satisfied, the overall optimal norm of production efficiency depends on the optimal rate of accumulation, given the workers' propensity to save from their earned income. On this equilibrium state path the rates of profit and accumulation can be computed. From equation (4.4.8) it is shown that the optimal rates of accumulation and profit are:

$$\xi^* = S_w \nu^* = S_w \left(\frac{Q^*}{K^*} \right) \tag{4.4.11}$$

Substituting equation (4.4.11) in equation (4.4.4), we immediately obtain the optimal rate of profit as

$$\rho^* = S_w \nu^* = \xi^* = r^* \tag{4.4.12}$$

which means that the proportion of total profit consumed is equal to the savings of the workers at the complete equilibrium. It is thus established that over the dynamic equilibrium path of Pasinettian capital accumulation system

$$m\epsilon K^* = m\epsilon I^* = r^* = S_w \nu^* = \rho^* = \xi^* \tag{4.4.13}$$

In the original Pasinetti formulation the rate of profit, in our notation, may be written as

$$\left. \begin{array}{ccc} \rho & = & \xi/S_c \\ \text{or} & & \\ \xi & = & S_c\rho \end{array} \right\}, \; \xi \neq S_w\nu \tag{4.4.14}$$

The condition $\xi \neq S_w\nu$ is inconsistent with our general result, wherein savings-investment constraint is satisfied over the optimal accumulation path. The reason is that the rate of profit path was not considered in the original Pasinettian exposition, which was more an analysis of income distribution than a theory of investment. We observe from the above that the higher the marginal propensity to save from profit (work) income, the greater (lower) is the overall norm of capital effectiveness, and vice versa.

4.5 ROBINSONIAN, KALDORIAN AND PASINETTIAN SYSTEMS COMPARED

A question arises as to whether there is any major difference among the specifications of Robinson, Kaldor and Pasinetti as viewed from the general neo-Keynesian system. The differences and similarities, if any, of these systems may be examined through the response functions. The Pasinettian system collapses to the Robinsonian system if savings are not allowed from work income (i.e., $S_w = 0$), as specified in equations (4.2.4) and (4.2.5). It collapses to the Kaldorian system if savings are allowed for workers but interest is not paid for the use of their savings (i.e., $S_w \neq 0, r = 0$). In the Robinsonian system, we start with a system of interdependent equations regarding profit and the volume of new investments. From the system of equations we derive the conditions for optimal capital and then analyze the conditions needed for the Keynesian savings-investment equality constraint to be met.

The Kaldorian and Pasinettian system begin with propositions about the savings. We then derive the conditions for the Keynesian equilibrium and analyze the requirement for optimal capital and hence optimal investment. In the Kaldorian system the income distribution at the equilibrium is such that the optimal rate of profit is equal to the product of the workers' marginal propensity to save and the output-capital ratio normalized by $(1 + S_w - S_c)$, while in the Pasinettian system the norm is one. A numerical example may be useful.

Example 4.5.1
Let $S_c = 2/3$, $S_w = 1/4$, and capital-output ratio be 3 ($K/Q = 3$). Then from equations (4.3.12) and (4.4.12)

$$\rho_K^* = \frac{(\frac{1}{4})(\frac{1}{3})}{1 + \frac{1}{4} - \frac{2}{3}} = \frac{1}{7} = 14\%$$

$$\rho_p^* = (\frac{1}{4})(\frac{1}{3}) = \frac{1}{12} = 8\%$$

where ρ_K^* and ρ_p^* are the optimal rates of profit in the Kaldorian and Pasinettian systems respectively.

In the Kaldorian and Pasinettian systems the accumulation functions have the same slopes but different intercepts. In other words, the autonomous investment induced by capital efficiency, v, is greater in the Kaldorian than in the Pasinettian system. As such, the two functions are simply parallel to one another, and hence the same optimal values can never be obtained for the dynamic equilibrium. From the functional forms of the Kaldorian and Pasinettian systems, what explicit statement can we make about the differences in the intercepts? For all values $S_w < S_c$ the intercept of the Kaldorian system will be greater than that of Pasinettian system. Hence

$$S_w v > S_w[r + (1 - rS_c\mu)v]$$

$$\Rightarrow v > r + (1 - rS_c)$$

$$\Rightarrow rS_c\mu v > r$$

(4.5.1)

$$\Rightarrow S_c > 1/v\mu \Rightarrow S_c > \frac{\dot{K}^*}{Q^*}$$

But from equation (4.4.10), $S_w = \dot{K}^*/Q^*$, and hence $S_c > S_w$. The implication is that the computed optimal rates will be lower in the Pasinettian system than the Kaldorian system when $S_w < S_c$. They will be equal when $S_w = S_c$.

Alternatively, the optimal values will be greater in the Pasinettian system than the Kaldorian system if it is assumed that $S_w > S_c$. They will be equal when $S_w = S_c$, as in equation $(4.5.1)$, where subscripts K and P refer to hypothetical functional relations that may be postulated from Kaldorian and Pasinettian specifications respectively.

Figure 4.5.1
Comparison between Kaldorian (K) and Pasinettian (P) Systems. Where
A = Rate of Profit Function and B = Rate of Accumulation Function

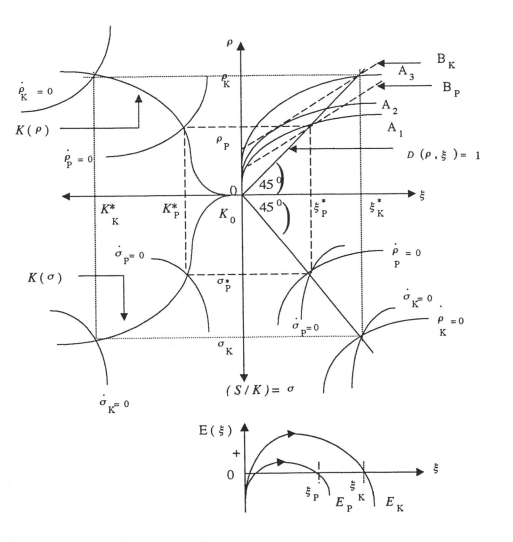

The reasons for higher values for the optimal rates of profit and accumulation in the Kaldorian system than in the Pasinettian system may be explained by either the presence or absence of interest-rate changes in the two specifications. The presence of interest payments for the use of workers' accumulated savings affects profit expectations negatively. Expectations are, therefore, more optimistic in Kaldorian system than the Pasinettian system. In this case, the profit functions A_1, A_2 and A_3 in Figure 4.5.1 will correspond to different interest rates of an order $r_1 > r_2 > r_3$ that will be consistent with the accumulation function, which together may induce an optimal investment process (note, $r_3 = 0$). The inference is that the rate of interest and the volume of new investment will move in opposite directions. This inference may be examined by investigating the effects of interest-rate changes on the volume of new investment in the Pasinettian system.

Let us consider equation (4.4.5) and assume that the investment function is analytic on the rate of interest. This also implies that the response function is analytic on the rate of interest. By taking variations of equation (4.4.5) with respect to r, we obtain

$$\frac{\partial I}{\partial r} = \frac{2 S_c S_w (1 - S_c \mu \nu) \xi}{\{\xi + \psi(\xi) - S_w [r + (1 - r S_c \mu) \nu]\}^2} [\prod(t)$$
$$+ \delta \int_0^t \prod(\tau; t) d\tau] \tag{4.5.2}$$

It may be established from equation (4.5.2) that since $S_c, S_w, \xi > 0$ and the denominator is positive,

$$\frac{\partial I}{\partial r} \lesseqgtr 0, \text{ if } S_c \gtreqless \frac{\dot{K}^*}{Q^*} \tag{4.5.3}$$

Since $S_w = \dot{K}^*/Q^*$, the share of new investment in output, the condition expressed in (4.5.3) may be stated as

$$\frac{\partial I}{\partial r} < 0, \ if \ S_c > S_w \tag{4.5.4}$$

But $S_c > S_w$ from equation (4.3.1). We conclude that

$$\frac{\partial I}{\partial r} < 0. \tag{4.5.5}$$

The following observation must not be overlooked in the analysis: the optimal investment path as a function of the rate of interest is derived by comparing alternative paths of capital accumulation as they relate to income distribution. By reasoning from equations (4.5.3-5) we conclude that the gross investment is inversely related to the rate of interest if the marginal propensity to consume out of profit is greater than the proportion of net investment to output. This translates into the statement that the marginal propensity to save out of profit must exceed the marginal propensity to save out of work income. It also follows from the analysis that variations in the rate of interest have no effect on accumulation if savings are not taken out of work income.

Whether $S_c > \dot{K}/Q$ is a statistical question; however, it is our conjecture that this is the case. Obviously, $S_c Q > \dot{K}$. However, $S_c \prod < \dot{K}$, and hence the total national income saved from profit falls short of net investment in both the Kaldorian and Pasinettian systems. Other sources of finance will consequently be needed to sustain the optimal rate of accumulation. The higher the rate of interest, the less attractive will such funds be for carrying on the new investment, since it tends to reduce profit expectations. As such, the rate of accumulation will be lower for those equilibrium paths with higher rates of interest. Such reduced rates of accumulation will lead to a lower demand for real loanable funds, thus forcing the rate of interest to equality with the rate of profit in the Pasinettian system.

As the rate of interest rises over different accumulation paths, the function for the rate of accumulation that satisfies the Keynesian saving-investment-equality constraint rotates leftwards, causing the rate of accumulation to fall for all rates of profit. On the other hand, the expectations about the potential effects of a rising interest rate and a falling accumulation cause the rate-of-profit function also to shift leftwards in a parallel way, thus registering lower optimal rates of accumulations and profit, with a corresponding lower level of capital stock that is optimally consistent with these values (see Figure 4.5.1).

Equations (4.2.4), (4.3.6), (4.3.7), (4.4.5) and (4.4.9) define different optimal investment processes and possible short-run equilibrium states. Given the structure of expectations about profit and accumulation rates, these paths are determined and fixed by the social psychology of savings from different income sources and the rate of interest payable on savings from real work income. For any given data, each investment path defines a short-run equilibrium process where the profit expectations are such as to induce an equality between the rate of investment and the rate of savings. For the attainment of the long-run dynamic equilibrium and for the optimal investment policy to be maintained, it is necessary not only that the rates of accumulation and profit be in the desired relation with one another but that the income distribution and the psychology of saving from each income cohort be correct. Over the path of long-run dynamic equilibrium, irrespective of the particular specification adopted, the optimal investment policy requires that on the aggregate

$$I(t) = \prod(t) + \delta \int_0^t \prod(\tau; t) d\tau \qquad (4.5.6)$$

where $\xi^* = \psi(\xi^*) = \rho^* = \phi(\rho^*)$ and either $S_c = 1$, $S_w = 0$ or $\prod = [S_w/(1 - S_c)]W$. The condition $\prod = [(S_w)/(1 - S_c)]W$ defines the optimal state of income distribution that is capable of generating sufficient aggregate savings to support the maximum capacity creation. The condition "investment equals aggregate profit," does not mean that all profits are invested. It simply means that for the greatest capacity creation an equivalent value of profit must be reinvested and that such aggregate profit must be equal to savings if the optimal accumulation process is to be internally sustainable.

At this optimal state, not only is the marginal efficiency of capital equal to the marginal efficiency of investment in the advancing economy but both are equal to the rates of profit, accumulation and interest. The volume of new investment defined by equation (4.5.6) is that which is needed to maintain the dynamic equilibrium path; $\prod(t)$ is the optimal profit that is being generated by the accumulated optimal stock, and $\delta \int_0^t \prod(\tau; t) d\tau$ is the accumulated depreciation needed to maintain the current level of the capital stock.

In concluding this section we ask whether an upper bound may be established over the volume of investment that is taking place and being maintained by the volume of profit that is being generated by the accumulated capital. From equations (4.4.10) and (4.5.1)

$$\left. \begin{array}{rcl} S_w Q & = & \dot{K} \\ S_c Q & > & \dot{K} \end{array} \right\} \tag{4.5.7}$$

from equation (4.5.7) we derive

$$\dot{K} \le \frac{1}{2}(S_w + S_c)Q \tag{4.5.8}$$

as the upper bound of the volume of new investments at any time point.

4.6 AN ILLUSTRATIVE NOTE

It will be useful at this point to provide an illustrative example by using specific linear, homogeneous, functional forms for equations (3.3.1) and (3.3.2). Let us suppose that for a given labor force, income distribution and technology, the profit that is being generated by the accumulated capital and maintained by the new investment may be written as

$$\prod = F(K, \dot{K}) = AK^{1-\theta}\dot{K}^{\theta}, \theta \in [0, 1] \tag{4.6.1}$$

Furthermore, let the volume of new investment that is supported by the profit flow and restricted by the current level of accumulated capital be also written as

$$\dot{K} = G(K, \prod) = BK^{1-\beta}\prod^{\beta}, \beta \in [0, 1] \tag{4.6.2}$$

where θ and β are the distributional weights of interdependency of profit and net investment.

The intensity forms of equations (4.6.1) and (4.6.2) may be written as

$$\rho = A\xi^{\theta} \qquad \text{(a)}$$

$$\xi = B\rho^{\beta} \qquad \text{(b)} \tag{4.6.3a}$$

74

The equilibrium process for the determination of optimal level of capital accumulation is obtained by simultaneously solving equation (4.6.3a). By subtracting (b) from (a) and algebraically manipulating the terms one can write

$$\frac{\xi}{\rho} = \frac{1 + B\rho^{\beta-1}}{1 + A\xi^{\theta-1}} \qquad (4.6.3b)$$

From equation (4.6.3a and b) one may write the net-investment process as

$$\dot{K} = [1 + B\rho^{\beta-1}][1 + A\xi^{\theta-1}]^{-1} \prod(t) \qquad (4.6.4)$$

where in this case

$$D(\rho, \xi) = [1 + B\rho^{\beta-1}][1 + A\xi^{\theta-1}]^{-1} \qquad (4.6.5)$$

By combining equations (4.6.5), (4.1.6) and (4.1.7) we obtain the gross-investment process as

$$I(t) = [1 + B\rho^{\beta-1}][1 + A\xi^{\theta-1}]^{-1} \prod(t) + \delta \int_0^t \prod(\tau; t)d\tau \qquad (4.6.6)$$

Alternatively,

$$I(t) = \frac{[1 + B^{\beta-1}][1 + A\xi^{\theta-1}]^{-1}}{\alpha S_w + S_c} S(t) + \delta \int_0^t S(\tau; t)d\tau \qquad (4.6.7)$$

By an alternative algebraic manipulation, it is possible to examine the condition for the long-run dynamic equilibrium where $D(\xi^*, \xi^*) = 1$ in terms of the parameters in equations (4.6.1) and (4.6.2). By simple substitution one can write

$$\rho = AB^\theta \rho^{\beta\theta}$$

and hence

$$\rho = [AB^\theta]^{1/(1-\beta\theta)} \qquad (4.6.8)$$

By substitution of equation (4.6.8) in (4.6.3a) we obtain

$$\xi = B[AB^\theta]^{\beta/(1-\beta\theta)} \qquad (4.6.9)$$

and hence

$$(\xi/\rho) = D(\rho, \xi) = [BAB^\theta]^{-(1-\beta)/(1-\beta\theta)} \qquad (4.6.10)$$

On the long-run dynamic equilibrium $D(\rho, \xi) = 1$, and hence

$$B[AB^\theta]^{-(1-\beta)/(1-\beta^\theta)} = 1$$

and the value of A may be written as

$$A = B^{(1-\theta)/(1-\beta)} \tag{4.6.11}$$

Equations (4.6.6) or (4.6.7) combines with equation (4.6.11) to define the volume of gross capital investment that is needed to maintain both the optimal level of accumulated capital and the corresponding optimal flow in dynamic equilibrium. By combining equation (4.6.11) with (4.6.1) we obtain the optimal profit flow as

$$\prod(t) = B^{\beta(1-\theta)/(1-\beta)} K^{1-\theta} \dot{K}^{\theta} \tag{4.6.12}$$

and the optimal rate of profit as

$$\rho^* = B^{\beta(1-\theta)/(1-\beta)} \xi^{\theta} \tag{4.6.13}$$

In the long-run equilibrium $\xi = \rho$, and hence

$$\rho^* = B^{\beta(1-\theta)/(1-\beta)\}^{1/(1-\theta)}} \tag{4.6.14}$$

$$\rho^* = B^{\beta/(1-\beta)} \tag{4.6.15}$$

Chapter 5

Fiscal Policy and Optimal Capital Accumulation

So far the problems of optimal aggregate capital and investment behavior have been analyzed under the assumptions of a closed economy, no taxation and no government expenditure. We shall now relax the assumptions of no taxation and no government expenditure; however, we shall retain the assumption of a closed economy. We would like to examine the effects of taxation and government savings on the path of optimal accumulation and capacity creation.

5.1 THE STRUCTURE OF SAVINGS-EQUAL-INVESTMENT FUNCTION

The analysis begins with a distributional identity

$$Q = W + \prod \tag{5.1.1}$$

Let T be total tax revenue, which may be specified as

$$T = t_w W + t_c \prod \qquad 0 \le t_w < t_c < 1 \tag{5.1.2}$$

where t_w and t_c are differential tax rates for wage and profit incomes, respectively. This allows us to define a disposable real income, Q^D, at each time point as

$$Q^D = (1 - t_w)W + (1 - t_c) \prod \tag{5.1.3}$$

Suppose workers do save from their work income and as a result receive interest income on the use of their savings from the capitalists. The profit income may, therefore, be divided between the workers and capitalists. Thus we specify

$$\prod = \prod_w + \prod_c; \prod_c > \prod_w \tag{5.1.4}$$

77

Substituting equation $(5.1.4)$ in $(5.1.3)$ we obtain

$$Q^D = (1 - t_w)W + (1 - t_c)\prod_c + (1 - t_c)\prod_w \qquad (5.1.5)$$

Total saving from work and profit income depends on the respective disposable incomes. Let $\mathbb{S}w$, $\mathbb{S}_c$ be the total savings from wages and profit; then

$$\mathbb{S}_w = S_w[(1 - t_w)W + (1 - t_c)\prod_w] \qquad (5.1.6)$$

$$\mathbb{S}_c = S_c(1 - t_c)\prod_c \qquad (5.1.7)$$

The total savings of the economy at each time point will be affected by the revenue-expenditure balance of the government budgetary behavior. Let G represent government expenditure; the government savings, $\mathbb{S}_G$, may be specified as

$$\mathbb{S}_G \;=\; \mathbb{T} - G$$

$$\;=\; t_w W + t_c \prod - G \qquad (5.1.8)$$

The total savings of the economy, $\mathbb{S}$, may then be specified as

$$\mathbb{S} = \mathbb{S}_w + \mathbb{S}_c + \mathbb{S}_G \qquad (5.1.9)$$

By substituting equations $(5.1.6)$, $(5.1.8)$ in $(5.1.9)$ we obtain:

$$\mathbb{S} \;=\; S_w(1 - t_w)W + S_w(1 - t_c)\prod_w + S_c(1 - t_c)\prod_c$$

$$+ t_w W + t_c \prod - G \qquad (5.1.10)$$

By substituting $W = Q - \prod$ and $\prod_w = \prod - \prod_c$ in equation $(5.1.10)$, and through a series of algebraic manipulations and simplifications we can write the aggregate savings as

$$\mathbb{S} \;=\; [S_w(1 - t_w) + t_w]Q - [S_w(t_c - t_w) + t_w - t_c]\prod$$

$$+ [(S_c - S_w)(1 - t_c)]\prod_c - G \qquad (5.1.11)$$

Can we say anything about G in order to conclude the specification of $\mathbb{S}$? We shall assume that at any given period G is some constant proportion, $\hat{\mu}$, of real output, Q. Thus

$$G = \hat{\mu}Q \qquad (5.1.12)$$

The government expenditures are devoted to military and nonmilitary activities, with a nonlinear distributional parameter of α and β, respectively. The proportion $\hat{\mu}$ is isoparametric in the $\alpha - \beta$ plane. Thus

$$\hat{\mu} = \hat{\mu}(\alpha, \beta), \ d\alpha/d\beta < 0 \tag{5.1.13}$$

Graphically, $\hat{\mu}$ is shown in Figure 5.1.1. For any given government budget the higher the proportion devoted to military activities the lower, of course, the

Figure 5.1.1
Government Iso-expenditure Proportion Curves

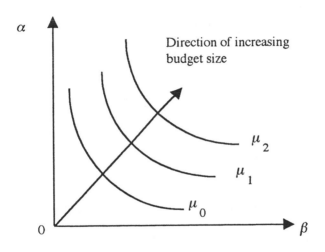

proportion devoted to nonmilitary activities. The government is not involved in any productive investment. Substituting (5.1.12) in (5.1.11) we can write the aggregate savings as

$$\mathbb{S} = [S_w(1 - t_w) + t_w - \hat{\mu}] \ Q - [S_w(t_c - t_w)$$

$$+ \ t_w - t_c] \prod + [(S_c - S_w)(1 - t_c)] \prod_c \tag{5.1.14}$$

The path of Keynesian equilibrium may be specified as $\dot{K} = \mathbb{S}$, and hence

$$\dot{K} = [S_w(1 - t_w) + t_w - \hat{\mu}] \ Q + [(1 - S_w)(t_c - t_w)] \prod$$

$$+ \ (S_c - S_w)(1 - t_c) \prod_c \tag{5.1.15}$$

79

We may obtain from equation (5.1.15) an expression for capitalist real income $\prod_c$, as a ratio of accumulated capital and current net investment:

$$
\begin{aligned}
\frac{\prod_c}{K} &= -[\frac{(1-S_w)(t_c-t_w)}{(S_c-S_w)(1-t_c)}]\frac{\prod}{K} \\
&+ \frac{[S_w(1-t_w)+t_w-\hat{\mu}]}{(S_c-S_w)(1-t_c)}\frac{Q}{K} \\
&+ [\frac{1}{(s_c-S_w)(1-t_c)}]\frac{\dot{K}}{K}
\end{aligned}
\tag{5.1.16}
$$

Dividing through equation (5.1.16) by $(\dot{K}/K)$ we can write an expression for the share of capitalist profit in net investment as

$$
\begin{aligned}
\frac{\prod_c}{\dot{K}} &= -[\frac{(1-S_w)(t_c-t_w)}{(S_c-S_w)(1-t_c)}]\frac{\prod}{\dot{K}} \\
&+ [\frac{S_w(1-t_w)+t_w-\hat{\mu}}{(S_c-S_w)(1-t_c)}]\frac{Q}{\dot{K}} \\
&+ -[\frac{1}{(S_c-S_w)(1-t_c)}]
\end{aligned}
\tag{5.1.17}
$$

An expression for the overall profit rate may also be developed. From equation (5.1.4) we may write, after dividing through by the total accumulated capital,

$$
\frac{\prod}{K} = \frac{\prod_w}{K} + \frac{\prod_c}{K}
\tag{5.1.18}
$$

We have an expression for the rate of capitalist profit, $\prod_c/K$, over the path of Keynesian equilibrium. We need to develop a corresponding expression for the profit rate that goes to the workers, $\prod_w/K$. Such an expression can be found by noting that the workers' profit share is equal to the interest earnings, which is assumed to be proportional to the real value of that part of capital, K_w, financed by the workers' savings. Thus

$$
\frac{\prod_w}{K} = \frac{rK_w}{K}
\tag{5.1.19}
$$

We now observe that on the path of Keynesian dynamic equilibrium

$$
\frac{K_w}{K} = \frac{\mathbb{S}_w}{\mathbb{S}} = \frac{S_w}{\dot{K}}
\tag{5.1.20}
$$

Substituting equation (5.1.6) in (5.1.20) we obtain

$$
\frac{K_w}{K} = \frac{S_w[(1-t_w)W+(1-t_c)\prod_w]}{\dot{K}}
\tag{5.1.21}
$$

Again, write $W = Q - \prod$ and $\prod_w = \prod - \prod_c$, and hence by substituting these values in equation (5.1.21) we obtain

$$\frac{K_w}{K} = \frac{S_w(1 - t_w)Q - S_w(t_c - t_w)\prod - S_w(1 - t_c)\prod_c}{\dot{K}} \tag{5.1.22}$$

Substituting the value of $\prod_c$ from equation (5.1.17) in (5.1.22), and by series of algebraic simplifications we can write

$$\frac{K_w}{K} = \frac{S_w[(1 - t_w)(S_c - S_w) + S_w(1 - t_w) + t_w - \hat{\mu}]}{(S_c - S_w)} \frac{Q}{\dot{K}}$$

$$+ \frac{S_w[(t_c - t_w)(1 - S_w) - (S_c - S_w)(t_c - t_w)]}{(S_c - S_w)} \frac{\prod}{\dot{K}} \tag{5.1.23}$$

$$- \frac{S_w}{S_c - S_w}$$

The stage is now set to specify fully the profit rate over the path of Keynesian dynamic equilibrium. First, the workers' rate of profit may be obtained by substituting equation (5.1.23) in (5.1.19), to obtain

$$\frac{K_w}{K} = \frac{rS_w[(1 - t_w)(S_c - S_w) + S_w(1 - t_w) + t_w - \hat{\mu}]}{S_c - S_w} \frac{Q}{\dot{K}}$$

$$+ \frac{rS_w[S_w(t_c - t_w)(1 - S_c)]}{(S_c - S_w)} \frac{\prod}{\dot{K}} \tag{5.1.24}$$

$$- \frac{rS_w}{S_c - S_w} = \frac{rK_w}{S_K}$$

Substituting equations (5.1.16) and (5.1.24) in equation (5.1.17) and making some algebraic simplifications, we can define the basic components of the profit rate as

$$P = P(S_w, S_c, t_w, t_c, r, \mu)$$

$$= (S_c - S_w)(1 - t_c) + (1 - S_w)(t_c - t_w)$$

$$- rS_w\mu[S_w(t_c - t_w)(1 - S_c)(1 - t_c)] \tag{5.1.25}$$

$$R = R(S_w, S_c, t_w, t_c, r, \mu, \hat{\mu})$$

$$= [\hat{\mu} - S_w(1 - t_c) - t_w] + rS_w\mu(1 - t_c)$$

$$[(1 - t_w)(S_c - S_w) + S_w(1 - t_c)] \tag{5.1.26}$$

where $\mu = K/\dot{K}$ is capacity effect, and $\nu = Q/K$, capital efficiency. By using equations (5.1.25) and (5.1.26) we can write the overall profit rate as:

$$\frac{\Pi}{K} = \frac{\nu R - r S_w(1 - t_c)}{P} + \frac{1}{P}\frac{\dot{K}}{K} \tag{5.1.27}$$

An alternative derivation of the rate of profit function is possible. In this alternative derivation we consider equations (5.1.16) and (5.1.24) and combine them. After a series of algebraic simplications we can write

$$\begin{aligned}
\frac{\Pi}{K} = &\frac{r S_w Z(1 - t_c)\{(1 - t_w)(S_c - S_w) + S_w(1 - t_w)}{(S_c - S_w)(1 - t_c)} \\
&+ \frac{t_w - \hat{\mu} + \pi[S_w(t_c - t_w)(1 - S_c)]}{(1 - S_c)(t_c - t_w)} \\
&- \frac{r S_w Z(1 - tc)\pi S_w(t_c - t_w)(1 - S_c)}{(S_c - S_w)(1 - t_c) + (1 - S_c)(t_c - t_w)} \\
&- \frac{(1 - t_c)\{r S_w + \nu[S_w(1 - t_w) + t_w - \hat{\mu}]\}}{(S_c - S_w)(1 - t_c) + (1 - S_c)(t_c - t_w)} \\
&+ \frac{1}{(S_c - S_w)(1 - t_c) + (1 - S_c)(t_c - t_w)}\frac{\dot{K}}{K}
\end{aligned} \tag{5.1.28}$$

Let

$$M = (S_c - S_w)(1 - t_c) + (1 - S_c)(t_c - t_w) \tag{5.1.29}$$

$$N = (1 - t_w)(S_c - S_w) + S_w(1 - t_w) + t_w - \hat{\mu}$$

$$+ \pi[S_w(t_c - t_w)(1 - S_c)] \tag{5.1.30}$$

$$H = (1 - t_c)\{r S_w + \nu[S_w(1 - t_w) + t_w - \hat{\mu}]\} \tag{5.1.31}$$

Substituting equations (5.1.29-5.1.31) in that of (5.1.28), we can write

$$\frac{\Pi}{K} = \frac{r S_w Z(1 - t_c)N - H}{M} + \frac{1}{M}\frac{\dot{K}}{K} \tag{5.1.32}$$

where $Z = Q/\dot{K}$ is the inverse of the share of net investment in output, $\pi = \Pi/Q$ is the share of total profit in output, and $\nu = Q/K$ is capital efficiency.

The neo-Keynesian dynamic equilibrium process for capital accumulation in its intensity form may be written as:

$$\rho = (R/P)\nu - \frac{r S_w(1 - t_c)}{P} + \frac{1}{P}\xi \tag{5.1.33}$$

$$\xi = \phi(\rho) \tag{5.1.34}$$

Alternatively,

$$\rho = \frac{rS_w Z(1 - t_c)N - H}{M} + \frac{1}{M}\xi \tag{5.1.35}$$

$$\xi = \phi(\rho) \tag{5.1.36}$$

A solution to the accumulation process specified in (5.1.33) and (5.1.34) yields

$$\xi = \frac{rS_w(1 - t_c) - \nu R}{P + 1} + \frac{P[\phi(\rho) + \rho]}{P + 1} \tag{5.1.37}$$

A similar expression may be derived for a solution to equations (5.1.35) and (5.1.36) as

$$\xi = \frac{H - rS_w Z(1 - t_c)N}{M + 1} + \frac{M[\phi(\rho) + \rho]}{M + 1} \tag{5.1.38}$$

Both equations (5.1.37) and (5.1.38) define a short-run dynamic equilibrium process. In the long-run dynamic equilibrium, $\phi^*(\rho) = \rho^* = \xi^*$. In a unit simplex, it may be demonstrated that there is ρ^* such that $\rho^* = \phi(\rho)$. Over the long-run equilibrium path, therefore, we can write

$$\xi^* = \frac{rS_w(1 - t_c) - \nu R}{P + 1} + \frac{2P\xi^*}{P + 1} \tag{5.1.39}$$

or

$$\xi^* = \frac{H - rS_w Z(1 - t_c)N}{M + 1} + \frac{2M\xi}{M + 1} \tag{5.1.40}$$

From equations (5.1.39) and (5.1.40) we can compute the equilibrium rate of capital accumulation as

$$\xi^* = \frac{\nu R - rS_w(1 - t_c)}{P - 1} \tag{5.1.41}$$

or

$$\xi^* = \frac{rS_w Z(1 - t_c)N - H}{M - 1} \tag{5.1.42}$$

Essentially, equation (5.1.41) specifies the equilibrium rate of capital accumulation, to be determined by the multiplier and capacity-creating effects of investment, given the society's savings habits from different income types, principles of effective demand, full employment and income distribution. The multiplier effect suggests to us the level of income that would be necessary to bring savings to equality with net investment at the assumed conditions. On the other hand, the capacity-creating effect reveals the rate at which the capital stock must grow in order to maintain the full-employment condition.

Equation (5.1.42) defines the equilibrium rate of capital accumulation, to be determined by the combination of the multiplier and the acceleration effects of investment. The multiplier effect plays the same role as in equation (5.1.41). The acceleration effect, however, suggests the rate of growth of income that would be necessary to ensure the continuity of equilibrium where saving-investment equality is maintained at the assumed full-employment condition. Thus the multiplier-capacity-creating effect and the multiplier-acceleration effect of investment interact and combine to generate the rate of capital accumulation under the assumed conditions. The conditions expressed by equations (5.1.41) and (5.1.42) reduce to an expression of equilibrium capital efficiency that depends on the capacity effect and interest rate given the tax structure, the share of government expenditure in output and savings preferences of the society from different income types for any given rate of capital accumulation. Hence

$$\nu^* = \frac{rS_w(1 - t_c) + (P - 1)\xi^*}{R} \tag{5.1.43}$$

with $\rho^* = \xi^*$, and

$$Z^* = \frac{H + (M - 1)\xi^*}{rS_w(1 - t_c)N} \tag{5.1.44}$$

Recall from equation (4.1.1) that

$$\dot{K} = (\xi/\rho) \prod \tag{5.1.45}$$

Hence the path of aggregate net investment process may be constructed by substituting equation (5.1.37) in (5.1.45) to obtain

$$\dot{K} = \left\{ \frac{rS_w(1 - t_c) - \nu R + P[\phi(\rho) + \rho]}{(P + 1)\rho} \right\} \prod \tag{5.1.46}$$

Alternatively, we can substitute (5.1.38) in (5.1.45) to obtain

$$\dot{K} = \{ \frac{H - rS_w Z(1 - t_c)N + M[\phi(\rho) + \rho]}{M + 1} \} \prod \tag{5.1.47}$$

where the response coefficient is

$$D(\rho, \xi) = \frac{rS_w(1 - t_c) - \nu R + P[\phi(\rho) + \rho]}{(P + 1)\rho} \tag{5.1.48}$$

or

$$B(\rho, \xi) = \frac{H - rS_w Z(1 - t_c)N + M[\phi(\rho) + \rho]}{M + 1} \tag{5.1.49}$$

The path of gross aggregate investment process, $I(t)$, may then be specified as

$$I(t) = \frac{rS_w(1 - t_c) - \nu R + P[\phi(\rho) + \rho]}{(P + 1)\rho}$$

$$\times [\prod(t) + \delta \int_0^t \prod(\tau; t)d\tau] \tag{5.1.50}$$

84

The path of gross investment can also be specified in terms of the aggregate savings process, where the total savings from work and profit incomes is equal to total profit, in the sense that maximum capacity buildup requires that an equivalent amount of profit equals savings is reinvested. Thus:

$$I(t) = \frac{rS_w(1 - t_c) - R\nu + P[\phi(\rho) + \rho]}{(P + 1)\rho}$$

$$\times [\mathbb{S}(t) + \delta \int_0^t \mathbb{S}(\tau; t)d\tau] \tag{5.1.51}$$

Alternatively, if we combine equation (5.1.49) with (4.1.8) and (4.1.11), we can write the path of gross investment as

$$I(t) = \frac{H - rS_w Z(1 - t_c)N + M[\phi(\rho) + \rho]}{(M + 1)\rho}$$

$$\times [\prod(t) + \delta \int_0^t \prod(\tau; t)d\tau] \tag{5.1.52}$$

or

$$I(t) = \frac{H - rS_w Z(1 - t_c)N + M[\phi(\rho) + \rho]}{(M + 1)\rho}$$

$$\times [\mathbb{S}(t) + \delta \int_0^t \mathbb{S}(\tau; t)d\tau] \tag{5.1.53}$$

Equations (5.1.50-5.1.53) define alternative specifications of the short-run equilibrium process of aggregate investment plans. The long-run Keynesian dynamic equilibrium requires that the savings-investment-equity condition hold in all equilibrium states. Hence

$$D(\rho, \xi) = \frac{rS_w(1 - t_c) - \nu R + P[\phi(\rho) + \rho]}{(P + 1)\rho} = 1 \tag{5.1.54}$$

and

$$B(\rho, \xi) = \frac{H - rS_w Z(1 - t_c)N + M[\phi(\rho) + \rho]}{(M + 1)\rho} = 1 \tag{5.1.55}$$

This is the condition that satisfies the dynamic savings-investment equality constraint as well as an equality between the rate of profit and the rate of accumulation, in a manner that ensures maximum rate of capacity creation.

5.2 NEO-KEYNESIAN DYNAMIC EQUILIBRIUM WITH INTEREST RATE, TAX AND GOVERNMENT-EXPENDITURE PARAMETERS

The complete set of conditions for long-run neo-Keynesian dynamic equilibrium of capital accumulation where the rates of profit, savings and net investment over accumulated capital are equalized may be stated in parametric terms as

$$
\begin{aligned}
\xi &= \frac{\nu R - r S_w(1 - t_c)}{P - 1} & \text{(a)} \\
D(\xi, \rho) &= 1 & \text{(b)} \\
\xi &= \phi(\rho) = \rho & \text{(c)}
\end{aligned}
\qquad (5.2.1)
$$

Alternatively,

$$
\begin{aligned}
\xi^* &= \frac{r S_w Z(1 - t_c)N - H}{M - 1} & \text{(a)} \\
B(\xi, \rho) &= 1 & \text{(b)} \\
\xi &= \phi(\rho) = \rho & \text{(c)}
\end{aligned}
\qquad (5.2.2)
$$

The conditions (a,b) in (5.2.1) imply (c). Similarly, conditions (a,b) imply (c) in (5.2.2). The conditions $D(\xi, \rho) = 1$ and $B(\xi, \rho) = 1$ imply instantaneous response and full adjustment of aggregate investment to aggregate profit on the dynamic equilibrium path for capital accumulation. The same conditions for instantaneous and complete adjustment of aggregate investment to aggregate saving are met when the total profit is equal to total savings, irrespective of the sources of saving.

From the parametric conditions for the long-run dynamic equilibrium as defined in either equation (5.2.1) or (5.2.2), we can derive expressions for the rate of profit in terms of other parameters specified by aggregate savings propensities of income classes and the propensities of government to tax and spend. We observe from equation (5.2.1a) that

$$
\nu^* = \frac{r S_w(1 - t_c) + (P - 1)\xi^*}{R}
\qquad (5.2.3)
$$

and from equation (5.2.2a) that

$$
Z^* = \frac{H + (M - 1)\xi^*}{N r S_w(1 - t_c)}
\qquad (5.2.4)
$$

On the long-run dynamic equilibrium path, $\rho^* = \xi^*$, which also implies that $\dot{K} = \prod$. If the total aggregate real saving is equal to the total profit, then $\sigma = \rho = \xi$ and $\mathbb{S} = \dot{K} = \prod$. This does not mean that all profit is saved.

It simply means that the total savings is equal to the total profit (or surplus over the workers' income). The interest rate is determined and computed at the equilibrium path of the accumulation process. From equations (5.2.1) and (5.2.2) we can derive expressions for the ratios of profit and capital accumulation in terms of known or estimated parameter over the long-run neo-Keynesian dynamic equilibria. From equations (5.2.1) and (5.1.54) we can compute the equilibrium rates of profit and accumulation as

$$\rho^* = \xi^* = \frac{\nu R - r S_w (1 - t_c)}{P - 1} \tag{5.2.5}$$

Alternatively, by combining equations (5.2.2) and (5.1.55) we obtain

$$\rho^* = \xi^* = \frac{r S_w Z (1 - t_c) N - H}{M - 1} \tag{5.2.6}$$

where in each case $\phi(\rho^*) = \rho^* = \xi^*$.

From the set of equilibrium conditions of equations (5.2.1) and (5.2.2) we can derive an expression between the rate of interest and the government's propensity to spend out of aggregate output, by utilizing $D(\xi, \rho) = 1$. After appropriate substitution of values in equation (5.1.54) and some algebraic simplification we can write

$$r = \frac{\rho \mathbb{F}_1 - \nu [S_w (1 - t_c) - t_w] + \nu \hat{\mu}}{S_w (1 - t_c) - \nu S_w \mu \mathbb{F}_2 - \rho S_w \mu \mathbb{F}_3 + S_w \nu \mu (1 - t_c) \hat{\mu}} \tag{5.2.7}$$

where

$$\mathbb{F}_1 = [1 - (S_c - S_w)(1 - t_c) - (1 - S_w)(t_c - t_w)] \tag{5.2.8}$$

$$\mathbb{F}_2 = (1 - t_c)[(1 - t_c)(S_c - S_w) + S_w (1 - t_c) + t_w] \tag{5.2.9}$$

$$\mathbb{F}_3 = S_w (t_c - t_w)(1 - S_c)(1 - t_c) \tag{5.2.10}$$

Furthermore,

$$\hat{\mu} = \text{the share of government expenditure in total output } (\hat{\mu} = G/Q)$$

$$\nu = \text{the capital efficiency measure } (\nu = Q/K)$$

$$\mu = \text{the capacity effect } (\mu = K/\dot{K})$$

Implicitly, we can write the rate of interest from equation (5.2.7) as a conditional function of government propensity to spend, as

$$r = f(\hat{\mu}; S_w, S_c, t_w, t_c, \nu, \mu, \rho) \tag{5.2.11}$$

The rate of interest also depends on the equilibrium rate of profit as seen from equation (5.2.7). Similarly, one can calculate r from the condition $B(\rho, \xi) = 1$ of equation (5.1.55). By appropriate substitution of values and algebraic simplications we can write

$$r = \frac{(1 - M)\rho - \nu(1 - t_c)[S_w(1 - t_w) + t_w - \hat{\mu}]}{S_w(1 - t_c)[1 - ZN]} \tag{5.2.12}$$

where M and N are as specified by equations (5.1.29) and (5.1.30). From equation (5.2.12) we can write an implicit function as

$$r = q(\hat{\mu}, S_w, S_c, t_c, t_c, Z, \pi, \rho, \nu) \tag{5.2.13}$$

Equations (5.2.7) and (5.2.12), or (5.2.11) and (5.2.15), are alternative expressions that define the long-run path of the equilibrium rate of interest. These alternative expressions highlight a connection between the equilibrium rate of interest and the income distribution parameter, π, in addition to the rate of profit, given all relevant parameters. The essential difference between the short-run and the long-run equilibrium interest rates is that while the long-run equilibrium rate of interest depends on the equilibrium rate of profit, in addition to all essential factors that determine the short-run equilibrium rate of interest rate, the short-run equilibrium rate is independent of the profit rate. Given the government's tax-expenditure behavior, societal attitude to save from different income types and the structure of income distribution, the short-run equilibrium rate of interest is determined by capital efficiency and capacity effect. These factors, in addition to the long-run profit rate, determine the long-run equilibrium rate of interest. Thus the long-run equilibrium rate of interest is determined by the long-run profit rate, given full capacity utilization and maximum production efficiency.

Generally, we can say that equations (5.2.11) and (5.2.13) suggest that if the rate of interest, r, is viewed as exogenously determined outside the real sector its behavior in the parametric space over the long-run equilibrium path depends on the proportion of income devoted to government expenditures, the savings psychology of the society with respect to different income types, average productivity of capital, the income distribution (represented by the profit share), the proportion of output devoted to increasing the level of accumulated capital and the rate of profit that is being generated by the accumulated capital and maintained by the current investment and accumulated capital, given the underlying tax structure. Given that all relevant parameters are fixed at their current levels in the parametric space, the behavior of the rate of interest in such a space depends in a nonlinear way on the proportion of national income devoted to government expenditures, for any given tax structure.

Equations (5.2.7) and (5.2.12) provide an important initial resolution to the debate as to whether the rate of interest depends on the behavior of government expenditure. In this essay we have established not only such a relationship but also an exact one, over the neo-Keynesian dynamic equilibrium path. These established relationships offer us an opportunity to raise new questions and conduct an analysis regarding the behavior of the rate of interest. For one thing, we can compute the exact effects of government expenditure changes on the behavior of the interest rate, if all other relevant parameters are known and the system is in an equilibrium state. We can also analyze the effects of either the government surplus or deficit on the rate of interest and accumulation. Furthermore, we can raise questions about the effects of changes in the tax structure on the rates of interest and accumulation as one examines the structure of social income distribution. An important assumption in this analysis is that the government does not invest in productive assets.

5.3 SENSITIVITY ANALYSIS

From the foregoing analysis a number of important questions emerge. Some of these questions may be stated for reflection.

1. What effect, if any, will an increase in the proportion of government expenditures in the national output have on the paths of gross aggregate investment and profit rate, when such expenditures are not in areas of productive investment?

2. What effect, if any, will changes in the tax structure and tax rates have on the time paths of optimal gross investment and profit rate in the closed economy?

3. What effect does deficit spending have on the paths of optimal gross investment and profit rate?

4. Does a balanced government budget have any effect on the path of optimal gross investment and the profit rate?

We shall examine these questions and related ones. The effects of parameter changes will affect the optimal time-path of investment, through their effects on the response functions of $D(\xi, \rho)$ and $B(\xi, \rho)$. The directions and magnitudes of changes in the response functions will provide us with the measures corresponding to particular parameter effects. These directions and magnitudes may be obtained by deriving sensitivity functions from the response functions.

5.3.1 Sensitivty Function: $\hat{\mu}$, Government Expenditure Changes

Let us consider the effect of changes in the government expenditure on the economy's accumulation response. The government expenditure is said to have changed if its share in real output changes. Our interest is on the effects of variations of the share of government budget in output, not its size. The share of government budget may decrease (or increase) though the size might have increased (decreased): it is the proportion, not the size, of government expenditure that counts, given the tax structure. The change can be computed and analyzed by taking the derivative of either $D(\xi, \rho)$ or $B(\xi, \rho)$ with respect to $\hat{\mu}$.

Let us recall from equations (5.1.54) and (5.1.55) that

$$D(\rho, \xi) = \frac{rS_w(1 - t_c) - \nu R + P[\phi(\rho) + \rho]}{(P + 1)\rho} = \frac{U}{(P + 1)\rho} \qquad (5.3.1.1)$$

and

$$B(\rho, \xi) = \frac{H - rS_w Z(1 - t_c)N + M[\phi(\rho) + \rho]}{(M + 1)\rho}$$

$$= \frac{X}{(M + 1)\rho} \qquad (5.3.1.2)$$

where $U = rS_w(1 - t_c) - \nu R + P[\phi(\rho) + \rho]$, and

$$X = H - rS_w Z(1 - t_c)N + M[\phi(\rho) + \rho]$$

Taking partial derivatives of equations (5.3.1.1) and (5.3.1.2) with respect $\hat{\mu}$ we obtain

$$\frac{\partial D}{\partial \hat{\mu}} = \frac{-\nu\rho(1 - P)[1 - r\mu S_w(1 - t_c)]}{[\rho(1 + P)]^2} \qquad (5.3.1.3)$$

$$\frac{\partial B}{\partial \hat{\mu}} = \frac{-\rho(M + 1)(1 - t_c)(rZS_w - \nu)}{[\rho(M + 1)]^2} \qquad (5.3.1.4)$$

Equations (5.3.1.3) and (5.3.1.4) in their absolute terms define the magnitude of the response effect of government expenditure changes relative to total real output. We, however, need additional information in order to determine the direction of change. Such information is provided by the subsequent lemma.

Lemma 5.3.1

$$R > 0, \ P > 0, \ M > 0, \ N > 0 \text{ and } H > 0$$

The proof of this lemma can easily be done, by term-by-term comparison.

Proposition 5.3.1

$$\frac{\partial D}{\partial \hat{\mu}} < 0$$

Proof

From equation (5.3.1.3) we have

$$\frac{\partial D}{\partial \hat{\mu}} = \frac{-\nu\rho(1 + P)[1 - rS_w(1 - t_c)]}{\rho^2(1 + P)^2}$$

Since $\rho^2(1 + P)^2 > 0$, we need only to show that the numerator is positive. Now, since $P > 0$ by lemma (5.3.1), $-\nu\rho(1 + P) < 0$. For all relevant values of r, S_w and t_c, $rS_w(1 - t_c) < 1$. This implies that $[1 - rS_w(1 - t_c)] > 0$, and hence $\frac{\partial D}{\partial \hat{\mu}} < 0$. Again, for all values of S_w and t_c, $r < \frac{1}{S_w(1-t_c)}$. This implies $[1 - rS_w(1 - t_c)] > 0$.

Proposition 5.3.2

$$\frac{\partial B}{\partial \hat{\mu}} \begin{cases} < 0, & \text{if} \qquad r < (\nu/SwZ) \\ \geq 0, & \text{elsewhere} \end{cases}$$

Proof

Since $M > 0$ by lemma (5.3.1), the proposition is demonstrated if $[rS_w Z - \nu] < 0$, which implies that $r < /S_w Z$.

Propositions (5.3.1) and (5.3.2) suggest that an increase in the proportion of government expenditure will reduce the magnitude of the aggregate investment response, given the structures of taxation, social income distribution and savings behavior out of income types. A reduction in the value of the government's propensity to spend out of the aggregate output should lead to an increase in the aggregate investment response to available savings. The analysis so far has not explicitly identified the source of financing for the government expenditure changes. It may be that the government budget over the accumulation process is always balanced or it may be either in deficit or in surplus. If the budget is in deficit, one may assume that it is taken care of from the accumulated and aggregate savings, and hence the deficit reduces the available savings for aggregate private investment. Budget surplus goes to increase the same aggregate savings available for aggregate private investment.

The results of propositions (5.3.1) and (5.3.2) do not permit one immediately to conclude their support for the phenomenon of crowding-out by government expenditure in the lending and borrowing space of the economy, in the neoclassical sense. In this framework, changes in the government's tax-expenditure propensities and behavior directly affect the value of social savings that make possible investment financing. Additionally they affect the value of real consumption. By directly changing the value of social savings, measured in either units of cost or consumption goods, changes in government's tax-expenditure propensities affect the path of optimal aggregate investment. If one wants to view this result in terms of crowding-out of private investment, then such crowding-out emerges in every socioeconomic system where there is a government with tax-expenditure behavior and the government does not invest in productive assets. This kind of constraint on aggregate private investment is different from the one that emerges out of government expenditure behavior that is supported by changes in government behavior in the borrowing and lending space. This point is important and must be noted.

The transmission mechanism of the former constraint is the income distribution parameters operating through the institutions of income distribution, with a third party, the government, added. The constraint, therefore, does not operate through the interest rate and the market. The transmission mechanism of the latter is the institution of the market, with interest rate as its vehicle. The former, therefore, is a direct phenomenon of income distribution as well as the social sector, held to be responsible for productive investment, while the latter is an indirect one, viewed in terms of cost of borrowing. The results of the government budgetary behavior may alter if either productive investments by the government are allowed or the productivity of private investment is either enhanced by government investment in the general social infrastructure, or both. In-fact, these are the cases which are not fully explored in this study.

5.3.2 Sensitivity Analysis: The Effects of Balanced Government Budget on the Accumulation Path

We shall now examine the effects of the government's balanced-budget behavior on the capital accumulation path, by considering the accounts of government savings from eqquation (5.1.8), where net government savings is

$$S_G = t_w W + t_c \prod - G$$

$$= (t_w - \hat{\mu})Q + (t_c - t_w)\prod$$

(5.3.2.1)

where

$$G = \hat{\mu}Q, \ W = Q - \prod$$

We can, by substitution into equation (5.3.2.1), immediately write the share of profit when the government budget is balanced as

$$\frac{\prod}{Q} = \frac{\hat{\mu} - t_w}{t_c - t_w}$$

(5.3.2.2)

Note that $\hat{\mu} > t_w, t_c > t_w$. From (5.3.2.2) we can also write

$$\rho^{**} = (\frac{\hat{\mu} - t_w}{t_c - t_w})\nu$$

(5.3.2.3)

where $\rho = \prod/K$ is profit rate and $\nu = Q/K$ is a measure of capital efficiency. Equation (5.3.2.3) defines the rate of profit consistent with a government balanced budget, given the tax structure and average productivity of capital. The profit rate, therefore, depends on the capital efficiency, given the government's tax-expenditure behavior.

Net investment under the conditions of balanced budget may be obtained by substituting equation (5.3.2.3) in either equations (5.1.46) or (5.1.47) to obtain

$$\dot{K} = \frac{rS_w(1 - t_c) - \nu R}{(P+1)[(\hat{\mu} - t_c)/(t_c - t_w)]\nu}$$
$$+ \frac{P\{\phi(\rho) + [(\hat{\mu} - t_w)/(t_c - t_w)]\nu\}}{(P+1)[(\hat{\mu} - t_c)/(t_c - t_w)]\nu}$$

(5.3.2.4)

Similarly, we can write the path of net investment as

$$\dot{K} = \frac{H - rS_w Z(1 - t_c)N}{(M+1)[(\mu - t_c)(t_c - t_w)]\nu}$$
$$+ \frac{M\{\phi(\rho) + [(\hat{\mu} - t_w)(t_c - t_w)]\nu\}}{(M+1)[(\mu - t_c)(t_c - t_w)]\nu}$$

(5.3.2.5)

From equation (5.3.2.3), an increase in average productivity of capital implies an increase in the profit rate. Over the path of balanced budget we can write, for $\pi = \prod / Q$, the government's propensity to spend as

$$\hat{\mu} = t_w + (t_c - t_w)\frac{\prod}{Q}$$

$$= t_w + (t_c - t_w)\pi \qquad (5.3.2.6)$$

Equation (5.3.2.6) suggests that the government balanced-budget "average propensity to spend" depends on propensity to tax from income types and the social distribution of income over the equilibrium capital accumulation. If $t_c > t_w$, the government can increase the balanced-budget propensity to spend as the profit share, π, increases. An alternative expression is possible from equation (5.3.2.6), just by observing that $\pi = (1 - w)$ where $w = W/Q$. The expression may be written as

$$\hat{\mu} = t_c - (t_c - t_w)w$$
$$\qquad (5.3.2.7)$$
$$= t_c + (t_w - t_c)w$$

In other words, the government average propensity to spend can increase as the wage share increases if $t_w > t_c$ and the budget is always in balance.

A further analysis will be useful. From equation (5.3.2.6) we have

$$d\hat{\mu} = \pi dt_c + (1 - \pi)dt_w \qquad (5.3.2.8)$$

Changes in the tax structure that maintain the balanced budget over the accumulation path given the social income distribution require a tax trade-off as

$$-\frac{dt_c}{dt_w} = \frac{1 - \pi}{\pi} = \frac{w}{\pi} \qquad (5.3.2.9)$$

where the trade-off depends on the income distribution. The revenue side of the government's budget, given the structure of income distribution, depends essentially on the government's propensity to tax from wage and profit incomes. Generally, the government's total revenue, as a proportion, ϕ, of output, depends on the profit tax rate, t_c, and tax rate, t_w, of work income, for any given income distribution and on any path of capital accumulation. Thus,

$$\phi = \phi(t_w, t_c) \qquad (5.3.2.10)$$

The value ϕ is the government's average revenue propensity. At any given ϕ,

$$-\frac{dt_c}{dt_w} = (\frac{\partial \phi}{\partial t_c})/(\frac{\partial \phi}{\partial t_w}) \qquad (5.3.2.11)$$

Thus there is a trade off between the tax rates such that higher tax rate on work income must be compensated by a lower profit tax rate, given the revenue propensity. From equation (5.1.13) we have

$$\hat{\mu} = \hat{\mu}(\alpha, \beta) \tag{5.3.2.12}$$

$$d\hat{\mu} = \frac{\partial \hat{\mu}}{\partial \alpha} d\alpha + \frac{\partial \hat{\mu}}{\partial \beta} d\beta \tag{5.3.2.13}$$

If the average propensity to save remains the same as we trade-off military, α, and nonmilitary, β, expenditures proportions, then $d\hat{\mu} = 0$, and

$$-\frac{d\alpha}{d\beta} = (\frac{\partial \hat{\mu}}{\partial \beta})/(\frac{\partial \hat{\mu}}{\partial \alpha}) \tag{5.3.2.14}$$

The equality occurs at the point of tangency of the revenue and expenditure propensities.

From equation (5.3.2.2) and for a given structure of taxation and government propensity to spend, a continually balanced budget requires that the income distribution be optimal given the tax structure. Hence

$$\frac{\dot{\Pi}}{\Pi} = \frac{\dot{Q}}{Q}$$

$$\frac{\dot{\Pi}}{\dot{Q}} = \frac{\Pi}{Q} \tag{5.3.2.15}$$

In other words, the share of increased profit in increased output must always be equal to the share of profit in output. The rate of growth of profit must be equal to the rate of growth of output when the structure of income distribution is optimal, in the sense that $\dot{\omega} = \dot{\pi} = 0$. Equations (5.3.2.9), (5.3.2.13) and (5.3.2.14) may be graphically represented as in Figure 5.3.2.1.

5.3.3 Sensitivity Analysis: Government Budget Deficit

Let us now consider what effect, if any, a government budget deficit has on the equilibrium path of aggregate capital. First, consider equation (5.3.2.1), and suppose $S_G < 0$, implying that the government budget is in deficit. Write

$$t_w W + t_c \prod - G = -D \tag{5.3.3.1}$$

Furthermore, suppose the budget deficit is some proportion, $\hat{\lambda}$, of aggregate output, where

$$D = \hat{\lambda} Q, \ \hat{\lambda} < \hat{\mu} \tag{5.3.3.2}$$

Figure 5.3.2.1
Geometry of Optimal Expenditure and Tax Distribution

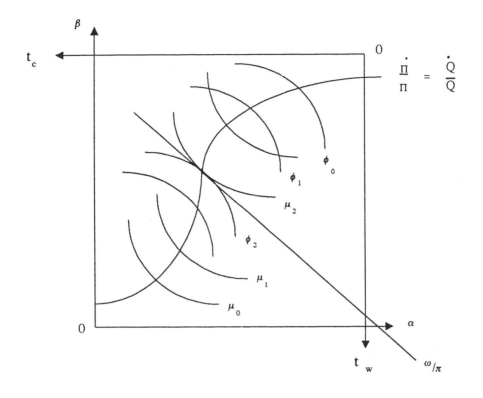

Similarly, $\hat{\lambda}$, propensity to overspend, depends on α and β. From (5.3.3.1) we obtain

$$t_w w + t_c \prod = (\hat{\mu} - \hat{\lambda})Q \qquad (5.3.3.3)$$

A few algebraic simplifications, where $W = Q - \prod$, $\nu = Q/K$ and $\pi = \prod/Q$, allow us to write the government's average propensity to spend in terms of propensity to overspend and propensity to tax different income types. Thus

$$\hat{\mu} = t_w + \hat{\lambda} + (t_c - t_w) \prod \qquad (5.3.3.4)$$

and alternatively,

$$\hat{\mu} = t_w + \hat{\lambda} + \frac{(t_c - t_w)\rho}{\nu} \tag{5.3.3.5}$$

We may now examine the effects of variations in government propensity to overspend on the path of aggregate gross investment. This may be done by substituting either equation (5.3.3.4) or (5.3.3.5) in the response functions defined by equations (5.3.1.1) and (5.3.1.2). The effects of variations in government deficit spending may be viewed through its effect on the total expenditure budget and how such variations in the total expenditure budget affect the private rate of accumulation. To examine the effects of variations in the budget deficit we compute the sensitivity function, of the form $\partial D/\partial \hat{\lambda}$. It is easily verified from equations (5.3.1.1), (5.3.1.2), (5.3.3.4) and (5.3.3.5) that

$$\frac{\partial D}{\partial \hat{\mu}} \frac{\partial \hat{\mu}}{\partial \hat{\lambda}} = \frac{\partial D}{\partial \hat{\mu}} = \frac{-\nu\rho(1 - P)[1 - rS_w(1 - t_c)]}{\rho^2(1 + P)^2} \tag{5.3.3.6}$$

since $\partial \hat{\mu}/\partial \hat{\lambda} = 1$. Similarly,

$$\frac{\partial B}{\partial \hat{\mu}} \frac{\partial \hat{\mu}}{\partial \hat{\lambda}} = \frac{\partial B}{\partial \hat{\mu}} = \frac{\rho(M + 1)(1 - t_c)[rS_w Z - v]}{(M + 1)^2 \rho^2} \tag{5.3.3.7}$$

Thus, the effects of deficit spending on the response function and the accumulation path are the same as those of variations on the aggregate budget. In other words, *variation in government budget* deficit proportion in output is in an *inverse* relationship with the path of *aggregate private accumulation*.

The analysis may easily be extended to the case where there is a budget surplus. In this case, we may write

$$\hat{\mu} = t_w - \hat{\sigma} + (t_c - t_w)\pi \tag{5.3.3.8}$$

or

$$\hat{\mu} = t_w - \hat{\sigma} + \frac{(t_c - t_w)}{\nu}\rho \tag{5.3.3.9}$$

where $\hat{\sigma}$ is the proportion of surplus as a share in the national income. The magnitude of the effects of surplus is the same as that of deficit, but in the opposite direction. In other words,

$$\frac{\partial D}{\partial \hat{\mu}} \frac{\partial \hat{\mu}}{\partial \hat{\sigma}} = -\frac{\partial D}{\partial \hat{\mu}} = \frac{\nu\rho(1 - P)[1 - rS_w\mu(1 - t_c)]}{\rho^2(1 + P)^2} \tag{5.3.3.10}$$

Similarly,

$$\frac{\partial B}{\partial \hat{\mu}} \frac{\partial \hat{\mu}}{\partial \hat{\sigma}} = -\frac{\partial B}{\partial \hat{\mu}} = -\frac{(M + 1)(1 - t_c)[rS_w Z - v]}{(M + 1)^2 \rho^2} \tag{5.3.3.11}$$

Proposition 5.3.3.1

$$\frac{\partial D}{\partial \hat{\sigma}} \begin{cases} > 0, & \text{if } \dfrac{\partial D}{\partial \hat{\mu}} < 0 \\[3mm] \leq 0, & \text{if } \dfrac{\partial D}{\partial \hat{\mu}} \geq 0 \end{cases}$$

$$\frac{\partial B}{\partial \hat{\sigma}} \begin{cases} > 0, & \text{if } \dfrac{\partial D}{\partial \hat{\mu}} < 0 \\[3mm] \leq 0, & \text{if } \dfrac{\partial B}{\partial \hat{\mu}} \geq 0 \end{cases}$$

Proof

The proof of the proposition is easily demonstrated from combining equations (5.3.3.10) and (5.3.3.11) with propositions (5.3.1) and (5.3.2).

5.3.4 Sensivity Function: The Effects of Deficit on Interest Rate

In Section (5.2) we established relationships between the rate of interest and government expenditure propensity, given other relevant structural parameters. These results establish only the magnitude of the relationship; they do not tell us the direction of effects as variations occur in government's expenditure propensity. Furthermore, we do not have an explicit relationship between the rate of interest and either a government budget surplus or deficit on the path of capital equilibrium. We shall establish this and then provide answers to questions regarding the effects of variations in either government surplus or deficit on the rate of interest.

5.3.4.1 *Sensitivity Function: Interest Rate and Government Expenditure Propensity*

Consider equations (5.2.11) and (5.2.13) from the general equilibrium conditions. We need to compute $\partial f/\partial \hat{\mu}$ and $\partial g/\partial \hat{\mu}$ and examine the directions of change by using equations (5.2.12) and (5.2.14), respectively. Let

$$L_1 = \rho[1 - (S_c - S_w)(1 - t_c) - (1 - S_w)(t_c - t_w)]$$

$$L_2 = \nu[\hat{\mu} - S_w(1 - t_c) - t_w]$$

$$L_3 = S_w(1 - t_c) - \rho S_w \mu[S_w(t_c - t_w)(1 - S_c)(1 - t_c)]$$

$$L_4 = S_w \nu \mu(1 - t_c)[(1 - t_c)(S_c - S_w) + S_w(1 - t_c) + t_w - \hat{\mu}]$$

Equation (5.2.13) may thus be written as

$$r = f(\hat{\mu}; \cdot) = \frac{L_1 + L_2}{L_3 - L_4} \tag{5.3.4.1.1}$$

We may now compute the partial derivative of r with respect to $\hat{\mu}$ to obtain

$$\frac{\partial r}{\partial \hat{\mu}} = \frac{\partial f}{\partial \hat{\mu}} = \frac{(L_3 - L_4)\frac{\partial L_2}{\partial \hat{\mu}} 2 - (L_1 + L_2)\frac{\partial L_4}{\partial \hat{\mu}}}{(L_3 - L_4)^2}$$

$$= \frac{\nu(L_3 - L_4) - S_w \nu \mu(1 - t_c)(L_1 + L_2)}{(L_3 - L_4)^2} \tag{5.3.4.1.2}$$

Alternatively, we can examine the relationship between the interest rate and variations in the government's propensity to spend from equation (5.2.13). Let

$$P_1 = (1 - M)\rho - \nu(1 - t_c)[S_w(1 - t_w) + t_w - \hat{\mu}]$$

$$P_2 = S_w(1 - t_c)[1 - ZN]$$

Hence

$$r = q(\hat{\mu}, \bullet) = P_1/P_2 \tag{5.3.4.1.3}$$

Taking derivate of r with respect to $\hat{\mu}$ we can write

$$\frac{\partial r}{\partial \hat{\mu}} = \frac{\partial g}{\partial \hat{\mu}} = \frac{P_2 \frac{\partial P_1}{\partial \hat{\mu}} - P_1 \frac{\partial P_2}{\partial \hat{\mu}}}{P_2^2}$$

$$= \frac{\nu(1 - t_c)P_2 + P_1 S_w(1 - t_c)Z\frac{\partial N}{\partial \hat{\mu}}}{P_2^2}$$

$$= \frac{\nu(1 - t_c)P_2 - P_1 S_w(1 - t_c)Z}{P_2^2} \tag{5.3.4.1.4}$$

In order to examine the direction of change we need to establish the qualitative value for L_1, L_2, L_3, L_4, P_1 and P_2.

Lemma 5.3.4.1

For values of $S_w < 1/4$, $t_w \leq 1/3$, and $t_c, S_c, \hat{\mu} > 2/5$.

$$(L_3 - L_4) > 0, \quad (L_1 + L_2) > 0, \quad P_1 > 0$$

and $P_2 > 0$ if $Z < N^{-1}$.

Proof

Consider $L_1 = \rho[1 - (S_c - S_w)(1 - t_c) - (1 - S_w)(t_c - t_w)]$. By substitution, it may easily be verified that $L_1 > 0$, since $\rho > 0$. Similarly, it may be established that $L_2 = \nu[\hat{\mu} - S_w(1 - t_c) - t_w] > 0$ for the values of $\hat{\mu}, S_c, t_c$ and t_w that satisfy the defined bounds. By the same substitution method, $L_3 > 0$ and $L_4 < 0$. Hence $(L_1 + L_2) > 0$, and $(L_3 - L_4) > 0$. The cases for P_1 and P_2 may be similarly established. By substitution $M < 1 \Rightarrow (1 - M)\rho > 0$, and $| [S_w(1 - t_w) + t_w] | < | \hat{\mu} |$. Hence $-\nu(1 - t_c)[S_w(1 - t_w) + t_w - \hat{\mu}] > 0$. Thus $P_1 > 0$. From $P_2 = S_w(1 - t_c)[1 - ZN]$, it follows that $P_2 > 0$ if $Z > 1/N = N^{-1}$.

Lemma 5.3.4.1 establishes that the rate of interest as computed in the equilibrium is positive over the established parametric bounds. We are now ready to examine the direction of $\partial f_o / \partial \hat{\mu}$ and $\partial g_o / \partial \hat{\mu}$.

Proposition 5.3.4.1

$$
\frac{\partial r}{\partial \hat{\mu}} = \frac{\partial f}{\partial \hat{\mu}}
\begin{cases}
> 0, & \text{if} \quad r < \dfrac{1}{S_w \mu (1 - t_c)} \\[2ex]
\leq 0, & \text{otherwise}
\end{cases}
$$

$$
\frac{\partial r}{\partial \hat{\mu}} = \frac{\partial g}{\partial \hat{\mu}}
\begin{cases}
> 0, & \text{if} \quad r < \dfrac{\nu}{S_w Z} \\[2ex]
\leq 0, & \text{otherwise}
\end{cases}
$$

Proof

The proof of this proposition follows by combining the lemma (5.3.4.1) and the computational value of r.

It must be pointed out that for all properly conceivable values where $S_c > S_w$, $t_c > t_w$ and $\hat{\mu} \geq t_c$, the proposition (5.3.4.1) may be demonstrated to hold. Thus the statement defines a general proposition that the rate of interest, r, paid to workers for indirectly owning part of capital through their savings is positively related to the government's average propensity to spend, given its propensity to tax, the structure of income distribution and the behavior of social savings over the neo-Keynesian dynamic equilibrium. Proposition (5.3.4.1) suggests that if we examine the data and adjust government expenditures for tax variations, we will find that the rate of interest is positively related to the share of government expenditure as a proportion of real domestic output. The economic rationale is found in the relationship between aggregate profit and government expenditure, viewed in terms of their contributions to aggregate savings and their relative roles on the path of capital accumulation, for any given income distribution.

For any given tax structure, income distribution and savings propensities, an increase in government average propensity to spend reduces total savings available for productive investment. This reduction in aggregate savings can be made up by increasing savings propensities from either wages or profits. When the savings behavior defined by the propensities to save from income types is examined, it is quickly found that there is no way to change the incentive to save from profit. Alternatively, by altering the interest rate paid to workers for the use of their savings as a claim to part of capital, we are able to change savings from work income. Thus changes in government's propensity to spend relate directly to the interest rate if the system is on path of optimal rate of accumulation. An increased (decreased) propensity of the government to spend must be accompanied by a similar increased (decreased) rate of interest in a manner that ensures sufficient savings to support the path of optimal rate of capital accumulation.

5.3.4.2 *Sensitvity Function:*
The Rate of Interest and Surplus
or Deficit Spending

We have derived and analyzed an explicit relationship between the real rate of interest and the government propensity to spend, given other relevant parameters. From such an established relationship we can derive others that explicitly relate the interest rate to either the budget deficit or surplus, specified as a proportion of real domestic output. Such relationships may be obtained by substituting either equation (5.3.3.4) or (5.3.3.5) and equation (5.3.3.8) or (5.3.3.9) in equations (5.2.7) and (5.2.12) to obtain

$$
r = \begin{cases} \dfrac{\rho \mathbb{T}_1 + \nu[\hat{\mu} - S_w)(1 - t_c) - t_w}{S_w(1 - t_c) - \mathbb{T}_2 - \rho S_w \mu[S_w(t_c - t_w)(1 - S_c)]} \\ \text{where} \quad \hat{\mu} = t_w + \hat{\lambda} + \dfrac{(t_c - t_w)\rho}{\nu} \\ \mathbb{T}_2 = \begin{aligned}[t] & S_w \nu \mu (1 - t_c)[(1 - t_c)(S_c - S_w) \\ & + S_w(1 - t_c) + t_w - \mu] \end{aligned} \\ \mathbb{T}_1 = 1 - (S_c - S_w)(1 - t_c) - (1 - S_w)(t_c - t_w)] \end{cases}
\tag{5.3.4.2.1}
$$

Alternatively we can write

$$
r = \begin{cases} \dfrac{(1 - M)\rho - \nu(1 - t_c)[S_w(1 - t_w) + t_w - \hat{\mu}]}{S_w(1 - t_c)1 - ZN} \\[2mm] \text{where } \hat{\mu} = t_w + \hat{\lambda} + (t_c - t_w)\pi \end{cases}
\tag{5.3.4.2.2}
$$

The sensitivity functions of r with respect to $\hat{\lambda}$ may easily be computed from equations (5.3.4.2) and (5.3.3.2). From equations (5.3.4.2.1) we have

$$
\begin{aligned}
\frac{\partial r}{\partial \hat{\lambda}} &= \frac{\partial r}{\partial \hat{\mu}} = \frac{\nu(L_3 - L_4) - S_w \nu \mu(1 - t_c)(L_1 + L_2)}{(L_3 - L_4)^2} \\
&= \frac{\partial f}{\partial \hat{\mu}} \frac{\partial \hat{\mu}}{\partial \hat{\lambda}}
\end{aligned}
\tag{5.3.4.2.3}
$$

Similarly, we can write

$$
\frac{\partial r}{\partial \hat{\lambda}} = \frac{\partial g}{\partial \hat{\mu}} \frac{\partial \hat{\mu}}{\partial \hat{\lambda}} = \frac{\partial r}{\partial \hat{\mu}} = \frac{\nu(1 - t_c)P_2 - P_1 S_w(1 - t_c)Z}{P_2^2}
\tag{5.3.4.2.4}
$$

Since $\partial r / \partial \hat{\lambda} = \partial r / \partial \hat{\mu}$, an analytical note becomes necessary. In the case of either equation (5.2.7) or (5.2.12), $\hat{\mu}$ is considered to be arbitrarily fixed by the government. In the case of either equation (5.3.4.2.1) and (5.3.4.2.2), the value of $\hat{\mu}$ is determined by certain economic variables and parameters, whose values may be determined by appropriate decision criteria and processes. As such the magnitudes of $\hat{\mu}$ and hence r in equations (5.2.7) and (5.3.4.2.1) may not be equal. Similarly those in (5.2.12) and (5.3.4.2.2) may also not be equal. The directional effects are, however, the same.

Proposition 5.3.4.2

$$\frac{\partial r}{\partial \hat{\lambda}} \gtreqless 0 \text{ as } \frac{\partial r}{\partial \hat{\mu}} = \frac{\partial f}{\partial \hat{\mu}} \gtreqless 0$$

Proof

The proof of the proposition follows from recognizing that $(\partial \hat{\mu} / \partial \hat{\lambda}) = 1$ and hence $(\partial r / \partial \hat{\lambda}) = (\partial r / \partial \hat{\mu})$. Consequently, Direct. $\partial r / \partial \hat{\lambda}$ =Direct. $\partial r / \partial \hat{\mu}$, where Direct. $\Rightarrow$ Direction of change. $\square$

Proposition (5.3.4.2) suggests that over the neo-Keynesian equilibrium path of capital accumulation, the rate of interest is positively related to the variations of government deficit, defined as proportion of real domestic output. This confirms the belief that an increase in the government's real deficit spending as a proportion of real output over the neo-Keynesian equilibrium path and for any given investment leads to an increase in the real rate of interest in a closed economy.

Let us now examine the case of budget surplus. In this case, the paths of the rate of interest may be obtained by combining (5.2.7) with (5.3.3.8), and (5.2.12) with (5.3.3.9). Thus we can write alternatively,

$$r = \begin{cases} \dfrac{L_1 + L_2}{L_3 - L_4} \\[2em] \text{where} \quad \hat{\mu} = t_w - \hat{\sigma} + \dfrac{(t_c - t_w)\rho}{\nu} \end{cases} \quad (5.3.4.2.5)$$

$$r = \begin{cases} \dfrac{(1 - M)\rho - \nu(1 - t_c)[S_w(1 - t_w) + t_w - \hat{\mu}]}{S_w(1 - t_c)[1 - ZN]} \\[2em] \text{where } \hat{\mu} = t_w - \sigma + (t_c - t_w)\pi \end{cases} \quad (5.3.4.2.6)$$

We may now examine the effect of variations in government surplus on the rate of interest payable for the use of savings from work income. This may easily be done by taking the partial derivative of either equation (5.3.4.2.5) or (5.3.4.2.6). Since $\hat{\mu}$ is related to $\hat{\sigma}$, we can write

$$\frac{\partial r}{\partial \hat{\sigma}} = \frac{-(\partial r)}{\partial \hat{\mu}} = \frac{-\nu(L_3 - L_4) + S_w \nu \mu (1 - t_c)(L_1 + L_2)}{(L_3 - L_4)^2}$$

$$= \frac{\partial f}{\partial \hat{\mu}} \frac{\partial \hat{\mu}}{\partial \hat{\sigma}} \quad (5.3.4.2.7)$$

Alternatively,

$$
\begin{aligned}
\frac{\partial r}{\partial \hat{\sigma}} &= -\frac{(\partial r)}{\partial \hat{\mu}} = \frac{-\nu(1 - t_c)P_2 + P_1 S_w(1 - t_c)Z}{P_2^2} \\
&= \frac{\partial g}{\partial \hat{\mu}} \frac{\partial \hat{\mu}}{\partial \hat{\sigma}}
\end{aligned}
\tag{5.3.4.2.8}
$$

Equations (5.3.4.2.7) and (5.3.4.2.8) suggest that the magnitude of effect of surplus is equal to that in the case of deficit. The proposition (5.3.4.3) shows that they have opposite signs over the path of neo-Keynesian optimal capital accumulation.

Proposition 5.3.4.3

$$
\frac{\partial r}{\partial \hat{\sigma}} \lesseqgtr 0 \text{ as } \frac{\partial r}{\partial \hat{\mu}} = \frac{\partial f}{\partial \hat{\mu}} \gtreqless 0
$$

Similarly,

$$
\frac{\partial r}{\partial \hat{\sigma}} \lesseqgtr 0 \text{ as } \frac{\partial r}{\partial \hat{\mu}} = \frac{\partial g}{\partial \hat{\mu}} \gtreqless 0
$$

Proof

The proof follows immediately, as one notes that $\partial \hat{\mu}/\partial \hat{\sigma} = -1$. The proposition is established by combining this result with proposition (5.3.4.1)□.

5.3.5 The Government Budget: A Reflection

So far we have constructed and analyzed the effect of government budget-policy behavior on the response adjustment of net investment to profit being generated by accumulated capital and maintained by it. We shall now reflect on the budget. From equation (5.3.3.4) and (5.3.3.5), the government budget as a proportion of real domestic output may be written as

$$
\hat{\mu} = t_w + \hat{\lambda} + \frac{(t_c - t_w)\rho}{\nu}
\tag{5.3.5.1}
$$

or alternatively, as

$$
\hat{\mu} = t_w + \hat{\lambda} + (t_c - t_w)\pi
\tag{5.3.5.2}
$$

Equations (5.3.5.1) and (5.3.5.2) are the same but place differential emphasis on economic factors that are themselves interdependent. Equation (5.3.5.1) emphasizes that the government propensity to spend depends on profit rate, capital efficiency and the government's savings behavior, given the propensities to tax from different income types. Equation (5.3.5.2) emphasizes the dependence of government's propensity to spend on income distribution, and government's savings behavior, given the distribution of tax rates over income types. The economic interpretations of the two different emphasis are reducible to one another, since the income distribution depends on the rate of profit and capital efficiency. We may thus state the following proposition.

Proposition 5.3.5.1

If $t_c > t_w$, a shift in the structure of social income distribution in favor of profit given the existing tax structure should lead to one of the following: (a) an increase in the government average propensity to spend; (b) a reduction in the government's deficit or (c) an increase in the governments savings. The corollary holds if $t_w > t_c$. We can also note that

$$\frac{\partial \hat{\mu}}{\partial t_c} = \begin{cases} \pi > 0, & \text{from equation (5.3.5.2)} \\ \\ \rho/\nu > 0, & \text{from equation (5.3.5.1)} \end{cases} \tag{5.3.5.3}$$

$$\frac{\partial \hat{\mu}}{\partial t_w} = \begin{cases} 1 - \pi > 0, & \text{from equation (5.3.5.2)} \\ \\ \dfrac{\nu - \rho}{\nu} > 0, & \text{from equation (5.3.5.1)} \end{cases} \tag{5.3.5.4}$$

$$\frac{\partial \hat{\mu}}{\partial \pi} = (t_c - t_w) \gtrless 0, \text{ as } t_c \gtrless t_w \tag{5.3.5.5}$$

In other words, the potential government budget, as a proportion of real domestic output, can be either increased or decreased by increasing or decreasing one or both of the tax rates.

One can easily establish a trade-off relationship between t_w and t_c for any given level of budget and social distribution of income. If the levels of budget and income distribution are given, then

$$d\mu = dt_w - \pi dt_w + \pi dt_c = 0 \tag{5.3.5.6}$$

$$\Rightarrow (1 - \pi)dt_w = -\pi dt_c$$

$$\Rightarrow -\frac{dt_c}{dt_w} = \frac{1 - \pi}{\pi} = \frac{\omega}{\pi}$$

This result may be illustrated by isobudget lines, as in Figure (5.3.5.1)

Figure 5.3.5.1
Government Iso-budget Lines with Fixed Income Distribution

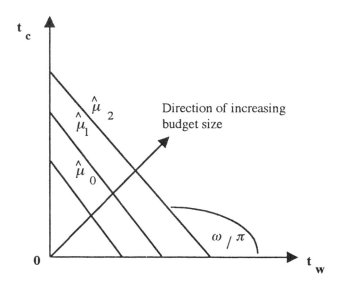

Similarly, one can establish a trade-off relationship between the budget deficit and the structure of income distribution between profits and wages for a given fixed structure of taxation and government budget as a proportion of real domestic output. In this respect, we can write

$$d\hat{\mu} \;\; = \;\; d\hat{\lambda} + (t_c - t_w)d\pi = 0$$

$$\Rightarrow \quad -\frac{d\hat{\lambda}}{d\pi} = (t_c - t_w) \tag{5.3.5.7}$$

Graphically, it is shown in Figure 5.3.5.2,

Figure 5.3.5.2
Government Iso-budget Line with Fixed Tax Structure

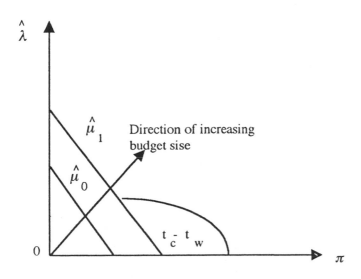

It is interesting to observe from the theoretical system that

$$\pi = (\rho/\nu) \tag{5.3.5.8}$$

Hence if the profit rate rises, it must be the case that the average productivity of capital has risen; otherwise, the structure of income distribution would have changed. In other words, a change in the profit rate must be accompanied by a corresponding change in the average productivity of capital, or the income distribution would have changed.

When one examines the structure of the budget as specified in equation (5.3.5.2), one immediately finds that all the parameters are government-budget decision variables except the parameter for income distribution. The government can substantially affect the optimal path of capital accumulation decision if it can, in addition, manipulate income distribution through an incomes policy. A complete analysis of the effects of incomes policy on aggregate capital

105

accumulation and government budgetary behavior can be carried on within the neo-Keynesian framework, as presented here.

We would like to point out some characteristics of this dynamic neo-Keynesian system of capital accumulation. The system is in dynamic equilibrium when aggregate savings is equal to aggregate profit and both are equal to the aggregate net investment. In this respect, the economic system is investing at its maximum where an equivalent value of profit is continually been invested, in that the investment goods sector is producing a value of investment goods that is equal to the value of profit with the satisfaction of effective demand, all measured in units of consumer goods or in cost units. Since this value is also equal to aggregate savings, the implication is that the consumer goods sector is producing consumption goods whose value is just equal to the total wage bill. Production is thus synchronized between demand for consumer goods and the supply of consumer goods, and between demand for investment goods and the supply of investment goods, satisfying the principle of aggregate demand equals aggregate supply. The income distribution between wages and profits is then computed at all equilibrium points on the path of maximum investment.

The propositions about government budgetary behavior and its effect on the path of interest rate and other relevant variables must be viewed in this setting. One can examine other propositions when the system is investing less than either the current aggregate savings or profit. One can examine the budgetary effects when the system attempts to invest more than the sustainable aggregate savings. All this can be done within the system of aggregate thinking as presented here. Within this neo-Keynesian framework a number of interesting conclusions present themselves to us, while new and challenging problems rise to the surface. Central to the framework is a demonstration of the dynamic and powerful role of income distribution in the capital-accumulation process and hence the growth of potential capacity building. The system is such that over the equilibrium path of maximum investment we can compute the parameters of income distribution as well as the rate of interest payable for the use of savings from work income, through their relationship to the accumulation process.

Given fixed income distribution over the optimal capital accumulation path, we can determine the optimal tax distribution between the two income types if we know the government preference distribution, as measured by a utility function. Let such a utility function depend on t_w and t_c (i.e., $U = U(t_w, t_c)$). The optimal tax rates may be obtained by maximizing $U(\cdot)$, subject to the government budget constraint from equation (5.3.2.6). The problem is simply

$$\left. \begin{array}{l} \max_{t_c, t_w} \quad U(t_w, t_c) \\[2ex] \text{S.T.} \quad \hat{\mu} = (1 - \pi)t_w + \pi t_c \end{array} \right\} \tag{5.3.5.9}$$

The solution reduces to

$$\frac{(\partial u / \partial t_w)}{(\partial u / \partial t_c)} = \frac{1 - \pi}{\pi} = \frac{\omega}{\pi} \tag{5.3.5.10}$$

Thus the rates of marginal utility of the government to tax differential income types must be equal to the rate of wage share to the rate of profit share in real output for any given structure of income distribution. The solution given by equation (5.3.5.10) is shown geometrically in Figure (5.3.5.3) where t_c^* and t_w^* are the optimal tax rates for profit and wage incomes respectively.

Figure 5.3.5.3
Optimal Tax Rates with a Given Budget and Income Distribution

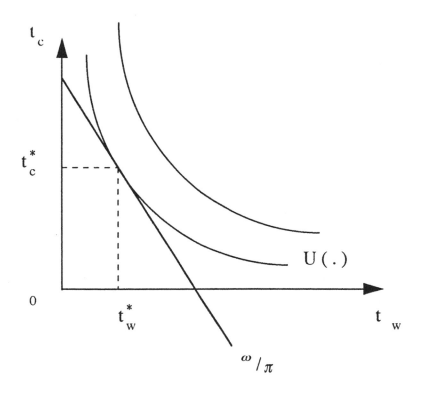

Similarly, we can compute optimal deficit and income distribution measured by the profit share, where both are choice variables that the government can affect by exercises of its power through the institutional arrangement. Let the government's preference over income distribution and deficit proportion be defined by a utility function, $U = U(\hat{\lambda}, \pi)$. The optimal decision is thus a simple optimization, given the tax structure. Thus

$$\left.\begin{array}{l} \max_{\hat{\lambda}, \pi} \quad U(\hat{\lambda}, \pi) \\[2em] \text{S.T.} \quad \hat{\mu} = \hat{\lambda} + (t_c - t_w)\pi \end{array}\right\} \qquad (5.3.5.11)$$

The solution yields the condition

$$\frac{\partial u/\partial \pi}{\partial u/\partial \hat{\lambda}} = (t_c - t_w) \tag{5.3.5.12}$$

In other words, the ratio of the government's marginal utility over income distribution to its marginal utility of deficit spending is equal to the difference between the two tax rates, given the tax distribution structure. The solution provided by equation (5.3.4.12) is illustrated graphically in Figure (5.3.5.4) where π^* and $\hat{\lambda}^*$ are the optimal income-distribution structure and deficit-spending propensity respectively.

Figure 5.3.5.4
Optimal Income Distribution with a Given Government Budget and Income Distribution

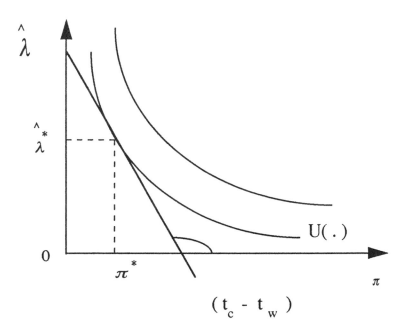

Chapter 6

The Theory of Aggregate Investment and Neo-Classical One-Sector Growth in a Closed Economy

In this chapter, we will reflect on some questions and results of basic neoclassical theory of one-sector growth. We shall then advance certain possible relationships that maybe established between fundamental results of the neoclassical growth theory and the neo-Keynesian theory of optimal capital accumulation in a closed economy, as we have presented it up to this point. Basically, the neoclassical growth theory may be viewed as a theory of aggregate investment that leads to the creation of new productive capacity and hence growth in potential output. It is in this light, I think, that one can appreciate the theoretical contribution and the applicational usefulness of the theory. The contributions must be seen in terms of the nature and behavior of the processes of aggregate investment and capital accumulation and in terms of how they influence the aggregate growth process, as well as how they help to determine the potential rate of growth of the aggregate output.

The initial works of Harrod and Domar are landmarks in the development of dynamic theory of aggregate economic behavior where capital accumulation is directly linked to the growth of output potential. These landmarks are the reference points for the development of the neoclassical and Cambridge modern theories of economic growth dynamics. The neoclassical and Cambridge theories of growth have a number of elements that are common to the neo-Keynesian theories of optimal aggregate capital accumulation and investment that we have advanced so far. A similar statement cannot be early made for the neoclassical theory of optimal capital accumulation and the subsequent investment analysis as they relate to aggregate growth dynamics. Generally, one would expect a logical continuity between theories on capital accumulation and aggregate growth; nonetheless, this does not seem to be the case with the neoclassical theories of capital accumulation and growth.

In fact, one encounters many theoretical difficulties as one attempts to establish a logical connection and continuity between the neoclassical growth theory and the currently accepted neoclassical theories of optimal capital accumulation and investment. There are doubts whether such a connection can even be established. However, the demands of logical consistency and continuity would require that a theory of optimal aggregate capital accumulation and investment must not only be an essential part of growth theory but must also account for the effects of income distribution and aggregate savings of the society. The flow of new aggregate investment goes to update the stock of accumulated aggregated capital; hence it widens the economy's productive capacity and increases the potential rate of aggregate growth, through the expansion of the potential production surface for any given technique and labor stock.

The set of conditions for constructing the optimal production surface (production-possibility frontier)at any moment of tiem suggests that a growth in any of the factors of capital stock, technology or labor stock should lead to an expansion of the optimal production surface and hence to the growth in the output potential. As such, one would expect that a theory of progressive changes in any one of these factors must also be an integral part of the growth theory. In this respect, the development of a theory of growth must have a logical connection, continuity and consistency with the development of a theory of progressive changes in any one of the key aggregate factors. This logical consistency, and a smooth connection between the neoclassical growth theory and neoclassical optimal capital dynamics, seem to be lacking. Whether an appropriate logical connection can be established or not is not a problem that concerns us here.

We simply want to point out that the approaches of both neoclassical and Cambridge economists to growth dynamics seem to support this logical line. The two approaches, however, have produced problems for reconciliation. Such problems have generated some interpretational and conceptual difficulties in various attempts to resolve some critical questions encountered in the study of economic dynamics. Furthermore the presence of an aggregate savings-investment-equality constraint that restricts capital accumulation and hence potential output growth is a characteristic of both the neoclassical growth theory and of the neo-Keynesian theory of aggregate capital dynamics that has been presented in this essay. This flow of resource constraint is clearly absent in the development of the neoclassical optimal capital dynamics. Another element that the neoclassical growth theory and the neo-Keynesian theory of capital dynamics have in common is that both are theories of aggregate behavior, where such behavior is constrained by the technology and the consumption psychology of the society. Furthermore, both theories are developed within the Keynesian aggregate framework rather than the micro-decision framework of either the classical or neoclassical thinking. As such, the results of both theories must be suspected to have some similarities and a logical connection.

To explore the similarities and the logical connection of the results of the two theories, let us examine the set of questions relevant to the neoclassical growth theory. Because of substantial emphasis of "steady state" properties of growth dynamics, the relevant questions seem not to be explicit in the foundations of neoclassical theory of growth. Let us begin by exploring the questions raised by Harrod and Domar leading to the Harrod-Domar growth theory [61] [113] and the neoclassical modifications [269] [666]. First we observe that both Harrod and Domar were working within the Keynesian system of aggregate thinking. Thus the Harrod-Domar consistency condition for steady-state growth is derived from the logical requirements of the Keynesian aggregate thinking. The consistency condition is obtained since both Harrod and Domar were answering two different but conceptually interrelated questions. Let us examine these questions and see how they relate to neo-Keynesian capital dynamics and neoclassical growth dynamics.

6.1   THE RELEVANT QUESTIONS OF HARROD AND DOMAR

In the Domar's original essay, a question is raised as to how much income should grow in order to maintain full-capacity utilization of a growing capital stock [114] [116]. To Harrod, the relevant question is how much income should grow so as to maintain planned aggregate investment to be equal to aggregate savings [273] [296]. The answer to Harrod and Domar's questions on the dynamic behavior of the economy is given by what Solow has called the *consistency condition* [274]. To obtain the consistency condition, both the Harrod and Domar analyses require that the Keynesian equilibrium conditions hold at each point in time. In addition, full factor employment is assumed from the initial time and is required to be maintained at all time points. The problem for Harrod and Domar is simply to find the conditions that would maintain the full factor employment in the Keynesian equilibrium. To abstract the required conditions Domar combines the Keynesian multiplier and capacity-creating effect of investment to obtain the consistency condition. Harrod, on the other hand, combines the Keynesian multiplier and the investment accelerator to derive the same consistency condition.

Domar's answer is obtained in terms of investment growth, which is translated into output growth. The answer by Harrod is directly obtained in terms of income growth. It must be noted that the assumed full-capacity utilization condition can be transformed into the conditions of the acceleration principle, since new investment has capacity-creating as well as employment-creating effect. In fact, the full-capacity utilization condition is also a requirement for the working mechanism of the acceleration principle. Both Harrod and Domar analytics require the Keynesian short-run equilibrium conditions to hold at each point of time. Furthermore, full factor employment is assumed from the initial time and hence the problem is simply finding the conditions that would maintain the system on the equilibrium path, where aggregate demand is equal to aggregate supply and aggregate savings is equal to aggregate investment. Since

111

full employment in addition to the labor force and its growth are given, the answers of Harrod and Domar are obtained in terms of capital accumulation and investment. Thus the Harrod-Domar approaches to optimal growth within the Keynesian framework constitute foundations for theories of aggregate capital and investment. If the questions of Harrod and Domar are to be illuminating, we must assume a given technique and hope that this technique will be the optimal one from the onset. This point will be examined a little closer later in this chapter.

The Harrod-Domar theory on growth is simply a theory of optimal aggregate capital and investment when it is properly interpreted and when the required logical connection is established to the process of capital accumulation and its role in capacity creation and in employment that lead to output growth. The logical validity of this statement can be found in the fundamental question of the neo-Keynesian theory of capital and investment that we have advanced in this essay. The question is, simply, what should the rate of aggregate savings be if the economy is to invest at the maximum rate and aggregate capital is to be always optimal (in a specific sense), such that the principle of effective demand is always satisfied and full employment of the labor force is maintained at a given technique? It is easy to see how this question is immediately related to those of Harrod and Domar. We should interperate the neoclassical growth theory in terms of this question.

We would like to point out that in dealing with aggregate growth dynamics, if technique is assumed in addition to labor force behavior, the theory that emerges can be nothing but capital theory. Alternatively, if we assume labor force behavior and capital stock, the theory that emerges is simply that of technological progress. On the other hand, if we assume an unlimited level of capital with a given technique, the theory that emerges is a theory of demography and labor force growth. Keeping these points in mind, we may examine the neoclassical growth dynamics.

One can explicitly state the relevant question of the neoclassical growth theory when the Harrod-Domar questions are extended into modern growth theory. Suppose we start from an initial position of full factor employment; what must be the optimal (in a specific sense) technique (properly defined) needed to maintain the full-capacity utilization of an endogenously growing capital stock and the full employment of an exogenously growing labor force, such that the Keynesian savings-investment equality constraint and the Harrod-Domar consistency condition are satisfied? To this question, the neoclassical answer is provided by that technique which corresponds to maximum "capital per worker," given the technological know-how of production and factor substitution, as represented by an aggregate production function.

Let us look at these questions and answers from the viewpoint of aggregate capital dynamics. From such a viewpoint, an alternative way of interpreting Harrod and Domar's questions and answers is possible. The questions may be stated and interpreted in terms of an economic environment where producers are profit (cost) maximizers (minimizers), in the sense of Joan Robinson [589]– i.e., producers always select the maximum profit (minimum cost) technique.

These questions may be stated on the condition that income distribution, social intertemporal consumption psychology and maximum profit technique are given. The income distribution and the consumption psychology determine the aggregate savings path of the society. The maximum profit technique, on the other hand, establishes the capital-output ratio, or the average capital productivity. Together, they determine the Harrod-Domar consistency conditions for steady-state growth. A change in the maximum profit technique (e.g., changes in the relative real factor cost structure of factor transformation know-how) can alter the relative value of the Harrod-Domar consistency condition, as implicitly interpreted.

These interpretations of the questions and answers of Harrod and Domar lead to results similar to those of the neoclassicals, under appropriate conditions. In light of these interpretations, the output-capital ratio, the multiplier, the capital-output ratio and the accelerator are specified to depend on the appropriate technique, given all the relevant information about production and relative prices. It must be noted that not all the neoclassical optimal growth paths are consistent with the maximum-profit technique. In fact, whether a particular neoclassical optimal growth path can be maintained when it is reached, given profit motives, must be examined. This examination will provide us with the required logical system to construct an aggregate investment path.

6.2   THE CONCEPTUAL FOUNDATION OF OPTIMAL AGGREGATE CAPITAL THEORY

The Harrod and Domar theories of growth present logical systems that allow aggregate investment and require capital level to be determined under the assumed growth conditions. One may reason as follows: the number of workers that can be employed per unit of output to be produced is fixed by a choice of technique; hence, given the initial conditions, if one knows the growth rate of the labor force, one can determine the output growth rate needed to maintain full-capacity utilization of the capital stock, which is growing in accordance with the behavior of aggregate savings, and at the same time fully employ the labor force, growing at a given constant rate. The optimal level of aggregate capital needed to employ fully the existing labor for the given technique is then determined. For the same given technique the additional aggregate capital (net aggregate investment) needed to employ fully the additional labor force is also determined.

Thus given the initial conditions, the determination of the full-employment output level and its growth rate allows one to determine the path of the desired level of aggregate capital and net investment that must take place, since in both Harrod and Domar's theories either capital level or investment is output determined. The conditions for the required growth of output are obtained and expressed in terms of the relationship between the social savings attitude, which can support net investment, and the production technology, expressed as either output-capital or capital-output ratio in such a way as to meet the requirements of the Keynesian savings-investment equality constraint.

From this viewpoint, the required value of aggregate capital and its growth (aggregate investment) are determined at any point in time by the level of labor force and its growth rate at the given "optimal" technique. The realization of these potential values are determined and maintained by the past and current behavior of real social savings. Such a volume of social savings is determined by the nature of income distribution and social consumption psychology implied in the assumed conditions.

In considering the Harrod-Domar systems as they relate to optimal capital accumulation, the optimal technique may be assumed to be given from the outset. In this line of aggregate thinking the profit rate and technique appear as a pair. They are determined outside the system. The collection of all the pairs of profit rates and techniques constitutes the blueprint. This blueprint of pairs of techniques and profit rates is contained in the information set for the aggregate decision process. We shall use this as a point of reference for examining the essential elements of optimal aggregate capital and investment theories that may be implied by the basic structure of the neoclassical theory of growth.

6.3 THE OPTIMAL AGGREGATE CAPITAL THEORY AND THE NEOCLASSICAL GROWTH THEORY

From the restatement of the Harrod-Domar questions, a different question arises as to whether the optimal technique and the corresponding profit rate can be endogenously determined. The search for an answer to this question will provide a contribution to capital theory implied in neoclassical growth theory. This contribution is seen from the neoclassical suggestion that the optimal (in a specific sense) technique and the profit rate must be determined through an internal decision logic of the theory. In its logical form the neoclassical growth theory shows that an optimal technique can be found through the method of factor substitution. Furthermore, the optimal technique selected by this method is shown to be consistent with the Harrod-Domar consistency condition as well as the Keynesian dynamic equilibrium condition. The neoclassical theoretical framework retains all the basic characteristics of the Harrod-Domar theories except the assumption of a "given optimal technique," which must be determined within the system's specification.

Given these questions of growth theory, can we establish similar characteristics and a possible logical link between the neoclassical growth theory and the neo-Keynesian theory of optimal capital accumulation that we have presented here? There are some interesting neoclassical results that may be compared and contrasted with the neo-Keynesian results that have been obtained in this treatise. For one thing, given the technological know-how, there is a set of neoclassical optimal techniques that will satisfy the Harrod-Domar consistency condition and the time-point Keynesian equilibrium condition. The elements of this set of techniques do not necessarily satisfy the neo-Keynesian dynamic equilibrium conditions where not only is the profit rate equal to the rate of accumulation but both are equal to the meI and meK and the rate of social savings. The neoclassical problem is simply to find either the *maximum* profit or *minimum* cost technique, for any given set of information about production and cost.

To show that the neoclassical system of growth dynamics leads us to a maximum profit technique, suppose s is the average propensity to save, Q the output, K, the capital stock and n a given growth rate of labor force. Then at the optimal technique

$$sQ = nK \tag{6.3.1}$$

Since the aggregate savings is instantaneously turned into aggregate net investment after replacement, we can write the net investment path, $\dot{K}(t)$, for $Q/K = \nu$ as

$$\dot{K} = sQ = nk \tag{6.3.2}$$

and $s\nu = n$ which meets the consistency condition. The interpretation of equation (6.3.2) is interesting. It states that for the Keynesian equilibrium to be maintained, over-time the net investment must be equal to the additional volume of capital needed to employ fully the added labor force, given the initial full-employment and full-capacity utilization conditions. The volume of capital at each point of time, given the social attitude to save, must generate enough social real savings to support the aggregate net investment that is taking place in these time points.

A question arises as to whether the business norms and motives of producers and investors would allow the use of the volume of aggregate capital at each point of time to generate the required savings given the path of production and cost information. Under the conditions of profit motives of producers, this question translates into a question as to whether enough aggregate profit would be forthcoming at each point of time to justify the continual existence and full-capacity use of such aggregate capital. Furthermore, given that the "wear and tear" is replaced, there is an added question as to whether the net aggregate investment taking place can generate enough increased aggregate profit to justify its creation, existence and use.

To answer these questions the neoclassicals evoke the conditions of "microeconomic competitive imputations," where factor payments are technologically determined under institutions of perfectly competitive markets and are equalized in all lines of production to aggregate marginal product. Thus if r, the rate of interest, is the *cost* of unit aggregate capital, and the aggregate production technology is linearly homogeneous with $K/L = k$, then

$$f'(k) = r = MP_K \tag{6.3.3}$$

where MP_K is the marginal product of capital, K, and $f(k) = F(K/L, 1)$ is a linearly homogeneous production function. With the assumption of a linearly homogeneous production function and institutions of perfectly competitive markets, one obtains within the neoclassical growth logic the condition that income distribution-to be specific, the distributive shares of factors - are technologically but not institutionally determined. Hence,

$$Q = rK + wL \tag{6.3.4}$$

and

$$Q = \prod + W \tag{6.3.5}$$

where $\prod = rK$, is the aggregate profit, $W = wL$ is the aggregate wage bill, and $Q = F(K, L)$. Equation (6.3.5) may be written in its intensity form as

$$\nu = \rho + \omega \tag{6.3.6}$$

where $\nu = Q/K$, $\rho = \prod/K$, and $\omega = W/K$. The profit rate may then be expressed as the difference between average capital productivity and the wage cost for operating a unit of the aggregate capital. Hence,

$$\rho = \nu - \omega \tag{6.3.7}$$

Given these assumptions about technology of factor use and the institutions of organization of production and distribution, the problem is to find the appropriate "steady state" technique among the set of admissible techniques. The appropriate technique must be one that would allow the economic system to generate enough aggregate savings, under profit motives, to maintain the accumulated aggregate capital and at the same time support the net aggregate investment taking place, so that full labor employment and full-capacity utilization of capital are dynamically maintained over the Keynesian equilibrium path.

The neoclassical answer is that technique which maximizes per-worker consumption. This is the celebrated "golden rule" of aggregate capital accumulation. In its basic form the golden rule establishes that if the technique is such that consumption per worker is maximum, the aggregate rate of interest, which is the price of aggregate capital, is equal to the exogenous growth rate of the labor force. Hence,

$$rK(t) = nK(t) \tag{6.3.8}$$

and hence from equation (6.3.2)

$$\dot{K} = rK = nK = sQ \tag{6.3.9}$$

This implies that $\dot{K}/K = r = s\nu = n$, where s is the aggregate propensity to save.

It is important to note that when the "maximum consumption per worker" technique is selected, aggregate profit is equal to aggregate savings, and both are equal to aggregate investment. This does not necessarily mean that all earned profits are saved and reinvested. It simply means that the economic system as a whole must save and invest a real value that is equivalent to the aggregate profit. This result is obtained under different conditions by Robinson [589]. Since $rK = \prod$ is the total profit, we immediately obtain (for $\xi = \dot{K}/K$)

$$\frac{\prod}{K} = \rho = r = \frac{\dot{K}}{K} = \xi = n \qquad (6.3.10a)$$

Thus

$$\rho = \xi = r = n \qquad (6.3.10b)$$

From equation (6.3.9), total profit is equal to total savings, and both are equal to net investment. Hence the rate of savings, $S/K = \sigma$, is equal to both the profit and accumulation rates. The most important results specified in equations (6.3.10a and b) are that the rate of profit is equal to the rate of accumulation and both are equal to the rate of savings on the golden-rule path. The same result is obtained in the neo-Keynesian optimal capital theory that we have presented so far. The essential difference lies in the response coefficient. The production technique consistent with such conditions is the *maximum profit rate technique*. The profit rate, $\rho = \prod/K$, is at maximum when $\dot{\rho} = 0$, which implies that $\dot{K}/K = \dot{\prod}/\prod$. Hence

$$\frac{\prod}{K} = \frac{\dot{\prod}}{\dot{K}} \qquad (6.3.11)$$

In this system we shall interpret $\prod/K$ as the measure of marginal efficiency of capital, while $\dot{\prod}/\dot{K}$ is the measure of marginal efficiency of investment. Thus the marginal efficiency of investment and marginal efficiency of capital are equal to the marginal product of capital, all of which are equal to the rates of accumulation and saving over the path of optimal accumulation. The theory of optimal aggregate capital accumulation within this setup suggests that the *path of optimal aggregate capital* is reached when the rates of profit, accumulation and savings are equal, and are equal to the marginal efficiencies of capital and investment as well as to the rate of growth of the labor force. On the optimal path of aggregate capital accumulation, the aggregate propensity to save equals the proportion of profit share. Furthermore, the system is such that $\dot{K} \neq 0$, contrary to what one finds in the case of the neoclassical theory of optimal capital accumulation, where $\dot{K} = 0$ when the optimal capital is reached in the microeconomic sense.

6.4 THE THEORY OF AGGREGATE INVESTMENT AND THE NEOCLASSICAL GROWTH THEORY

Beginning with the model of optimal aggregate capital accumulation we can specify the path of aggregate net investment between the less-than-maximum profit technique paths as

$$\dot{K} = (\rho/\xi) \prod(t) \tag{6.4.1}$$

where $\rho = \prod/K$ and $\xi = \dot{K}/K$. By combining the conditions of competitive imputation and the linear homogeneous aggregate production function we can write equation (6.4.1) as:

$$\dot{K} = \frac{f'(k)}{\xi} \prod(t) \tag{6.4.2}$$

The path of net investment may be linked to the savings propensity by substituting equations (6.3.2) and (6.3.7) in (6.4.2) to obtain

$$\dot{K} = \left(\frac{\nu - \omega}{s\nu}\right) \prod(t) \tag{6.4.3}$$

where $\xi = s\nu$. The degree of responsiveness, $[(\nu - \omega)/s\nu)]$, of the net investment path to the profit path is fixed by average capital productivity, the structure of wage cost (income distribution) and general social attitude to thriftiness. Alternatively, the response coefficient of the profit path may be written in terms of the technique, k, to obtain

$$\dot{K} = \frac{\nu + k f'(k) - f(k)}{\xi} \prod(t) \tag{6.4.4}$$

If $I(t)$ is the gross investment path, then

$$I = \dot{K} + \delta K(t) \tag{6.4.5}$$

where δ is some measure of the real rate of aggregate depreciation. By substituting equations (6.4.2-6.4.4) in (6.4.5) we can write

$$I(t) = \frac{f'(k)}{\xi}[\prod(t) + \delta \int_0^t \prod(\tau; t)d\tau] \tag{6.4.6}$$

$$I(t) = \frac{\nu - \omega}{\xi}[\prod(t) + \delta \int_0^t \prod(\tau; t)d\tau] \tag{6.4.7}$$

$$I(t) = \frac{\nu + k f'(k) - f(k)}{\xi} \tag{6.4.8}$$

$$\times [\prod(t) + \delta \int_0^t \prod(\tau; t)d\tau]$$

where

$$K(t) = \int_0^t \dot{K}(\tau; t)d\tau = \int_0^t \prod(\tau; t)d\tau \tag{6.4.9}$$

defines the past history of capital accumulation.

The profit adjustment coefficients in all the equations define the degree to which investment responds to the profit flow as the techniques, k, varies over the set of profit rates. At the maximum profit technique, an equivalent value of aggregate profit is instantaneously invested, since at that time the profit rate is equal to the rate at which capital accumulates. In this respect, $f'(k^*)/\xi = 1$, from equation (6.4.2), and hence,

$$\dot{K} = f'(k^*)K^*(t) \tag{6.4.10}$$

and the path of gross investment, $I(t)$, may be written as

$$I(t) = f'(k^*)K^*(t) + \delta K^*(t) \tag{6.4.11}$$

or

$$I(t) = (r + \delta)K^*(t) \tag{6.4.12}$$

where $r^* = \rho^* = \xi^* = f'(k^*)$. In terms of aggregate profit, $\prod(t)$, and savings, $S(t)$ one can write

$$I(t) = (r + \delta) \int_0^t \prod(\tau;t)d\tau \tag{6.4.13}$$

or

$$I(t) = (r + \delta) \int_0^t S(\tau;t)d\tau \tag{6.4.14}$$

Equations (6.4.11-6.4.14) establish a proposition that given an income distribution and social attitude to save, the optimal path of gross investment that will maintain the Keynesian dynamic equilibrium is determined by the profit rate and capital durability (measured by the rate at which capital depreciates). This proposition holds only over the golden-rule path. Since the rate of profit $(\rho^* = r^*)$ is equal to the labor force growth rate, the statement translates to the proposition that the rate of growth of the labor force and capital durability determine the optimal gross investment path that will keep capital and labor fully employed, with consumption per worker at its maximum. Finally, it may be added that the kind of profit-maximizing behavior consistent with this golden-rule path is that of maximization of the profit rate, where the maximum profit technique is selected among the set of techniques that meet the Harrod-Domar consistency condition.

Equations (6.4.6-6.4.9) define the path of aggregate investment when the system is not on the path of maximum-profit-rate technique. Equations (6.4.13) and (6.4.14) define the optimal aggregate investment policy that would maintain the golden-rule path when it is reached. Together these equations define investment functions that are profit instigated and hence provide supports for the profit principle as well as the aggregate savings principle. This interpretation of the neoclassical growth result in terms of capital accumulation yields results similar to those of the neo-Keynesian capital accumulation, when expectations are always realized and adjustments are instantaneous. The rate of profit over capital is equal to the marginal product of capital; both are equal to the rate of accumulation that is supported by them, if all profits are saved and all wages are consumed, as in the Robinsonian system.

In the Kaldorian system the conditions for an equivalent result with the neoclassical aggregate capital dynamics require that the optimal technique, k, defined in term of capital per worker, depends on the rate of profit and capital efficiency at the margin, given the distribution of societal savings behavior over income types. This statement may easily be abstracted from the adjustment coefficient defined in equation (6.4.8), where $vk = f(k)$ and

$$v = \frac{\xi - kf'(k)}{1 - k} \tag{6.4.15}$$

By combining equation (6.4.15) with equation (4.3.10) we obtain the stated result

$$k = \frac{(1 - S_c)\rho}{(1 - S_c) + S_w[1 - f'(k)]} \tag{6.4.16}$$

where $S_c > S_w \neq 0$. More simply, the choice of the optimal path of k, the technique, depends on the profit rate and the efficiency of capital at the margin of production.

A similar condition may be derived for the neoclassical optimal technique, as viewed in the logical framework of the Pasinettian system. This can be done by combining equation (6.4.15) with equation (4.4.8a) to obtain the value of k

$$k = \frac{(1 - S_c)\rho - (1 - \rho S_c\mu)rS_w}{\rho(1 - S_c) + S_w(\rho - r) - S_w(1 - rS_c\mu)f'(k)} \tag{6.4.17}$$

The neoclassical k, interpreted in terms of equivalent solution in the Pasinettian system, depends on the rate of profit and capital efficiency at the margin, adjusted for the interest rate paid for the use of the workers' finance for capital goods, given the distribution of societal savings behavior over income types. On the optimal path of instantaneous adjustment of investment to profit, where the rate of profit on capital is the same irrespective of the source of ownership, such that the rate of interest is equal to the rate of profit, we have $v = \rho/S_w$, from equation (4.4.10). Thus, we can combine equations (4.4.10) and (6.4.15) to obtain

$$k = \frac{(1 - S_w)\rho}{\rho - S_w f'(k)}, \quad S_c > S_w \neq S_w v \tag{6.4.18}$$

Thus the optimal technique of the neoclassical construct must depend on the rate of profit and capital efficiency at the margin, given social attitude to save from work income in the Pasinettian system.

6.5 OPTIMAL INVESTMENT PATH AND OUTPUT EFFECT

It was developed in section (6.4) that the path of net optimal investment between technique equilibria is some multiple of the profit path. Gross optimal investment, on the other hand, depends on the whole current and past history of profit flow, with a proportionality factor. In a closed economy, the proportionality factor (also known as the profit coefficient) cannot exceed one. The implication of the development in section (6.4) is that both net and gross investment can be studied in the profit space, whether it is on the equilibrium path or between equilibria.

By a simple transformation, however, the behavior of both net and gross investment paths can be studied in the output space. By specifying an appropriate link between profit and output, equations (6.4.6), (6.4.7) and (6.4.8) may be transformed into output principle. Let the profit path be defined as

$$\prod(t) = \pi(t)Q(t) \tag{6.5.1}$$

where $\pi(t)$ is the path of profit share, which may or may not be constant. The path of the past history of profit flow may be written as

$$\int_0^t \prod(\tau;t)d\tau = \int_0^t \pi(\tau;t)Q(\tau;t)d\tau \tag{6.5.2}$$

By substituting equation (6.5.1) and (6.5.2) in equations (6.4.6), (6.4.7) and (6.4.8), we obtain an output principle of the form

$$I(t) = \frac{f'(k)}{\xi}[\pi(t)Q(t) + \delta \int_0^t \pi(\tau;t)Q(\tau;t)d\tau] \tag{6.5.3}$$

$$I(t) = \frac{\nu - \omega}{\xi}[\pi(t)Q(t) + \delta \int_0^t \pi(\tau;t)Q(\tau;t)d\tau] \tag{6.5.4}$$

$$I(t) = \frac{\nu + kf'(k) - f(k)}{\xi} \tag{6.5.5}$$

$$\times [\pi(t)Q(t) + \delta \int_0^t \pi(\tau;t)Q(\tau;t)d\tau]$$

These three equations specify the optimal interequilibrium investment path, where the speed of adjustment depends on the output coefficient. The difference between the profit and output principles is that the output coefficient is a weighted value of the profit coefficient, where such a weight is the share of profit in output.

On the optimal path, however, profit is equal to savings, and both of them are equal to net investment, leading to optimal gross investment paths as specified by equations (6.4.13) and (6.4.14). By substituting equation (6.5.2) in (6.4.13) we obtain

$$I(t) = (r + \delta) \int_0^t \pi(\tau; t) Q(\tau; t) d\tau \qquad (6.5.6)$$

where $\pi(\tau; t)$ may be viewed as the income distribution factor. It must be noted that on the optimal path, aggregate savings is equal to the aggregate profit. The share of savings in output is the same as the share of profit in output. Hence a combination of equations (6.5.2) and (6.4.14) yields the same structure as (6.5.6).

Since at the optimal technique consumption per worker in the neoclassical system is optimal, with the rate of interest, r, equaling the rate at which the labor force is growing, the optimal gross investment path is fixed by the labor force growth rate and capital durability specified by the rate of real depreciation. The path, however, is affected by the distribution of income between profit and wages. An incomes policy that disturbs $\pi(\tau; t)$ will affect the optimal investment path in the neoclassical system.

All these neoclassical results are obtained within the neo-Keynesian theory of optimal capital accumulation that we have presented. These results are inconsistent with the neoclassical optimal capital theory which requires that when the optimal capital is reached, net investment must be zero ($\dot{K} = 0$). In the system presented here, the optimal aggregate capital is reached when the profit rate is equal to the accumulation rate, both of which can be shown to be equal to the savings rate. Criticism and discussion of the neoclassical optimal capital and investment theories will be offered in Chapter 7. To conclude this chapter we must point out that the logical structure has established a proposition that given that income distribution is technologically and market determined, in addition to by the social attitude to save, the equilibrium path of gross investment is determined by the profit rate and capital durability (measured by the rate at which capital depreciates). Since the rate of profit ($\rho = r$) is equal to the labor force growth rate on the path of the golden rule, the statement translates to the proposition that the labor force growth rate and capital durability determine the optimal gross investment path that will keep labor fully employed, with the consumption per worker at its maximum. Finally, it may be added that the kind of profit-maximizing behavior consistent with the results that we have obtained and analyzed is the maximization of the profit rate. We will return to this point in Chapter 7.

6.6 NEOCLASSICAL OPTIMAL GROWTH, AGGREGATE INVESTMENT AND FISCAL POLICY

We may now extend the effects of fiscal policy on capital accumulation into the framework of neoclassical growth dynamics. The implicit and explicit argument in Chapter 5 is that in the system of production, distribution and accumulation, the government's fiscal actions indirectly affect the aggregate capital accumulation through their impacts on aggregate savings. Thus given that production is synchronized in such a manner that effective demand is always satisfied, changes in the tax and expenditure propensities of the government will tend to affect the optimal path of aggregate capital accumulation.

The fiscal action-induced optimal path of aggregate capital accumulation under the neoclassical growth framework is obtained by combining equations (6.4.4) and (5.2.3). Thus

$$\dot{K} = \left\{ \frac{rS_w(1 - t_c) + (P - 1)\xi + [kf'(k) - f(k)]R}{rR} \right\} \prod(t) \qquad (6.6.1)$$

The corresponding gross investment path may be specified as

$$I(t) = \left\{ \frac{rS_w(1 - t_c) + (P - 1)\xi + [kf'(k) - f(k)]R}{rR} \right\}$$

$$\times [\prod(t) + \delta \int_0^t \prod(\tau; t)d\tau] \qquad (6.6.2)$$

Given the social attitude to save from different income types and the propensity of government's fiscal behavior, we seek the technique within the neoclassical framework that would be consistent with equality between the rate of accumulation and the rate of profit, such that total net investment is equal to total profit. This requires an instantaneous adjustment of investment to profit over the required accumulation path. The value of technique over such accumulation path is such that from equations (6.6.1) and (6.6.2)

$$k^* = \frac{rR - rS_w(1 - t_c) + (P - 1)\xi^*}{(\xi^* - \nu)R} \qquad (6.6.3)$$

where $f'(k^*) = \rho^* = \xi^*$. This technique is that which is consistent with the capital accumulation where an equivalent value of total profit is always reinvested in a closed economy.

Chapter 7

A Methodological Critique and Appraisal of the Neoclassical Theory of Investment

In the preceding chapters we presented the neo-Keynesian theory of optimal aggregate capital accumulation and investment in closed systems. We analyzed the properties of the optimal paths of aggregate capital accumulation and investment decisions. The effects of parameter variations on the optimal paths were also examined. From the conditions of equilibrium we were able to derive some important relationships among some key aggregate parameters. The theory of capital accumulation and investment presented here is not the only one about the aggregate capital accumulation of an economy.

Many other theoretical attempts have been made to provide explanations for the aggregate investment behavior. Such explanations are cast in terms of the determinants and evolution of optimal capital stock and its rate of change. Among such attempts are the neoclassical theories of optimal capital accumulation and investment behavior [329] [541], the acceleration theory in varied forms [137] [393], the profit theory in different settings [357] [393] and the flow of funds theory [504] [505], etc. While each of these approaches in the study of aggregate investment attempts to illuminate the difficult problems of constructing a theory of aggregate capital accumulation, they invariably get entangled, one way or the other, in logical difficulties in the analysis of dynamic behavior of economic aggregates. As such, some if not all of these approaches have become mired by a number of theoretical inconsistencies as they attempt to relate the theoretical structures to the path of capital aggregate that goes to raise the potential output.

Of all these theories, the neoclassical version has become the dominant theory for the study and prediction of determinants and trends of micro and aggregate investment behaviors. In its origin [325] [329] and modified forms [219] [321] [461] [462] [541] [728] [729] [731], it has acquired an enviable respect in the literature on the subject and among capital-investment theoreticians. Such respect is not without questions and doubts as have been expressed by Eisner and others [145] [152] [762]. From the foundations of the neo-Keynesian framework, in terms of the core of the theory of aggregate investment behavior that has been outlined above, it seems useful to examine the neoclassical capital-investment theory and compare and contrast its structure and form within the framework provided here. Such comparative analysis requires us to examine particular logical and theoretical obstacles in the use of the neoclassical framework for the study of aggregate capital accumulation and investment. The motivations to examine these logical and theoretical obstacles stem from a basic concern with the "acceleration" interpretation of the neoclassical results [144] [154] and the use of this theoretical framework for empirical analysis of aggregate investment [254] [327] [333] [393]. We shall then suggest that the proper empirical analysis of the neoclassical investment theory must be done in the price space, at both microeconomic and macroeconomic levels of analysis. Furthermore, at least an indication must be made as to how the microeconomic capital accumulation and investment relate to the macro economic ones.

The concerns and criticisms raised here about the neoclassical theory of optimal capital accumulation and investment are quite different from those raised about the neoclassical theory of growth in Chapter 6. The concerns and criticisms are not about assumed conditions that allow an macroeconomic analogue to be constructed from the results of microeconomic theory of capital accumulation, such that an adequate representation and description of capital accumulation and investment behavior can be made at the macroeconomic level within the neoclassical framework. Of course, the acceptance of the required assumptions is an open question. The criticisms and questions cannot be answered simply by the introduction of adjustment costs that would allow delayed adjustments of actual to the desired capital stock, as well as finite investment.

The criticisms and questions raised are methodological ones. In the neoclassical framework, the method of analysis is the flexprice, where the microeconomic capital accumulation is on the optimal path at each point of time when the present value is the criterion index. It is precisely on this optimal path that the relevant prices (shadow prices) are computed and demand and supply equations are constructed. With the flexprice approach, prices are flexible in both directions. The quantity of goods and services on the aggregate cannot be obtained simply by summing up the monetary values. By the very nature of its logical construct the flexprice technique leads to a microeconomic representation of capital accumulation. Under what set of conditions, if any, can the neoclassical microeconomic representation of capital accumulation have a macroeconomic analogue such that the Keynesian equilibrium is attained, with or without a maximum rate of accumulation? Furthermore, what role does income distribution play in the accumulation of aggregate capital, and how does the accumulation relate to potential and actual output and its growth? Let us consider the basic form of the neoclassical capital-investment theory. The concerns and questions raised about the basic form are also held to apply to the extended forms, such as adjustment costs [119] [219] [461] [728]. In this respect, the Q-theory of investment [28] [293] [694] [724] cannot escape the same criticisms and concerns. We shall concentrate on the basic form of the neoclassical theory.

7.1 THE NEOCLASSICAL CAPITAL-INVESTMENT THEORY IN A CLOSED ECONOMY

By the very flexprice approach, the neoclassical theories of capital accumulation and investment behavior proceed from the particular to the general. This approach and the framework represent a basic methodological departure from the neo-Keynesian framework, where the analysis proceeds from the general to the particular, with fixprice analytics. Even though this difference is methodological, it has important implications regarding the form and content of the theories constructed. In the neoclassical system, the central elements of explanation are individual behavior with respect to investment activities and how such behavior may be translated into aggregate behavior of the economy. In the neo-Keynesian framework, the emphasis of the explanation is placed on the aggregate behavior of the economy's capital accumulation and investment process. While an explanation of the microeconomic behavior is not necessary, the existence of individual production data is required in the construction of the theory. Examination of the details of the underlying micro-structures becomes necessary only when either the aggregate variables are constructed at the relevant time point or the aggregate behavior fails to meet expectations about the economy's accumulation as revealed by the theory, so as to provide a guide to design discretionary policy options.

As in the neo-Keynesian theory, the driving force of general capital accumulation and investment activities in the neoclassical system of explanation is the individual profit motive—profit maximization in a specific sense over time. The individual profit in the neoclassical system at each time point is specifically defined as revenue less the wage bill and capital expense, made up of interest cost and depreciation expense in addition to other relevant capital expense deductions, given the market value of the producer's assets and flexible prices. Alternatively, the individual investment decisions may be guided by an objective of present value optimization. The general process of accumulation is, however, derived from the basic postulate of utility maximization of the stream of individual consumption under appropriate conditions, within the neoclassical framework [124] [193] [329].

The concept of profit maximization is interpreted differently in the neo-Keynesian system. Profits under the fixprice method are maximized in the sense that more profitable technique of production will be selected from the available set of techniques that are socially admissible and technically feasible for producing each and every output type in the economy. Every investment good is, therefore, designed to embody the highest profit-rate technique, given the structure of income distribution. In the neo-Keynesian system that has been constructed, profits are sought by firms to promote their growth and development, rather than their growth being sought to promote profit, given the structure of income distribution. It may be pointed out that in the neo-Keynesian system, income distribution is institutionally determined, instead of technically determined as in the neoclassical system of accumulation. The maximization of the rate of profit is the choice criterion.

Under a given, fixed set of flexible prices, inputs and output in the neoclassical system, the attainment of the paths of optimal capital stock and the corresponding optimal capital cost require that the individual firm maximize the present value of the enterprise at a given set of inertial conditions. Alternatively, the firm may maximize the integral of discounted stream of profit, given the asset value. In each case the optimization is constrained by appropriate technical possibilities and an equation of motion that governs the system's evolution [219] [329] [462]. The present-value maximization plays the role of providing the largest possible budgets that allow individual investors to reach the highest possible utility level over time, under the conditions of utility maximization.

From the constraints of the technical possibilities and the equation of motion governing the system of individual capital accumulation, an individual investment demand function is derived in the parameter space consisting of prices and other relevant parameters, including the discount rate under appropriate conditions. The problems of evolution of individual capital accumulation, choice of optimal investment path and the corresponding solution are characterized by the following optimal control system:

$$\max_{I,L} \int_0^\infty \alpha(t)R(t)dt$$

$$S.T. \qquad F(K,L,Q) \;=\; 0$$

$$I - \dot{K} - \delta K \;=\; 0$$

$$\alpha(t) - e^{-rt} \;=\; 0 \qquad\qquad (7.1.1)$$

$$R(t) - R(K,L,Q;p,w,q) \;=\; 0$$

The conditions for optimal capital accumulation require that
(a) $F(Q,L,K) = 0$,
(b) $\partial Q/\partial L = w/p$
(c) $\partial Q/\partial K = C/p$ \qquad and

128

(d) $C = C(q, r, \delta, \dot{q})$

The optimal investment path is obtained as

$$I \;=\; \dot{K} + \delta K^*, \qquad K^* = K(w, C, p) \tag{7.1.2}$$

$$I \;=\; I(w, C, p, \dot{w}, \dot{C}, \dot{p})$$

If the functional representation of technical conditions of production is linearly homogeneous, the optimal distribution of income is such that

$$Q(t) = L(t)(w/p) + K(t)(C, p) \tag{7.1.3}$$

where Q, L and K are real output, labor-service and capital service inputs, with, $F(\cdot)$ a description of the technical possibilities. The w and p are the prices of L and Q, while I is the volume of investment with q as its price, and r is the discount rate and C is the shadow price of capital [11] [329]. As a dynamic-choice problem, the system can be complicated in many directions [12] [118] [416], including constraining the equation of motion that describes the speed of capital accumulation by some index of profit or available finance. Nonetheless, the basic neoclassical theoretic structure of investment analysis remains the same.

Given the solution to the individual accumulation decision problem, one is faced with the problem of how to obtain the paths of aggregate capital stock and investment, and how to examine the conditions for the satisfaction of the Keynesian equilibrium. Within the neoclassical framework, the individual investment function resulting from the solution to the investment decision problem is taken as a good structual representation of the economy's aggregate investment under certain defined conditions. On the basis of the microeconomic structure, hypotheses are derived about the behavioral trend of the aggregate investment and its responsiveness to parameter variations [16] [111] [124] [306].

As long as the theoretical and empirical analysis remain at the level of microeconomic behavior, one can accept with some comfort the theoretical and empirical results of the neoclassical theory on capital accumulation and investment. One cannot say the same when the analysis is projected to the economy as a whole. There are some important logical difficulties in utilizing the neoclassical framework to analyze the economy's aggregate investment behavior. First, there is the problem of aggregation of the underlying microeconomic relations as one moves to the macroeconomic. To resolve this problem, restrictive assumptions are usually made, either implicitly or explicitly, that allow the individual investment-demand function to be postulated as a good representation of the structure of the aggregate investment [327]. In other words, under an appropriate set of assumptions one can construct, it is claimed, a macroeconomic analogue of the set of microeconomic results. Epistemologically, therefore, what is theoretically true on the microeconomic level is also true on macroeconomic level, under an appropriate set of assumptions. These assumptions may lead, but not necessarily, to a case where the macroeconomic analogue is true by assumption. Some implications of appropriateness and realism in assumptions and of the results of economic theorizing are discussed in [123]. We want only to point out that assumptions are critical to the alternative results obtained by the neoclassicals and neo-Keynesians from the analysis of general-macroeconomic-model representation of the economy.

Interesting examples are the neoclassical characterizations of acceleration and stock adjustment principles for the economy [254] [327]. They work by interpreting the neoclassical theory of investment to conform to the acceleration principle, whereby it is claimed that underlying the accelerator is the relative price. This neoclassical approach has been criticized by Eisner [150] [152]. By taking the technical possibilities to be described, on the aggregate, by a linearly homogeneous function of the Cobb-Douglas type, the gross-investment function is usually written in general as

$$I(t) = \sigma_2(p/c)\dot{Q} + \delta K \qquad (7.1.4)$$

where the optimal capital stock

$$K = \sigma_2(p/c)Q, \ 0 < \sigma_2 < 1 \qquad (7.1.5)$$

Given that σ_2 is a constant capital distributive share in production, the relative prices must be constant in order for equations (7.1.4) and (7.1.5) to represent either the linear or nonlinear acceleration principle. At this point, things become a little troublesome. To move from equation (7.1.5) to (7.1.4), a change is made from the flexprice to fixprice method. The justification of this methodological switch is usually not explained. We have pointed out, however, that the flexprice method has a tendency to go into microeconomic modeling, and the fixprice method usually goes macroeconomic. The reason may be that one advantage of the fixprice method is to facilitate aggregation by summing up monetary values of qualities of goods and services, where monetary values become the volume index. Furthermore, it allows us to trace changes in real values without the problem of price distortion, since changes in prices may alter the structure of income distribution, as it is held by the neo-Keynesians, and hence violate the assumption of a given income distribution.

Additionally, many other disturbing questions emerge out of this neoclassical approach to the explanation and analysis of an economy's aggregate investment behavior. How should the dynamic choice problem and the marginal conditions for individual optimality be interpreted at the aggregate level? Does the maximization of the present value of individual firms imply the maximization of the economy's present value, on the basis of which the economy's optimal capital stock and its net investment are obtained, given the existence of an aggregate production function? If an aggregate production function is not assumed, shall the aggregate investment be interpreted as the effective sum of the microeconomic results? Finally, while the present-value optimization is claimed to yield the largest possible budget for the individual who uses it as an objective of optimal capital policy and investment decisions, it is not clear whether this individual present-value optimization will aggregatively lead to the largest possible budget for the economy as a whole. In other words, does this criterion lead to the largest possible real income to the society?

From purely the framework of the neoclassical extension of the classical system of thought, the derivation of the acceleration principle and the use of such an acceleration principle to study and analyze individual and aggregate investment demand seems inappropriate. In this framework, the derived investment demand as a function of output is inconsistent, and perhaps a mis-specification in the classical system. For after the optimal capital stock has been obtained under the conditions of flexprice, the nature of the optimal investment must be constructed and studied in the price space in order to be consistent with the classical definition of demand as a price-quantity relation, for an optimal behavior and use of information. The empirical validity of the neoclassical theory of optimal capital accumulation and the corresponding investment demand function must also be examined and tested in the price space. In fact, Jorgenson's original micro-investment function was constructed and analyzed in the price space [236] [329]. Unfortunately, however, most of the econometric analysis of investment from the neoclassical theoretical framework has been done in either output or input space [153] [154] [327].

From the viewpoint of decision analysis, given the information structure a choice of the optimal control variable determines the path of the state of the system. When the optimal state is reached, both the control and state variables are basically functions of the information set. Changes in this information set will alter both the optimal control and the state of the system. Precisely, this is the logical foundation for comparative dynamics, sensitivity and simulation analysis. The optimal control (in this case, investment) is a function of the information set (in this case, prices and other relevant parameters that constitute the incentive structure of choice). The control variable is optimal only relative to the information set. Thus the behavior of the optimal control variable must be studied in the information space. This technique and method of inquiry are logically true for all decision problems. From this perspective, let us examine the neoclassical capital-investment problems.

Using the Cobb-Douglas production function it immediately follows from the flexprice method in the neoclassical framework that

$$\frac{\dot{K}}{K} = \alpha_1 \frac{\dot{w}}{w} + \alpha_2 \frac{\dot{C}}{C} + \alpha_3 \frac{\dot{p}}{p} \tag{7.1.6}$$

where the signs of α_i are governed by the nature of the classical system of factor demand. By the use of Maclaurin expansion around the optimal values and a linear approximation equation (7.1.6) holds for decreasing and increasing returns for a linear homogeneous production function of the Cobb-Douglas type. From equation (7.1.6), the rate of accumulation at the optimal path depends essentially on the price system. Thus changes in the optimal capital stock and the corresponding investment are studied in the price space, as required by the flexprice method and the conditions of classical demand theory, but not in the output space, as we are led to believe by some authors [327] [333] [462]

[541]. From the background of the classical demand theory and its neoclassical extensions, a serious objection is raised here and in [119] [149] [156] [251b] against transforming the neoclassical theory of investment decisions to conform to the acceleration principle for the analysis of either aggregate or individual investment behavior.

These objections are often responded to by the neoclassicals through the epistemological position of the instrumentalists [123] [125]. They argue that the acceptability and value added of the theory do not rest on the assumptions and liberty of the deductive reasoning from the logical gaps in the model's structure. They claim the theory is acceptable if the set of deduced conclusions provide an adequate description of capital-investment behavior at the macroeconomic level. Additionally, they suggest that there is no alternative theory superior to that of the neoclassicals for the analysis of aggregate investment behavior. The epistemological position of the instrumentalists is not adequate to answer the criticisms, and the latter explanation may lead to a condition of theoretical laziness. Let us examine these theoretical concerns and objections a little more closely.

7.2   THEORETICAL PROBLEMS OF THE NEOCLASSICAL VERSION OF THE ACCELERATION PRINCIPLE

We shall examine the objection raised in section (7.1) in detail. If the production function of equation (7.1.1) is in the Cobb-Douglas class, then the optimal aggregate capital stock, K, under profit or present value maximization is obtained as:

$$K = \frac{\sigma_2 PQ}{C} = \frac{\sigma_2 Q}{C/p} \tag{7.2.1}$$

Alternatively, it may be written as

$$K = \left(\frac{\sigma_2 w}{\sigma_1 C}\right)^{\sigma_1/\mu} \left(Q^{1/\mu}\right) \tag{7.2.2}$$

where $\mu = \sigma_1 + \sigma_2$ and

$$L = \left(\frac{\sigma_1 C}{\sigma_2 w}\right) K \tag{7.2.3}$$

If $\mu = 1$ then equation (7.2.2) becomes

$$K = \left(\frac{\sigma_2}{\sigma_1} \frac{w}{C}\right)^{\sigma_1} Q \tag{7.2.4}$$

It is then argued that if either the real user cost of capital or relative factor prices or both remain constant, contrary to the flexprice method, we obtain forms of the acceleration principle where either constant user costs of capital or

132

relative factor prices and distributive shares of factors underlie the acceleration. Equations (7.2.1) and (7.2.4) express the linear form of acceleration principle, while (7.2.2a) expresses a form of the nonlinear accelerator. From the solution to the problem of the optimal factor input decision, if K is optimal, so also Q. The output, Q, is that which is optimally producible, given an optimal choice of capital and labor services. So long as prices either remain constant or change in the same proportion leaving the relative prices unchanged, there will be no need for the optimal choice of K and L to change and hence Q to change endogenously on the optimal path.

In other words, the optimal capital stock, K^*, and the optimally producible output, Q^*, are constant with time. The optimality is in the sense of profit. One can also say that K^*, L^* and Q^* are informationally optimal for each given time point, where such information is summarized by the set of prices. The constancy of K^*, L^* and Q^* is easily seen by noting that K^* and L^* are specified by prices and distributive shares. For example

$$K^* = \left[\frac{C}{\sigma_2 p}\right]^{(\sigma_1-1)/(1-\mu)} \left[\frac{w}{\sigma_1 p}\right]^{-\sigma_1/1-\mu} \tag{7.2.2b}$$

The constancy of K, L and Q will remain into indefinite future so long as prices remain the same. The values of K^* and Q^* are illustrated in Figure (7.2.1).

Figure 7.2.1
Neoclassical Capital Equilibrium

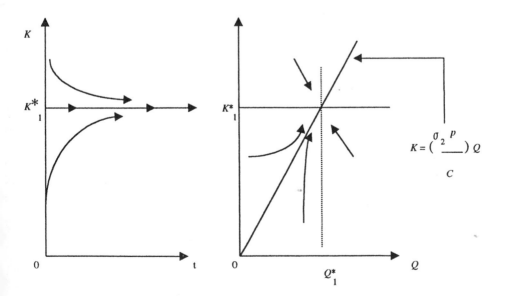

133

The optimal capital stock, K_1^*, is that consistent with an information set $(\sigma_2 p/C)_1$ or $[\sigma_2 w/\sigma_1 C]_1^{\sigma_1}$.

Let us suppose that the prices depend on time. The relative prices are not constant, and the path of optimal capital depends on relative prices. In other words, the path of optimal capital is of the form

$$K^* = \left(\frac{\sigma_2 p}{C}\right) Q \tag{7.2.5}$$

where K^* is an increasing function of (p/C). An increase in (p/C) for the given optimal conditions will leave K^* informationally suboptimal. This will lead to an increased level of the optimal capital stock through adjustments, given that the real wages remain unchanged. This may be explained by Figure 7.2.2 where $(\sigma_2 p/C)_1$ increases to $(\sigma_2 p/C)_2$ with optimal capital stock increasing from K_1^* to K_2^*. The corresponding optimal net investment will then be $\dot{K} = K_2^* - K_1^*$.

Figure 7.2.2
Variations in Neoclassical Capital Equilibrium Showing the Relationships among Optimal Capital, Constant Real Shadow Price of Capital and Output

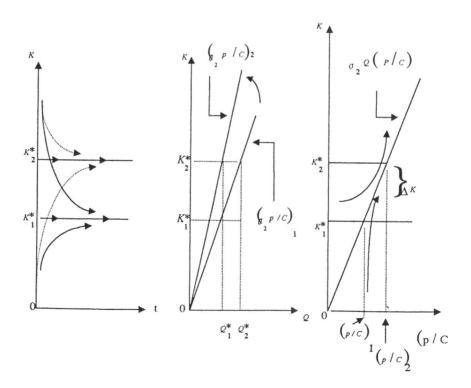

Changes in the real user cost of capital leading to changes in the optimal capital stock need not increase the optimal output that can be sustained by the optimal profit under the new price information. Generally, the optimal net investment as an addition to the optimal capital stock may be computed from equation (7.2.5) as

$$\dot{K} = \frac{\sigma_2 C(p\dot{Q} + Q\dot{p}) - \sigma_2 pQ\dot{C}}{C^2} \qquad (7.2.6)$$

Net investment as specified in equation (7.2.6) consists of *output effect* and *price effect*. Since the optimal output Q is fixed at the optimal profit, $\dot{Q} = 0$, and hence from (7.2.6).

$$\dot{K} = \frac{\sigma_2 Q[C\dot{p} - p\dot{C}]}{C^2} \qquad (7.2.7)$$

It is immediately deduced that

$$\dot{K} \gtrless 0, \ \text{if} \ \frac{\dot{p}}{p} \gtrless \frac{\dot{C}}{C} \qquad (7.2.8)$$

where $\dot{p}/p$ is the rate of *revenue effect* and $\dot{C}/C$ is rate of *capital cost effect*. Thus given the path of optimal output, new net investment depends on relative difference between revenue effect and capital cost effect. As long as revenue effect outweighs the capital cost effect, new investment will take place.

Obviously, if one assumes that the price information does not change and that there is an arbitrarily time-induced change of the optimally producible output, $\dot{p} = \dot{C} = 0$, with zero price effect and hence

$$\dot{K} = \frac{(\sigma_2 p)}{(C)}\dot{Q} \qquad (7.2.9)$$

It is immediately observed that $\dot{K} \gtrless 0$, if $\dot{Q} \gtrless 0$. In this case, $\dot{Q} = Q_2^* - Q_1^*$ from Figure 7.2.2, as measured along the ray $(\sigma_2 p/C)_1 Q$. The net investment path of equation (7.2.7) is price induced and price supported. The net investment path described by equation (7.2.9) is output-induced and output-supported.

In order for the net-investment path that is output induced to coincide with that which is price induced in the neoclassical framework, it must be the case from equations (7.2.7) and (7.2.9) that

$$\frac{\dot{Q}}{Q} = \frac{\dot{p}}{p} - \frac{\dot{C}}{C}, \ \frac{w}{p} \ \text{fixed.} \qquad (7.2.10)$$

This can also easily be seen and computed from Figure (7.2.2), in that the net price effect must be equal to the output effect, all of which are expressed as rates of changes.

135

The condition expressed in equation (7.2.10) may be rearranged into elasticities to obtain

$$\frac{\dot{Q}/Q}{\dot{p}/p} = 1 - \frac{\dot{C}/C}{\dot{p}/p} \qquad (7.2.11)$$

In other words, for the output changes to induce the same investment path as the price changes, the sum of price-output and price-user cost elasticities must be unity. The path of optimal net investment as described by equation (7.2.6) is not, and cannot be, the same as either the one described by equation (7.2.7) or equation (7.2.9). From equation (7.2.6) we can establish the following condition for the net-investment path:

$$\dot{K} \gtreqless 0 \text{ if } \frac{\dot{Q}}{Q} + \frac{\dot{p}}{p} \gtreqless \frac{\dot{C}}{C} \qquad (7.2.12)$$

In terms of elasticities equation (7.2.12) may be stated as

$$\dot{K} \gtreqless 0 \text{ if } 1 + \frac{\dot{Q}/Q}{\dot{p}/p} \gtreqless \frac{\dot{C}/C}{\dot{p}/p} \qquad (7.2.13)$$

The justification of equations (7.2.7), (7.2.12) and (7.2.13) stems from the fact that the negative user-cost effect restricts the revenue effect, composed of output-price effects. The end result is that $Q_1 \leq Q_3 \leq Q_2$ and $(p/C)_1 \leq (p/C)_3 \leq (p/C)_2$. As (p/C) changes, $(\sigma_2 P/C)$ rotates, while the investors, on the aggregate, move along the line of rotation. We do not think these conditions are consistent with the structure of the acceleration principle. They are graphically illustrated in Figure 7.2.3.

In a restricted sense of the acceleration principle, equation (7.2.9) is not the same as the acceleration theory, which is based on optimal expectations about demand conditions. Thus while K in equation (7.2.1) and (7.2.4) is optimal in the sense of profit, it may not be optimal relative to demand expectations. Similarly, the level of output needed to satisfy optimal demand expectations at each point of time may not satisfy the profit-maximizing output. The analysis will, however, be different if we consider an output maximizing system. Among the objections being raised here is that there are logical gaps in the neoclassical framework that prevent an inductive process from the microeconomic structure to the macroeconomic representation, and that attempts to fill them seem to lead to inconsistencies.

7.3   PRESENT VALUE, SAVINGS-INVESTMENT-EQUALITY CONSTRAINT AND THE PRINCIPLE OF EFFECTIVE DEMAND

Let us turn our attention to the role that Keynesian savings-investment-equality constraint and the principle of effective demand play in the capital accumulation process, and the problems that they present to the neoclassical theory as we attempt a logical move from the microeconomic representation to the macroeconomic one. Here there is an important logical gap that must be observed. Suppose that we start with an optimal state where the control system of equation (7.1.1) yields a solution where the optimal output to be produced and supplied is $Q*s$, with optimal level of capital K^*, for the given set of information, J. Let us suppose that Q_S^*, is equal to $Q_{d_1}^*$, the quantity that would be demanded under the same information set. Now suppose an arbitrary increase in the quantity that would be demanded at the same information set, J, from $Q_{d_1}^*$ to $Q*d_2$. From the control decision problem, $Q_{d_1}^*$ can be produced with the assumed technological possibilities only when either K or L increases, or both, to new levels $K_2^* \geq K_1^*$ or $L_2^* \geq L_1^*$. Investment therefore must increase by the amount $K_2^* - K_1^*$; such investment will not be forthcoming, since K_2^* and L_2^* are both informationally sub-optimal and their acquisitions will lead to a reduction in the optimal value of the objective function.

Figure 7.2.3
The Relationships among Optimal Capital, Real Shadow Price of Capital and Output Where $A_i = (\sigma_2 p/C)_i$ and $B_i = \sigma_2 Q (P/C)_i$ $X_i = (P/C)_i$

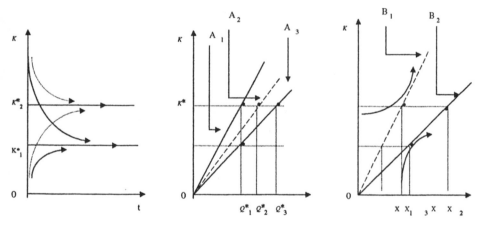

The argument being advanced here is simple, in the sense there is no logical way to derive the acceleration principle from the conditions of optimization without postulating that the time path of output price be dependent on either expected or prevailing demand. Such an assumption will endogenize external shocks on the information set, causing changes in the choice-decision behavior. At best the acceleration principle, from the framework of individual optimal-control decision process on the basis of which aggregate result is derived, indicates to us only the extra volume of capital services that would be needed if an indicated higher level of demand is to be met by production. But whether such an extra volume of capital services would be acquired by producers based on the established optimal decision process will depend on induced changes in the information set and the relative changes in the elements of the information set. The acceleration theory of investment is a demand-oriented argument, while the present-value optimization is a supply-decision argument. The empirical verification of the main propositions of the neoclassical theory of investment based on the present-value optimization, therefore, must not follow the statistical specification of the acceleration principle, except when one can demonstrate that there exists isomorphic structure between the deduced results of the supply-decision argument and those of demand-decision argument, and that such isomorphism is maintained as one logically moves from the micro-structure to the macroeconomic structure.

Now let us turn our attention to the criterion for choice of the path of the optimal capital. The method of present-value optimization is a formidable one for the analysis of the capital-accumulation process of individual enterprises. Many important difficulties, however, are encountered when the present-value criterion is used to analyze the evolution of the economy's aggregate capital accumulation. For one thing, the sum of the individually optimized present values may not be equal to the optimized present value of the economy if aggregation is admissible. Some of the reasons may be due to economic and structural interdependencies that are usually not accounted in the individual cases but become important constraints when the present value of the economy is optimized. This theoretical difficulty cannot easily be removed. A further problem exists even if this difficulty can be removed to allow the present-value approach to be accepted for the analysis of aggregate investment behavior. The neoclassical theory accounts only for private accumulation and its rate of change in the economy. As such, it neglects the component of aggregate investment that may be due to governmental activities, to the extent that it is specified by the economic size of the government expenditure. Such investment activities may include military arsenals, social infrastructure and other important non-private investments. While it is possible to incorporate relevant taxes as constraints in the framework for examining the evolution of private accumulation, government investment activities cannot similarly be handled, as one examines the evolution of aggregate capital within the neoclassical framework based on present-value optimization. This does not negate the statement that government investments can be analyzed separately within the same framework, with different criteria.

An additional question arises within the neoclassical framework. This question involves the role that aggregate savings plays or must play in the logical construct of macroeconomic representation of microeconomic results. Under the neoclassical optimal conditions for present-value optimization, the individuals may be in optimal states with respect to the levels and rates of capital accumulation, while the economy's capital stock and its investment may not be optimal in the sense of neo-Keynes or Keynes. In the neoclassical optimal state, it is possible for the economy as a whole to be investing less than it is saving on the aggregate; yet the aggregate and individual investments and the levels of capital accumulation would be said to be optimal in the neoclassical sense. This defines a state where aggregate savings exceeds aggregate investment. As such, the neoclassical optimal capital and investment policies may be suboptimal in the sense of Keynes when the economy is considered as a unit. In this respect, the aggregate saving rate may exceed the rate at which the economy is investing, in a closed economy.

A counter-argument may be that the difficulty may be removed by setting either equation (7.2.7) or (7.2.9) equal to the total aggregate saving, $S = sQ$, as it is in a number of texts. In this case, by combining equation (7.2.9) with the simple saving function, we obtain

$$\frac{\sigma_2 p}{C}\dot{Q} = sQ \tag{7.3.1}$$

and hence

$$\frac{\dot{Q}}{Q} = \frac{s}{\sigma_2}\frac{C}{p} \tag{7.3.2}$$

If the neoclassical version of acceleration principle is logically accepted, equation (7.3.2) defines the condition required for aggregate saving to be completely invested, and hence savings equal investment. Even if the condition expressed by equation (7.3.2) satisfies the saving-investment equality constraint, one of the neo-Keynesian conditions may not be met. This is the condition where the aggregate rate of profit is equal to the aggregate rate of accumulation, and both are equal to the rate of aggregate savings. In order for the neo-Keynesian condition to be met, it must be the case that the volume of aggregate saving is equal to the volume of profit, and hence

$$\prod = sQ \tag{7.3.3a}$$

$$\prod/K = s/\nu$$

and

$$\prod/K = \dot{K}/K = \dot{Q}/Q = s/\nu \tag{7.3.3b}$$

where $\nu = Q/K$ and $\prod/Q = s$.

On the other hand, if one uses equation (7.2.7), then

$$\frac{\sigma_2 Q[C\dot{p} - p\dot{C}]}{C^2} = sQ \tag{7.3.4}$$

and hence

$$\frac{\dot{p}}{p} - \frac{\dot{C}}{C} = \frac{sC}{\sigma_2 P} = s/\nu \qquad (7.3.5)$$

By combining equation (7.3.5) with equation (7.3.4) we can write

$$\frac{\dot{p}}{p} - \frac{\dot{C}}{C} = \frac{sC}{\sigma_2 p} = s/\nu = \frac{\dot{K}}{K} = \frac{\Pi}{K} \qquad (7.3.6)$$

where aggregate profit is equal to total aggregate saving. Conditions of equations (7.3.3b) and (7.3.6) yield the same result if that of equation (7.2.10) holds.

Now let us suppose that the optimal path of net investment depends on output effect and price effect, which is made up of revenue effect and capital-cost effect such that net investment is equal to aggregate savings. Using equation (7.2.6) we can write

$$\frac{\sigma_2 C[p\dot{Q} + Q\dot{p}] - \sigma_2 p Q \dot{C}}{C^2} = sQ \qquad (7.3.7)$$

By rearranging terms we obtain

$$\frac{\dot{Q}}{Q} + \frac{\dot{p}}{p} - \frac{\dot{C}}{C} = \frac{sC}{\sigma_2 p} = s/\nu \qquad (7.3.8)$$

Dividing equation (7.2.6) by (7.2.5) and substituting the value of K/Q from equation (7.2.1) we immediately obtain

$$\frac{\dot{Q}}{Q} + \frac{\dot{p}}{p} - \frac{\dot{C}}{C} = \frac{sC}{\sigma_2 p} = s/\nu = \frac{\dot{K}}{K} = \Pi/K = \frac{S}{K} = \xi = \rho \qquad (7.3.9)$$

where total aggregate profit is taken to be equal to total savings. Obviously, the rate of output growth cannot be abstracted from equation (7.3.6) without further assumptions. It is also clear from equation (7.3.9) that the growth rate of output, $\dot{Q}/Q$, is lower than rates of aggregate profit, capital accumulation and saving as normalized by accumulated capital. The questions that arises is which of these three conditions must be accepted as consistent with the neoclassical framework of analysis.

There is another troublesome problem in using the neoclassical capital theory to study aggregate capital investment. If the economic organization is such that a second-hand capital-goods market exists, it is possible for some individual enterprises to record optimal net positive investments while no net positive investment is registered by the system as a whole. Such a problem can be dealt with only within a logically proper aggregation process, if such a process can be constructed such an aggregative process is difficult if not impossible to construct.

7.4 THE PRESENT-VALUE CRITERION, THE KEYNESIAN MARGINAL EFFICIENCIES AND CAPITAL EQUILIBRIUM

In the neo-Keynesian framework, as it has been outlined above, a closed economy is in the long-run equilibria with respect to its capital stock when the rate of aggregate capital accumulation is equal to the rate of aggregate profit and hence the aggregate profit is equal to aggregate investment. The investment is said to be the optimal one on the aggregate if the rate of profit generated by accumulated capital and maintained by such investment is not only equal to the rate of accumulation but it is also equal to the rate of savings. In this state, aggregate savings are equal to aggregate profit. The rate of profit is equal to the marginal efficiency of capital, which is equal to the marginal efficiency of investment. All of them are equal to the rate of interest on aggregate real funds that go to finance the optimal level of capital as well as maintain the optimal investment that is taking place. The economy is investing an equivalence of its aggregate profit. In other words, "all profits" are being reinvested, and the principle of effective demand is also satisfied.

Interestingly, some authors [254] [446b] [700] comparing the Keynesian system of aggregate thinking to that of the neoclassicals have argued, contrary to Jorgenson's claim [329], that on the optimal path of firm's capital accumulation, the neoclassical marginal-productivity-stopping rule coincides with the Keynesian rule of marginal efficiency of investment. It is argued that if p and q are constant prices of output, $Q = F(K, L)$ and investment, I, then on the optimal path of capital accumulation

$$q = \int_0^\infty \alpha(t) F_K(K^*, L^*) dt \qquad (7.4.1)$$

where $\alpha(t) = Exp[-(\delta + r)t]$, F_K is the marginal product of capital, K, and L is labor.

The claim can only be maintained at the level of highly restrictive conditions and definitions. Let us examine it in a little more detail. First, the marginal product of capital must be viewed as the rate of return on individual capital needed to replace and maintain the existing optimal level of capital stock [254], properly defined. It is thus viewed as a marginal replacement concept. Over the optimal path of evolution of capital accumulation, it is argued that one may write $q = C/(r + \delta)$, where C is the user cost of capital and

$$[C/(r + \delta)] = \int_0^\infty \alpha(t) C(t) dt \qquad (7.4.2)$$

The investment good is either rented or used for an indefinite future where intertemporal arbitrage relations at optimal conditions equate the unit price of investment good with the present value of rental over the period. In the long run, the conditions of optimal choice require, the argument continues, that $C =$

$pF_K(K^*, L^*)$ and hence

$$q = \int_0^\infty \alpha(t)pF_K(K^*, L^*)dt \qquad (7.4.3)$$

as in (7.4.1) - which, the argument claims, coincides with the Keynesian rule.

Certain logical difficulties arise, and other theoretical problems emerge from such an important link. Over the optimal path, for the given set of information the value of the marginal product is constant, and the prospective yield from the marginal unit of the optimal capital stock is also constant over time. For the marginal productivity rule to coincide with the Keynesian marginal efficiency rule, we must be able to write

$$q = \int_0^\infty R(t)Exp[-F_K(K^*, L^*)d]dt \qquad (7.4.4)$$

where $F_K(K^*, L^*)$ is the real rate of return on capital that equates the present value of stream of earnings from capital asset to its replacement cost for a given fixed set of prices. For equations (7.4.4) to coincide with the marginal efficiency imputation, it is sufficient that $F_K(K^*, L^*) = m = \prod/K = \prod/\dot{K} = \hat{r}$, where $\hat{r}$ is the rate of amortization on investable fund in such optimal state. In order for equation (7.4.3) to be consistent with equation (7.4.4), it is sufficient that $R(t) = pF_K(K^*, L^*)$ and

$$F_K(K^*, L^*) = m = (\delta + r) = \hat{r} \qquad (7.4.5)$$

The optimal conditions of the neoclassical dynamic system require that

$$F_K(K^*, L^*) = [q(r + \delta)]/p \qquad (7.4.6)$$

where prices are given and constant, and hence $F_K(\cdot)$ is constant, so long as the prices remain constant.

Equations (7.4.5) and (7.4.6) are equivalent if $q/p = 1$. This condition is met if the system is assumed to be a one-product economy, where the same output is used for both investment and consumption. In this case, the prices of both output and investment goods are the same. Now if investment goods are assumed to last forever without depreciation, $m = r = \hat{r}$, which looks like the marginal efficiency rule. The theoretical difficulty that arises is that the nondepreciation assumption contradicts the internal logic of the argument from the viewpoint of replacement cost. Thus the argument seems to have a logical gap in supporting the claim that the marginal productivity and marginal efficiency rules coincide in the analysis of project selection. This difficulty increases when the claim is extended to macroeconomics of capital accumulation and investment behavior.

Perhaps a useful claim would be not the coincidence of the neoclassical marginal productivity and Keynesian marginal efficiency rules but that the neoclassical theory of optimal capital process allows one to compute what the value of marginal efficiency of capital would be in the optimal state of the individual capital accumulation at a given initial set of market information. In this case, the concept of marginal efficiency is defined only in equilibrium states. Its value in a one-product world is given by equation (7.4.5) at the level of the firm, where the current value of the future stream of capital's contribution to production must account for depreciation and the real discount rate.

If we assume that the micro-production functions are linearly homogeneous almost everywhere, we can assume that under a set of conditions an aggregate production function may be constructible. If an acceptable method of aggregation can be found within the neoclassical system, then the aggregate profit at a continuous time may be written as

$$\prod = K F_K(K^*, L^*) \qquad (7.4.7)$$

and hence

$$\rho = \prod / K = F_K(K^*, L^*) \qquad (7.4.8)$$

which is the rate of aggregate profit at the optimal path. The evolution of the system is such that

$$\dot{\rho} = \frac{K\dot{\prod} - \prod \dot{K}}{K^2} = \frac{\prod}{K}(\frac{\dot{\prod}}{\prod} - \frac{\dot{K}}{K}) = 0 \qquad (7.4.9)$$

since $F_K(K^*, L^*)$ is constant over the optimal path. Thus the rate of profit is also optimal, and hence since $(\prod / K) \neq 0$ one can write from (7.4.9)

$$\dot{\prod} / \prod = \dot{K} / K \qquad (7.4.10a)$$

or

$$\dot{\prod} / \dot{K} = \prod / K \qquad (7.4.10b)$$

These results are equivalent to those in (4.4.1.3). If $\dot{\prod} / \dot{K}$ and $\prod / K$ are interpreted as the measures of marginal efficiencies of investment and capital respectively, the neoclassical framework yields the same results as the neo-Keynesian framework as outlined above, conditional on the set of assumptions. In this state, total profit is specified as total revenue less the total wage bill, where profit is considered as capital's share in output. The system as described by (7.4.9) and (7.4.10a) is represented by phase diagrams in Figure 7.4.1. There is another disturbing problem. In the neo-Keynesian system, the rate of profit is optimal in equilibrium states. This implies that $\dot{\rho} = 0$ and that $\prod / K = \dot{K} / K$. In other words, the neo-Keynesian equilibrium implies the criterion of optimizing the internal rate of return, $\prod / K$, where $\dot{\prod} / \prod = \dot{K} / K$. We have also shown that in the neo-Keynesian equilibrium states all the key aggregate variables

Figure 7.4.1
Capital Equilibrium, Rates of Profit and Accumulation

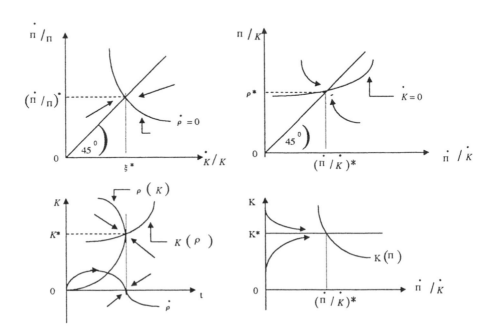

involved in the capital accumulation process are growing at the same rate. In the neoclassical capital-equilibrium states, $\dot{K} = 0$. Thus for any given information set, there is only one situation where the marginal productivity rule coincides with the marginal efficiency rule, if the logic of the coincidence is accepted: when $\rho = \xi = 0 = \dot{K} = \dot{Q}$ in other words, when all the aggregate variables are growing at zero rate. This is one of the many possible equilibrium states in the neo-Keynesian system of capital accumulation that has been constructed here. This state of zero rates is essentially equivalent to the classical stationary state. The system may be represented in a phase diagram as in Figure 7.4.2.

Figure 7.4.2
Neo-Keynesian and Neoclassical Capital Equilibrium Where the Marginal Productivity Rule Coincides with Keynesian Marginal Efficiency Rule and Output and Capital are Growing at Zero Rates. It is equivalent to the Classical Stationary State

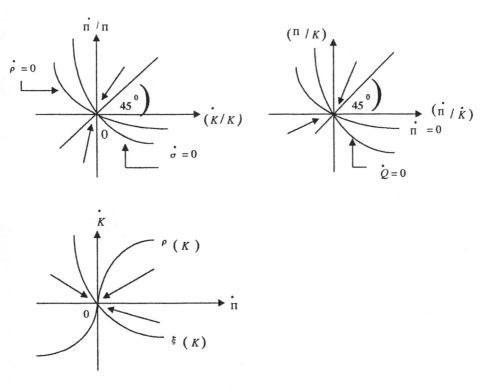

7.5 OTHER ALTERNATIVE THEORIES OF AGGREGATE INVESTMENT

There are alternative approaches to the study of investment besides the neoclassical theory under Fisherian conditions. Prominent among them is the neoclassical theory of investment under the Wicksellian conditions [756] [758]. Like the Fisherian version, the version of the neoclassical theory under Wicksellian conditions is microeconomic in its methodological approach and analytical construct. It therefore suffers from many of the theoretical difficulties (especially the problems of aggregation) that have been discussed above concerning the neoclassical theory under the conditions of Fisher. However, it must be observed that the central question that the Wicksellian version attempts to answer is analytically different from the question to which an answer is sought in the Fisherian framework. The essentials of the question of the Wicksellian version may be stated as: What are the optimal capital policies of the individual entrepreneurs, and what are the effects of their capital accumulation on the relative price structure of the rate of interest and wage rate, where the rate of interest is conceived as the price of capital [358] [467]? In comparison, the version of the neoclassical theory under Fisherian conditions attempts to answer the question as of what the optimal investment policies of entrepreneurs are, and what the effects of variations in interest rate are on such optimal policies.

These are inherent theoretical difficulties that make us ill at ease with the version under the Wicksellian conditions, given the general neoclassical analytics. Within the Wicksellian logic of accumulation, it is possible to determine the individual optimal capital policy, conditional on the given data. Thus for any data set there will correspond a unique optimal capital policy. However, a derivation of a testable investment-demand function linking optimal capital policies at varying data cannot be meaningfully constructed. The difficulty is embedded in the use of the method of comparative statics to deal with a problem that is basically and analytically dynamic in form. This difficulty in the synchronization of method and problem for analysis of investment has led to much confusion and conclusions that are not only contradictory but deny the possibility of any meaningful construction of a microeconomic investment-demand function under the neoclassical conditions, including those of Fisher [236] [329] [541] [762]. Even if an investment demand function can be constructed from the neoclassical conditions in the sense of Wicksell, the problem of a channel through which one may move from the micro to macro relationship still remains.

Finally, there is the Eisner-Strotz [144] [155] approach, which is basically a modification of the neoclassical approach where the firms are assumed to act rationally by optimizing the integral of the discounted stream of "the rate of investment cost" where the investment cost corresponds to what has come to be known in the neoclassical theory of investment as "adjustment costs." This approach also has the analytical problems of the neoclassical approach, in the sense of Fisher, in dealing with the analysis of aggregate investment. In fact, the approach uses implicit information that makes it difficult if not impossible to construct from the analytical framework an explicit investment-demand function that is directly testable.

From the Keynesian aggregate logical framework, other alternative theories of aggregate investment have been advanced. One version of this approach is based on profit realization [142] [163] [327] [714]. This has come to be known in the literature as the "profit principle". While many versions of the profit principle may differ in structural specifications, they are conceptually the same. There is Tinbergen's formulation, where aggregate investment is made to depend linearly on either current profit or last-period profit [713]. This belongs to the category of naive profit theory of investment. There is also the Kaleckian version, where aggregate investment in fixed capital is made to depend linearly on total gross saving, the time rates of change in profit and capital stock [357] [361]. This may be classified under the flexible profit theory of investment. Any other version of the profit theory of investment may be put in one of the two categories [142] [152] [163] [358].

There are some basic problems with these formulations of the profit principles that make one feel ill at ease. First, they say nothing about the nature of optimal capital policy or optimal capital stock; neither do they offer within their analytical framework any process through which such an optimal capital policy or stock can be determined. In all these cases, the analytical frameworks fail to integrate a process where the rate of interest can be incorporated as a determinant, or to develop a process where an optimal path (optimal in a specific sense) of capital accumulation can be selected by examining alternative paths of accumulation. This was Jorgenson's challenge, of course, with a specific interpretation of meI [329]. Nonetheless, these formulations of the profit principles fall short in providing a consistent theory of optimal aggregate capital accumulation and investment within the Keynesian logical framework, where income distribution is essential.

Furthermore, it seems that most of the versions of the profit principles are more empirical analyses rather than internally consistent theories of explanation. As such, they are based on highly simplified structures and tend to avoid judicious use of internally consistent theoretical constructs, which are essential for a marriage between theory and empirical work. There is, therefore, a tendency of these analyses to be victims of prematured empirical generalizations. It is precisely these problems that the neo-Keynesian theories of optimal aggregate capital accumulation and investment that have been presented above have sought to carefully avoid, in that the optimal aggregate capital accumulation is obtained by comparing alternative paths of capital accumulation.

The acceleration principle is another attempt to formulate a theory of aggregate investment within the Keynesian aggregate analytic framework [104] [144] [383] [393] [463]. But just as the volume of investment is not necessarily logically linked to profit levels so also there are no a priori reasons to believe that output may form a logically causal connection that may be observed with the aggregate volume of investment. Even if it has statistically been ascertained that the past history of output is correlated with the history of aggregate investment, or vice versa, such a correlation cannot be taken as a seriously causal explanation of aggregate investment behavior. A proper theoretical framework must be constructed to allow an effective link between the empirical relationship and an abstract theoretical explanation. Furthermore, we are not provided with a logical process through which the path of an optimal aggregate capital stock may be derived from the logic of the output-principle approach to the explanation of aggregate investment, even though such an optimal capital stock is an important reference value against which the actual is examined. Thus the output principle as we know it suffers from the same analytical problems as the profit-principle approach. One is likely to cite the neoclassical profit-maximizing approach as a counterexample; however, it has been argued above that such an approach has logical problems and hence one is likely not to dwell on it.

From classical demand logic, changes in the choice pattern in the commodity space are induced by changes in the information set, which in a market setting is summarized by a set of prices and other relevant parameters. The schedule of units of commodity demand is a unique function of the information set. Thus given the goals and preferences of the economic units, the changes in the pattern of optimal demand behavior are studied in the parameter space. This may be done by using either the method of comparative statics or dynamics. The study of investment based on the elements of classical system of thought, such as the neoclassical one, cannot be exempted. Thus within the classical system of thought, the behavior of optimal investment demand must be studied in the parameter space but not in the output space. The reason may be found in the role that information processing plays in establishing the basis for making and changing optimal decision. It therefore remains to be seen whether an aggregate investment demand function based solely on classical demand logic can be constructed from the neoclassical framework in any internally consistent manner that accounts for aggregate saving and for the problem of income distribution that may come to affect the path of aggregate accumulation, an idea which is also embedded in classical thinking.

7.6 BUDGET DEFICIT, INTEREST RATE AND INTERNATIONAL INDEBTEDNESS

A major concern in recent times is the effect of the size of the government budget deficit and its increase on the level of aggregate economic activity. A related major concern is the effect of fiscal deficit and its change on the real rate of interest in a closed economy. Another major concern emerges when the system is opened. In the open economic system the concern is not only on the effects of government domestic indebtedness but also on the country's international indebtedness and risk of default. All these factors that generate concern may affect, one way or the other, a country's capital accumulation and investment process, which in turn may affect the short-run stability and the long-run growth process of the country's economy.

When it comes to analysis of the effects of a government fiscal deficit on aggregate capital accumulation and investment, the neoclassical capital accumulation and investment theories have a number of theoretical difficulties. There is no convincing way within the logic of neoclassical analytics of capital accumulation to examine the merits of these concerns without superimposing the neoclassical system on the Keynesian system of aggregate thinking.

It is either analytically impossible or extremely difficult at best to derive a nontrivial relationship between the rate of interest and the government fiscal budget deficit solely within the setting of the neoclassical logic of capital accumulation, a relationship that allows us to examine the effect of budget deficit or surplus on the behaviors of aggregate investment and interest rate in the economy. If the possibility exists, it has not been shown yet, or the presentation has logical gaps. This is another challenge to the neoclassical theory of investment. It has been shown within the neo-Keynesian capital dynamics that this is not only possible but natural.

By opening the system up, we can also established a channel within the neo-Keynesian framework of capital dynamics through which one can examine the effects of international indebtedness on aggregate capital accumulation, investment and the rate of interest. The neoclassical framework is not flexible enough to accommodate this. Furthermore, we can argue within the neo-Keynesian framework that the role of effects of international indebtedness is to alter the system's investment response to the path of aggregate profit flow, savings or finance.

Since income distribution is institutionally determined, the profit path is fixed for any given path of output. The effects of profit flow on the path of aggregate investment depend on the response function if the neo-Keynesian equilibrium is to be attained and maintained. This is precisely one of the strengths of neo-Keynesian framework for the analysis of aggregate capital accumulation and investment, where one of the requirements of dynamic equilibrium is that an equivalence of aggregate profit be invested in the long run. The size of the proportion of equivalent value of aggregate profit that is invested at short-run equilibrium states depends on the adjustment coefficient, which depends not on relative prices but rather on income distribution, societal savings behavior and capital efficiency. Within the neo-Keynesian framework the adjustment coefficient acts as accelerator coefficient or the profit coefficient, which is theoretically derived but not assumed. This strength of the neo-Keynesian logical framework cannot be found in the neoclassical theory of capital accumulation and investment, at least as we currently know it.

An alternative neoclassical framework has been used in examining the deficit-interest rate relations [43] [67] [104] and also to examine the external indebtedness and aggregate capital accumulation relative to labor force. The problem within the neoclassical analytical framework is that explicit path of aggregate investment is hard to construct. Even if certain aspects of the framework is accepted, one immediately observes that a reliance on certain aspects of Keynesian aggregate thinking is necessary to complete the neoclassical logic in so far as aggregate thinking is concerned. This is because the flexprice method has the tendency to go micro-analysis.

Chapter 8

Concluding Remarks
and Reflections

The study is now logically complete with respect to its objectives. One cannot, however, claim that it is conceptually complete when one considers the host of problems of aggregate capital accumulation in an economy and how such capital accumulation relates to economic growth and subsequent economic development. The study advances a theoretical construct of how the economic system generates forces that incessantly transform it, through capital accumulation. Capital accumulation, viewed as a distinct process, composed of capital widening and deepening, is endogenous to the economic system and hence takes place within the economic system itself. As such, the logic of the theory is to develop an explanation that relies principally on internal factors, so as to understand the capital accumulation process and how such capital accumulation relates to output growth. It is this respect that the assumption of a closed economy is made.

It is suggested that the study of capital accumulation must examine the relative growth rates of productive and nonproductive assets. A substantial portion of the total accumulated inventories are nonproductive assets, as the economy evolves over time. Additionally, there are also nonproductive assets, such as national defense equipment, monuments, etc. The Keynesian equilibrium conditions are indifferent to these components, as one conceives the evolution of aggregate capital. The analysis of growth and development of the industrial base of the economy, however, cannot be indifferent to the relative magnitudes of these capital components.

For any given path of real aggregate savings, there will always be a trade-off between productive and nonproductive assets, such that the aggregate savings are allocatively exhaustive over the Keynesian equilibrium path. The greater the

151

growth of nonproductive assets, such as defense equipments, the slower will be the rate of growth of productive assets and hence the growth of the industrial base, including retooling and modernization, over the Keynesian equilibrium path. The hypothesis implied by changes in the relative composition of productive and nonproductive assets in the capital accumulation process is that more rapid growth of the rate of nonproductive assets, particularly military munitions, will lead to an erosion of the economy's competitive edge in the international system of markets over the Keynsian equilibrium path. That will be true when the economic system is closed with respect to both savings and capital accumulation, in the sense that the economic system is capable of generating enough savings and has available to it technological know-how to support investment-goods creation for all investment possibilities. Similarly, if the economic system is "savings open," in the sense that the economic system is not generating, or is incapable of generating, enough savings in support of available investment possibilities, and international loans are acquired in support of capital creation and development, then an increase in the growth rate of nonproductive assets will erode the growth rate of productive assets and hence will retard the growth rate and modernization of the industrial base. The output growth will thus be affected, to the extent to which the size of accumulated capital relates to the level of output. Similarly, the growth of total factor productivity on the aggregate will be affected to the degree to which modernized industrial base, viewed in terms of improvements in techniques and know-how, relates to productivity.

The set of theoretical conclusions arrived at in this study is based on the fix-price method of analysis which allows us to discount the possible distortions of price effect and thus concentrate on effects of changes in real factors. The equilibrium process of the system is induced by the Keynesian savings-investment equality condition, while the system is propelled by the resolution of disparities between the rate of profit and the rate of accumulation. The concepts of profit and savings are carefully constructed so that the total savings are always equal to the total inventories that must be transformed into productive and nonproductive capital, given the level of the economy's technological know-how. Total profit on the other hand, is the excess of total wage bill over total output, in such a manner that total output is distributionally exhaustive. As presented, the concept and measurement of total savings are exactly equal to the concept and measurement of the excess of total consumption over total output. The concept and measurement of total profit are linked to the structure of income distribution, which is taken to be institutionally determined. The magnitudes of the essential variables are measured either in the units of labor cost or in the units of consumption goods.

The maximum-profit technique, from the set of techniques at the given level of technology, is assumed and unchanging throughout the analysis. The principle of effective demand is satisfied over the neo-Keynesian equilibrium path, where there is a complete synchronization between demand and supply in both consumption and capital-goods sectors and total saving is equal to total profit. On the neo-Keynesian equilibrium path of capital accumulation, the rate of profit is at the maximum when the growth rate of profit is equal to the rates of growth of capital accumulation and savings.

This path is one of the many Keynesian equilibrium paths where savings-investment equality is maintained. It is the path where there is full employment, and profit rate is at the maximum. On this maximum-profit-rate equilibrium path, marginal efficiency of investment is equal to the marginal efficiency of capital, and both of them are equal to the rate of profit on accumulated capital. With full employment, maximum-profit technique in use, profit rate at maximum, marginal efficiencies of investment and capital equalized and savings rate equal to accumulation and profit rates, there is no incentive to change the accumulation path. The accumulation system is moving on the path of a golden age.

The analytical procedure to arrive at this capital accumulation path is to combine the multiplier and capacity-creating effects of investment to determine the appropriate level of aggregate income that would be necessary to bring about internally equality between savings and investment, as abstracted, while at the same time identifying the rate of capital accumulation at the maximum-profit-rate technique that would ensure the full employment condition as assumed. When the savings-equal-investment path is reached at the maximum-profit-rate technique, the multiplier and acceleration effects are combined to determine the growth rate of real income that would continually maintain such an equilibrium path at a given structure of income distribution and societal propensity to save, at current data. The effects of the maximum-profit-rate technique and income distribution are combined to isolate the savings-equal-investment path, on which the rate of profit is equal to the rate of savings in a closed economy.

A closed economy, however, may have a savings-deficit or savings-surplus accumulation system. The system may be limitative, or limitational, in those internal factors required to reach and maintain an accumulation path that is supportive of a predetermined path or rate of output growth. When the economic system is factor limitational or limitative in the process of capital accumulation, it may be enhanced by opening it up. The opening up of the capital accumulation system to the global environment of production cannot be construed to mean that the process of capital accumulation becomes external to the economy. In an open capital accumulation system with either savings or technological limitative or limitational, the path of the desired output growth may be supported with international loans and technology. These situations may be fully examined in a theoretical system of capital and output dynamics in open macroeconomic systems.

The logical structure of this study is both derived from and is a generalization of the works of such Cambridge economists such as Joan Robinson, Kaldor, Pasinetti, and Champernowne. As presented, there are a number of optimal aggregate-investment behaviors over the path of the neo-Keynesian capital equilibrium that would sustain it. All of them are related to the size of aggregate profit allowed by the conflict in the prevailing structure of income distribution. Current investment is always adjusted to current profit, in line with the adjustment coefficient. The adjustment coefficient is endogenous and depends on the economic system's internal profit rate, income distribution and societal savings habits from different income types. An equality among the rates of accumulation, savings and profit implies a perfect adjustment, in which case the investment adjustment coefficient to profit is one.

Four different adjustment coefficients that can maintain a continual existence of the path of neo-Keynesian equilibrium are constructed. They are the general, Robinsonian, Kaldorian and Pasinettian adjustment coefficients. The Robinsonian adjustment coefficient is the propensity to save out of profit, which is unity for perfect adjustment. In the case of Kaldor, optimal adjustment requires the structure of income distribution to be related to the societal attitude to save, in a specific form. The relationship of the structure of income distribution for instantaneous adjustment of net investment to profit is such that the rate of profit in the equilibrium must be proportional to average capital efficiency. The proportionality is determined by the relative differential savings propensities from income types. The resulting effect of Kaldor's analytics is a generalization of a type of accelerator and capacity principles of investment. The Kaldorian optimal investment policy implies that in the neo-Keynesian capital equilibrium states, consumption out of profit must be equal to savings out of wages.

The Pasinettian optimal investment policy, where net investment is instantaneously adjusted to profit, is an extension of that of Kaldor. Here a balance must be made between the aggregate rate of profit, on one hand, and on the other the average capital efficiency, adjusted by the rate of interest paid to workers for the use of their savings. In the Pasinettian system, with instantaneous adjustment of investment to profit, the rate of profit is analytically dependent on overall capital efficiency, the share of investment in output and societal propensity to save from different income types, for any given structure of income distribution and maximum-profit-rate technique. On the path of greatest accumulation, the rate of profit is proportional to the average capital efficiency, where the proportionality is the average propensity to save out of wages.

The structures of the Robinsonian, Kaldorian and Pasinettian systems were developed without the government sector. A general theoretical system is here constructed from the systems of Robinson, Kaldor and Pasinetti and is extended to the government sector, with the system still closed. The government structure is characterized by differential income taxes from income types and government expenditures, on the basis of which the effects of government fiscal policy on the accumulation process are examined. The analysis lead to a number of propositions. The rate of interest payable to workers depends on the profit rate, capital efficiency, government budgetary behavior (taxes and expenditure) and societal savings habits from different income types. The fiscal behavior (taxation and expenditure) of the government affects the path of capital accumulation through changes in the adjustment coefficient of investment to profit. Positive (or negative) variations in the government expenditure proportion in aggregate output negatively (positively) change the adjustment coefficient toward unity.

In the analysis of the effects of government fiscal behavior on capital accumulation, it is the share of government expenditures in output that is critical to the capital dynamics, not simply the size of the government expenditure given the tax structure. In this respect, variations in the government's expenditure

154

proportion are in a positive relationship with the rate of interest payable to workers for the use of their savings in the capital accumulation process, as long as the inverse of the rates of accumulation and profit exceed a multiple of the rate of interest, where the proportion is the ratio of marginal propensity-to-save to the proportion of untaxed profit in a closed economy, where output is completely divided between workers, capitalists and government.

An increase in the proportion of the government expenditure at any equilibrium state and at a balanced budget implies a reduction in either disposable wages or profit shares in output. At any given social attitude to save from income types, this means a reduction in the total savings available for private productive investment. To motivate investment of an equivalent value of profit requires increasing the rate of interest payable on savings from wage income. Thus the interest rate payable on workers' savings is positively related to the proportion of government expenditure in output. This interest-rate relationship with government-expenditure proportion is based on a different argument from that used to explain the crowding-out effect of the financial sector through government borrowing. The current argument is basically the income distributional one, from the real sector.

From the logical background of the neo-Keynesian theory of capital accumulation and investment, the basic propositions of the neoclassical one-sector growth dynamics are examined. Given the assumption of full employment of factors, a question arises in the neoclassical framework as to what price method underlies the analysis. The adjustment mechanism in the growth process cannot be based on the flexprice, unless the neoclassicals are willing to concede the theoretical view that variations in prices lead to changes in prevailing income distribution and thus changes in aggregate savings at a given structure of expectation-formation and societal attitude to save. A reinterpretation and analytical rearrangement of the basic structure lead us to suggest that the neoclassical growth theory is a theory of aggregate capital accumulation and investment. The logical structure of the theory is, however, different from the accepted neoclassical theory of optimal capital and investment, which is based on individual optimal decisions to accumulate at any given set of time paths of prices.

The structure of aggregate capital and investment process implied by the neoclassical growth theory is similar to that of the neo-Keynesian theory of aggregate capital and its adjustments. The difference is only in the adjustment coefficient that propels investment to equality with profit. Within the neoclassical logical growth structure and on the path where the rate of profit equals the rate of investment over accumulated capital, the average propensity to consume is equal to the wage share, and hence total savings are equal to total profit, with instantaneous adjustments. This is a neo-Keynesian twist, and with it the capital accumulation and growth processes in the neoclassical framework may be extended to analyze the effects of government fiscal actions.

In the development of the neo-Keynesian framework for capital accumulation, the maximum-profit-rate technique is always assumed. Thus we are always on the path of the market-efficient technology of production. The direct decision process in arriving at this technologically efficient path of capital accumulation is not discussed; this belongs to the special area of technology, capital accumulation and growth. There are sources from which one may attempt to abstract insights into the problem within the neo-Keynesian framework; Examples are the works of Kaldor and Mirrlees [352], Robinson [601b] and Dobb [110]. Additionally, one may enter the neoclassical growth framework to examine how the capital labor ratio (viewed as technique) is selected.

Here, as we have pointed out, the response coefficient in adjusting capital from disequilibrium is influenced by technique, which is related to real factor prices. Thus with prices fixed, the initial selection will put us on the path of efficient technique. The implication in terms of the neo-Keynesian framework is that we will stay on this technologically efficient path as long as the structure of income distribution, as given by the institutions of production and consumption, remains unchanged. Changing prices amounts to altering the structure of income distribution for any given expectation formation and hence changing the capital adjustment coefficient through changes in technique.

The manner in which capital accumulation proceeds and how capital accumulation affects economic growth and employment in theoretical constructs will depend essentially on the way in which technology and its progress are introduced in the analysis for a closed macroeconomic system. Added complications tend to arise when capital accumulation and growth are examined for open macroeconomic systems. The complications involves comparative analysis of productivity and growth rates and how the productivity and growth rates relate to technology capital accumulation and employment.

In all economies, we are confronted with situations where countries have deficiencies in many areas of capital accumulation and production. These deficiencies reveal themselves in terms of degrees of limitativeness and limitationality of essential factors. Some economies are either savings limitational or limitative; others have either limitationality or limitativeness in technology; and so forth. The degrees to which these deficiencies show themselves in capital and growth dynamics can be examined in models of capital accumulation only when the economic systems are open. Thus the neo-Keynesian framework must be extended from closed economic systems to those that are open. Here we must drop the assumption of closed economy. The resulting analysis, while extremely important is beyond the logical confines of this volume and hence is left as another project to all.

Development of the theory of neo-Keynesian aggregate capital dynamics and examination of the neoclassical theory of growth require us to take a look at the structure of the neoclassical theories of capital accumulation and investment within the neo-Keynesian framework. Consequently, it is argued that the flex-price method used in neoclassical framework demands that the acceleration principle's approximation to the empirical analysis of investment is inconsistent with its methodological foundation. Furthermore, the set of assumptions required to obtain the aggregate investment from the underlying micro-investments is too restrictive, where the empirical results may be true by assumptions.

The neoclassical capital accumulation and investment theory, it is argued, must be studied in the price space, where given the decision criterion, disparities between revenue effect (composed of output effect and price effect) and capital cost effect are the motivating factors of capital adjustment. Furthermore, the adjustment and the internal dynamics of the theory do not offer any correspondence to the neoclassical theory of output growth; neither do they convincingly offer an analytical channel for establishing the needed logical correspondence. In its logical setup, the resulting rates of individual and aggregate output growth are established by the net difference between the rates of price effect and capital cost effect.

Another important shortcoming of the neoclassical optimal capital approach to the study of aggregate capital accumulation and investment is its complete neglect of the role that the economy's total savings play in aggregate capital formation. There is also the question as to whether investment ranking by present-value optimization can be used to analyze the aggregate capital accumulation and investment of the economy, and whether enough aggregate savings would be forthcoming to support such capital aggregate formation. When the Keynesian and neo-Keynesian savings-investment-equality conditions are grafted onto the neoclassical present-value process of capital accumulation, three different conditions emerge. These conditions relate the profit rate to output growth rate and the rate of net revenue effect, such that the rate of output growth is lower than the rates of accumulation and profit. The important theoretical point argued here is that there is a closer logical relationship between the neo-Keynesian theory of aggregate capital accumulation and the neoclassical growth theory than between the neoclassical theory of capital accumulation and its theory of output growth. For logical consistency, this perhaps should not be the case. But it is.

Finally, we may add that the theoretical insights and derived propositions of the neo-Keynesian theory of aggregate capital accumulation and investment may be used to design a planned growth rate for open and closed economic systems where the economy may be constrained by availability of finance and technology. The overall design may require for some economics a strategic and tactical use of backlog and diffusion of international technological knowledge and innovation to attain a rate of capital accumulation that cannot be internally supported.

References

[1] Abramowitz, M., *Thinking about Growth*, Cambridge, U.K., Cambridge University Press, 1989.

[2] Aczel, J., *On Application and Theories of Functional Equations*, Basel, Birkhauser Verlag, 1969.

[3] AEIBC Economics, *International Debt, Banks and LDC's* 1977-1983, Special Papers, AMEX Bank Review, London 1984.

[4] Agency for International Development (USA), *Loan Terms, Debt Burden and Development: A Study*, Washington, D.C., USAID, April 1965.

[5] Agenor, P.R., et al., *Development Macroeconomics*, Princeton, N.J., Princeton University Press, 1996.

[6] Alexander, S.S., "The Accelerator as a Generator of Steady Growth," *Quarterly Journal of Economics*, Vol. 67, 1949, pp. 174-197.

[7a] Alexander, S.S., "Mr. Harrod's Dynamic Model," *Economic Journal*, Vol. 60, 1950, pp. 724-739.

[7b] Allais, M., "Some Analytical and Practical Aspects on the Theory of Capital," in [480], pp. 64-107.

[8] Almon, S., "The Distributed Lag between Capital Appropriations and Expenditures," *Econometrica*, Vol. 33, 1965, pp. 178-196.

[9] Anchisklin, A., *The Theory of Growth of a Socialist Economy*, Moscow, Progress Publishers, 1977.

[10] Arrow, K.J., "Optimal Capital Policy with Irreversible Investment," in [763], pp. 1-20.

[11] Arrow, K.J., "Optimal Growth with Irreversible Investment in a Ramsey Model," *Econometrica*, Vol. 38, 1970, pp. 333-346.

[12] Arrow, K.J., "Optimal Capital Policy, the Cost of Capital and Myopic

Decision Rules," *Annals of the Institute of Statistical Mathematics,* Vol. 16, 1964, pp. 21-30.

[13] Arrow, K.J., et al., "Capital-Labor Substitution and Economic Efficiency," *Review Economic Statistics,* Vol. 43, 1961, pp. 225-250.

[14] Arrow, K.J., et al., "Optimal Expansion of the Capacity of a Firm," in K.J. Arrow et al. (eds.), *Studies in the Mathematical Theory of Inventory and Production,* Stanford, Calif., Stanford University Press, 1959, pp. 92-105.

[15] Arrow, K.J., "Optimal Capital Adjustment," in K.J. Arrow et al. (eds.), *Studies in Applied Probability and Management Science,* Stanford, Calif., Stanford University Press, 1962, pp. 1-17.

[16] Arrow, K.J., and M. Kurz, "Optimal Public Investment Policy and Controllability with Fixed Private Savings Ration," *Journal Economic Theory,* Vol. 1, 1969, pp. 141-177.

[17] Arrow, K.J., and M. Kurz, *Public Investment, the Rate of Return and Optimal Fiscal Policy,* Baltimore, Md., Johns Hopkins University Press, 1970.

[18] Auerbach, A., "Taxation, Corporate Financial Policy and the Cost of Capital," *Journal of Economic Literature,* Vol. 21, 1983, pp. 905-940.

[19] Auerbach, A.J., "Wealth Maximization and Cost of Capital," *Quarterly Journal of Economics,* Vol. 93, 1979, pp. 433-446.

[20] Auerbach, A.J., "The Optimal Taxation of Heterogeneous Capital," *Quarterly Journal of Economics,* Vol. 93, 1979, pp. 589-612.

[21] Aukrust, O., "Investment and Economic Growth," *Productivity Measurement Review,* Vol. 16, 1959, pp. 35-53.

[22] Avramovic, D., *Economic Growth and External Debt,* Baltimore, Md., John Hopkins University Press, 1964.

[23] Bade, R., "Optimal Growth and Foreign Borrowing with Restricted Mobility of Foreign Capital," *International Economic Review,* Vol. 13, 1972, pp. 544-552.

[24] Bailey, M.F., "Formal Criteria for Investment Decisions, *Journal of Political Economy,* Vol. 67, 1959, pp. 476-488.

[25] Balass, B. and R. Nelson (eds.), *Economic Progress, Private Values and Public Policy,* New York, North-Holland, 1977.

[26a] Barna, T., "On Measuring Capital," in [467], pp. 75-94.

[26b] Barro, R. and X. Sala-i-Martin, *Economic Growth,* McGraw-Hill, New York, 1995.

[26c] Barro, R. and X. Sala-i-Martin, "Public Finance in Models of Economic Growth," *Review of Economic Studies,* Vol. 59, 1992, pp. 645-661.

[27] Baumol, W., "On the Social Rate of Discount," *American Economic Review,* Vol. 58, 1968, pp. 788-802.

[28] Becker, G.K. et al., "Economic Growth, Human Capital and Population," *Journal of Political Economy,* Vol. 98, 1990, S12-S137.

[29] Benassy, J.P., "Neo-Keynesian Disequilibrium Theory in a Monetary Economy," *Review of Economic Studies,* Vol. 42, 1975, pp. 503-523.

[30] Bensusan-Butt, D.M., *On Economic Growth: An Essay in Pure Theory,* Oxford, Oxford University Press, 1960.

[31] Bhaduri, A., "The Concept of Marginal Productivity of Capital and Wicksell Effect," *Oxford Economic Papers*, Vol. 18, 1966, pp. 284-288.

[32] Bhaduri, A., "On the Significance of Recent Controversies in Capital Theory: A Marxian View," *Economic Journal*, Vol. 79, 1969, pp. 532-539.

[33] Bhagwati, J., *Essays in International Economic Theory, Vol. 1: The Theory of Commercial Policy*, Cambridge, Mass., MIT Press, 1983.

[34] Bhagwati, J., *Essays in International Economic Theory, Vol. 2: International Factor Mobility*, Cambridge, Mass. MIT Press, 1983.

[35] Bhagwati, J. (ed.), *The New International Economic Order*, Cambridge, Mass., MIT Press, 1983.

[36] Bhagwati, J. et. al. (eds.), *Trade, Balance of Payments and Growth*, Amsterdam, North-Holland, 1971.

[37] Bhagwati, J. (ed.), *Import Competition and Response*, Chicago, NBER, University of Chicago Press, 1982.

[38] Bhandari, J.S., et al. (eds.), *Economic Interdependence and Flexible Exchange Rates*, Cambridge, Mass., MIT Press, 1984.

[39] Bierwag, G.O., and M.A. Grove, "Aggregate Koyck Functions," *Econometrica*, Vol. 34, 1966, pp. 828-832.

[40] Bischoff, C.W., "The Effect of Alternative Lag Distribution," in [196], pp. 61-130.

[41] Black, J., "Optimal Savings Reconsidered, or Ramsey without Tears," *Economic Journal*, Vol. 72, 1962, pp. 360-366.

[42] Blackhouse, R.E., "Keynesian Unemployment and One-Sector Neoclassical Growth Model," *Economic Journal*, Vol. 91, 1981, pp. 174-187.

[43] Blanchard, J.O., and S. Fischer, *Lectures on Macroeconomics*, Cambridge, Mass., MIT Press, 1990.

[44] Blaug, M., *The Cambridge Revolution: Success or Failure?* London, London Institute of Economic Affairs, 1974.

[45] Bliss, C.J., "On Putty Clay," *Review Economic Studies*, Vol. 35, 1968, pp. 105-132.

[46] Bliss, C.J., *Capital Theory and Distribution of Income*, Amsterdam, North-Holland, 1975.

[47] Bohm-Bawerk, E. von, *Positive Theory of Capital*, New York, Stecherx, 1930.

[48] Bohm-Bawerk, E. von, *Capital and Interest*, London, Macmillan, 1890.

[49] Boltyanskii, V.G., *Mathematical Methods or Optimal Control*, New York, Holt, Rinehart and Winston, 1971.

[50] Boltyanskii, V.G., *Optimal Control of Discrete Systems*, New York, Wiley, 1978.

[51] Boot, J.C.G., and G.M. Deklit, "Investment Demand Empirical Contribution to Aggregation Problem," *International Economic Review*, Vol. 1, 1969, pp. 3-30.

[52] Bort, G.H., "A Theory of Long-Run International Capital Movements," *Journal of Political Economy*, Vol. 72, 1964, pp. 341-359.

[53] Bourneuf, A., "Manufacturing Investment, Excess Capacity and Rate of Growth of Output," *American Economic Review*, Vol. 54, 1964, pp. 607-

625.

[54] Bradford, D.F., "The Economics of Tax Policy toward Savings," in [199], pp. 11-71.

[55] Brechling, F.P., *Investment and Employment Decisions,* Manchester, U.K., Manchester University Press, 1975.

[56] Brockie, M.C., et al., "The Marginal Efficiency of Capital and Investment Programming," *Economic Journal,* Vol. 66, 1956, pp. 662-675.

[57] Brown, M., *The Theory and Empirical Analysis of Production, Studies in Income and Wealth,* Vol. 31, New York, Columbia University Press, 1967.

[58] Brown, M., et al. (eds.), *Essays in Modern Capital Theory,* Amsterdam, North-Holland, 1976.

[59] Burmeister, E., "A Synthesis of the Neo-Austrian and Alternative Approaches to Capital Theory," *Journal of Economic Literature,* Vol. 13, pp. 413-456.

[60] Burmeister, E., *Capital Theory and Dynamics,* Cambridge, U.K., Cambridge University Press, 1980.

[61] Burmeister, E., and A.R. Dobell, *Mathematical Theories of Economic Growth,* New York, Macmillan, 1970.

[62] Burmeister, E., and P. Taubman, "Labour and Non-Labour Income Saving Propensities," *Canadian Journal of Economics,* Vol. 2, 1969, pp. 78-89.

[63] Cass, D., and M.E. Yaari, "Individual Saving, Aggregate Capital Accumulation and Efficient Growth," in [657], pp. 233-268.

[64] Cass, D., "Optimal Growth in an Aggregative Model of Capital Accumulation," *Review of Economic Studies,* Vol. 32, 1965, pp. 233-240.

[65] Cass, D., and J.E. Stiglitz, "The Implication of Alternative Savings and Expectation Hypothesis for Choices of Technique and Patterns of Growth," *Journal of. Political Economy,* Vol. 77, pp. 586-627.

[66] Cass, D., et al. (eds.), *Macroeconomics and Capital Theory,* Cambridge, Mass., MIT Press, 1974.

[67] Cavaco-Silva, A.A., *Economic Effects of Public Debt,* New York, St. Martin's, 1977.

[68] Cave, D.W., et al., "The Economic Theory of Index Numbers and the Measurement of Input, Output, and Productive," *Econometrica,* Vol. 50, 1982, pp. 1393-1414.

[69] Chakravarty, S., *Capital and Development Planning,* Cambridge, Mass., MIT Press, 1969.

[70] Champernowne, D.G., "A Dynamic Growth Model Involving a Production Function," in [467], pp. 223-244.

[71] Champernowne, D.G., "A Note on John v. Neumann's Article on 'A Model of General Economic Equilibrium'," *Review of Economic Studies,* Vol. 12, 1945, pp. 10-18.

[72] Champernowne, D.G., "The Production Function and the Theory of Capital: A Comment," *Review of Economic Studies,* Vol. 21, 1953, pp. 112-135.

[73] Champernowne, D.G., "Capital Accumulation and the Maintenance of Full Employment," *Economic Journal,* Vol. 58, 1958, pp. 211-244.

[74] Champernowne, D.G., "The Stability of Kaldor's 1957 Model," *Review of Economic Studies,* Vol. 38, 1971, pp. 112-135.

[75] Champernowne, D.G., "Some Implications of Golden Age Conditions When Savings Equal Profits," *Review of Economic Studies,* Vol. 29, 1962, pp. 235-237.

[76] Champernowne, D.G., and R.F. Kahn, "The Value of Invested Capital," *Review of Economic Studies,* Vol. 21, 1953-1954, pp. 107-111.

[77] Chenery, H.B., "Overcapacity and the Acceleration Principles," *Econometrica,* Vol. 20, 1952, pp. 1-28.

[78] Chenery, H.B., et al., *Foreign Assistance and Economic Development,* USAID Discussion Paper #7, Washington, D.C., USAID, 1965.

[79] Chenery, H.B., *Structural Change and Development Policy,* New York, Oxford University Press, 1981.

[80] Chiang, A.C., *Elements of Dynamic Optimization,* New York, McGraw-Hill, 1992.

[81] Chick, N., *Macroeconomics After Keynes,* Cambridge, Mass., MIT Press, 1983.

[82] Christensen, L.R. and D.W. Jorgenson, "The Measurement of Real Capital Input 1992-1967," *Rev. of Income and Wealth,* Series 15, no. 4, 1969, pp. 293-320.

[83] Clark, C., *The Conditions of Economic Progress,* London, Macmillan, 1940.

[84] Clark, J.B., *The Distribution of Wealth,* London, Macmillan, 1899.

[85] Clark, J.B., *Essentials of Economic Theory as Applied to Modern Problems of Industry and Public Policy,* London, Macmillan, 1907.

[86] Clark, J.M., "Business Acceleration and the Law of Demand," *Economic Journal,* Vol. 25, 1917, pp. 217-235.

[87] Clower, R.W., "An Investigation into the Dynamics of Investment," *American Economic Review,* Vol. 44, 1954, pp. 64-81.

[88] Clower, R.W., "The Keynesian Counter-Revolution: A Theoretical Appraisal," in [248], pp. 103-125.

[89] Cobb, C.W., and P.H. Douglas, "A Theory of Production," *American Economic Review* (Supplemental), Vol. 18, 1928, pp. 139-165.

[90] Coddington, A., "Keynesian Economics: The Search for First Principles," *Journal of Economic Literature,* Vol. 14, 1976, pp. 1258-1273.

[91] Coen, R.M., "Investment Behavior, The Measurement of Depreciation and Tax Policy," *American Economic Review,* Vol. 65, 1975, pp. 59-74.

[92] Coen, R.M., "The Effect of Cash Flow and the Speed of Adjustment," in [196], pp. 131-196.

[93] Coen, R.M., "Effects of Tax Policy on Investment in Manufacturing," *American Economic Review,* Vol. 58 (May), 1968, pp. 200-211.

[94] Coen, R.M., "Tax Policy and Investment Behavior: Comment," *American Economic Review,* Vol. 59, 1969, pp. 370-377.

[95] Conlisk, J., "A Neoclassical Growth Model with Endogenously Positioned Technical Change Frontier," *Economic Journal,* Vol. 79, 1969, pp. 348-362.

[96] Craine, R., "Investment, Adjustment Costs and Uncertainty," *International Economic Review,* Vol. 16, 1975, pp. 648-661.

[97] Cripps, T.F., and R.J. Tarling, *Growth in Advanced Capitalist Economies, 1950-1970,* New York, Cambridge University Press, 1973.

[98] Cuthbertson, K., *Macroeconomic Policy,* New York, Wiley, 1979.

[99a] Denison, E.F., "Theoretical Aspects of Quality Change, Capital Consumption, and Net Capital Formation," in *Problems of Capital Formation, Studies in Income and Wealth,* Vol. 19, Princeton, N.J., Princeton University Press, 1957, pp. 215-261.

[99b] Denison, E.F., *Why Growth Rates Differ: Postwar Experiences in Nine Western Countries,* Washington, D.C., Brookings Institution, 1967.

[100] Denny, M., and M.A. Fuss, "The Use of Approximation Analysis to Test for Separability and Existence of Consistent Aggregates," *American Economic Review,* Vol. 67, 1977, pp. 404-418.

[101] Dewey, D., *Modern Capital Theory,* New York, Columbia University Press, 1965.

[102] Dhrymes, P.J., "Some Extensions and Tests for CES Class of Production Functions," *Review of Economic Statistics,* Vol. 47, 1965, pp. 357-366.

[103] Diamond, P.A., "National Debt in a Neoclassical Growth Model," *American Economic Review,* Vol. 55, 1965, pp. 1126-1150.

[104] Diamond, P.A., and J. Mirlees, "Optimal Taxation and Public Production," *American Economic Review,* Vol. 61, 1971, pp. 8-27.

[105] Diewert, W.E., "Aggregation Problems in the Measurement of Capital," in D. Usher (ed.), *The Measurement of Capital,* Chicago, Chicago University Press, 1980, pp. 433-528.

[106] Diewert, W.E., "Hicks Aggregation Theorem and the Existence of Real Value-Added Function," in M. Fuss et al. (eds.), *Production Economics,* Vol. 2, Amsterdam, North-Holland, 1978, pp. 17-70.

[107] Dixit, A.K., *The Theory of Equilibrium Growth,* New York, Oxford University Press, 1976.

[108] Dixit, A., "The Accumulation of Capital Theory," *Oxford Economic Papers,* Vol. 29, 1977, pp. 1-29.

[109] Dobb, M., *Theories of Value and Distribution Since Adam Smith,* Cambridge, U.K., Cambridge University Press, 1973.

[110] Dobb, M., *An Essay on Economic Growth and Planning,* New York, Modern Reader, 1969.

[111] Dobb, M., *Political Economy and Capitalism,* London, Routledge, 1940.

[112] Dobb, M., "The Sraffa System and Critique of the Neo-Classical Theory of Distribution," *De Economist,* Vol. 4, 1970, pp. 347-362.

[113] Domar, E.D., "Capital Expansion, Rate of Growth and Employment," *Econometrica,* Vol. 14, 1946, pp. 137-147.

[114] Domar, E.D., *Essays in the Theory of Economic Growth,* New York, Oxford University Press, 1957.

[115] Domar, E.D., "Depreciation, Replacement and Growth," *Economic Journal,* Vol. 63, 1953, pp. 1-32.

[116] Domar, E.D., "Expansion and Employment," *American Economic Review,*

Vol. 37, 1947, pp. 34-55.

[117a] Dompere, K.K., "Technical Progress and Optimal Supply Price," *International Journal of Production Economics*, Vol. 32, 1993, pp. 365-381

[117b] Dompere, K.K., *The Theory of Aggregate Investment in Closed and Open Economic Systems*, Working Mongraph, Department of Economics, Howard University, Washington, D.C., 1984.

[118] Dompere, K.K., "The Inventory Control Problem and Optimal Supply Price Micro-theoretic," *Engineering Costs and Production Economics*, Vol. 20, 1990, pp. 51-64.

[119] Dompere, K.K., "The Internal Structure and Functional Representation of Capital-Adjustment Costs," *Engineering Cost and Production Economics*, Vol. 18, 1989, pp. 105-115.

[120a] Dompere, K.K., "A Fuzzy-Decision Theory of Optimal Social Discount Rate: Collective-Choice-Theoretic," *Fuzzy Sets and Systems*, Vol. 58, 1993, pp. 279-301.

[120b] Dompere, K.K., *Theoretical Basis for the Construction of External Trade Indices of Botswana: A Manual on Methods*, Gaborene, Botswana, Central Statistical Office of Ministry of Finance, Government of Botswana, 1989.

[121a] Dompere, K.K., *An Integrated Industrial Statistical System of Botswana: A Manual on Methods*, Gaborene, Botswana, Central Statistical Office of Ministry of Finance, Government of Botswana, 1989.

[121b] Dompere, K.K., "The Theory of Fuzzy-Decisions, Cost-Distribution Principle in Social Choice and Optimal Tax Distribution," *Fuzzy Sets and Systems*, Vol. 53, 1993, pp. 241-252.

[122] Dompere, K.K.,"The Theory of Approximate Prices: Analytical Foundations of Experimental Cost-Benefit Analysis in a Fuzzy-Decision Space," *Fuzzy Sets and Systems*, Vol. 87, 1997, pp. 1-26.

[123] Dompere, K.K., and M. Ejaz, *Epistemics of Development Economics: Toward a Methodological Critique and Unity*, Westport, Conn., Greenwood Press, 1995

[124] Dompere, K.K., and K.O. Nti, "Learning By Doing and Optimal Factor Demand," *International Journal of Production Economics*, Vol. 22, 1991, pp. 67-79.

[125] Dompere, K.K., "On Epistemology and Decision-Choice Rationality," in R. Trappl (ed.), Cybernetics and Systems Research, New York, North-Holland, 1982, pp. 219-228.

[126] Dompere, K.K., "The Theory of Fuzzy Decisions," in M.M. Gupta and E. Sanchez (eds.), *Fuzzy Information and Decision Processes*, New York, North-Holland, 1982, pp. 365-379.

[127] Dorfman, R., "An Economic Interpretation of Optimal Control Theory," *American Economic Review*, Vol. 59, 1969, pp. 817-831.

[128] Dornbusch, R., *Open Economy Macroeconomics*, New York, Basic Books, 1980.

[129] Douglas, P.A., "Are There Laws of Production?" *American Economic Review*, Vol. 38, 1948, pp. 1-41.

[130] Douglas, P.H., "The Cobb-Douglas Production Function Once Again: Its

History, Its Testing, and Some Empirical Values," *Journal of Political Economy,* Vol. 84, 1976, pp. 903-916.

[131] Drandakis, E.M., "Factor Substitution in the Two-Sector Growth Model," *Review of Economic Studies,* Vol. 30, 1963, pp. 217-228.

[132a] Drandakis, E.M., and E.S. Phelps, "A Model of Induced Invention, Growth and Distribution," *Economic Journal,* Vol. 76, 1966, pp. 823-840.

[132b] Dreze, J.H. (ed.), *Allocation Under Uncertainty: Equilibrium and Optimality,* New York, Wiley, 1974.

[133] Duesenberry, J.S., *Business Cycles and Economic Growth,* New York, McGraw-Hill, 1958.

[134] Duesenberry, J.S., et al. (eds.), *Brookings Quarterly Econometric Model of the United States,* Chicago, Rand McNally, 1965.

[135a] Eatwell, J., "Irving Fisher's 'Rate of Return over Cost' and the Rate of Profit in a Capitalist Economy," in [58], pp. 77-96.

[135b] Eatwell, J., et al. (eds.), *Capital Theory,* The New Palgrave Series, New York, Norton, 1990.

[136] Eatwell, J., et al., *Keynes' Economics and the Theory of Value and Distribution,* New York, Oxford University Press, 1983.

[137] Eckaus, R.S., "The Acceleration Principle Reconsidered," *Quarterly Journal of Economics,* Vol. 67, 1953, pp. 209-230.

[138] Eckstein, O., "Investment Criteria for Economic Development and the Theory of Intertemporal Welfare Economics," *Quarterly Journal of Economics,* Vol. 71, 1957, pp. 56-85.

[139] Eckstein, O., "Manufacturing Investment and Business Expectations: Extensions of de Leeuw's Results," *Econometrica,* Vol. 32, 1965, pp. 420-424.

[140] Eichhorn, W., et al., *Production Theory,* Berlin, Springer-Verlag, 1974.

[141] Eichner, A.S., et al., "An Essay on Post-Keynesian Theory: A New Paradigm in Economics," *Journal of Economic Literature,* Vol. 13, 1975, pp. 1293-1314.

[142] Eisner, R., "Capital Expenditures, Profits and the Acceleration Principle," in *Models of Income Determination: NBER Studies in Income and Wealth,* Vol. 28, Princeton, N.J., Princeton University Press, 1964, pp. 137-176.

[143] Eisner, R., "Capital and Labor in Production: Some Direct Estimates," in *The Theory and Empirical Analysis of Production: Studies in Income and Wealth,* Vol. 31, New York, Columbia University Press, 1967 pp. 210-293.

[144] Eisner, R., "A Distributed Lag Investment Function," *Econometrica,* Vol. 28, 1960, pp. 1-29.

[145] Eisner, R., "On Growth and the Neo-Classical Resurgence," *Economic Journal,* Vol. 68, 1958, pp. 707-721.

[146] Eisner, R., "A Permanent Income Theory for Investment," *American Economic Review,* Vol. 57, 1967, pp. 363-390.

[147] Eisner, R., "Realization of Investment Anticipations," in J. Duesenberry et

al. (eds.), *The Brookings Quarterly Econometric Model of the United States,* Chicago, Rand McNally, 1965, pp. 95-128.

[148] Eisner, R., "Tax Policy and Investment Behavior: Comment," *American Economic Review,* Vol. 59, 1969, pp. 378-387.

[149] Eisner, R., "The Aggregate Investment Function," in *The International Encyclopedia of Social Sciences,* Vol. 8, London, Macmillan, 1968, pp. 185-194.

[150] Eisner, R., "Investment and the Frustrations of Econometricians," *American Economic Review,* Vol. 59 (May), 1969, pp. 50-64.

[151] Eisner, R.,"Components of Capital Expenditure: Replacement and Modernization Versus Expansion," *Review of Economic Statistics,* Vol. 54, 1972, pp. 297-305.

[152] Eisner, R., *Factors in Business Investment,* Cambridge, Mass., Ballinger, 1978.

[153] Eisner, R., and M.I. Nadiri, "Investment Behavior and the Neoclassical Theory," *Review of Economic Statistics,* Vol. 58, 1968, pp. 216-222.

[154] Eisner, R., and M.I. Nadiri, "Neoclassical Theory of Investment Behavior: A Comment," *Review of Economic Statistics,* Vol. 52, 1970, pp. 216-222.

[155] Eisner, R., and R.H. Strotz, "Determinants of Business Investment," in *Commission on Money and Credit: Impacts of Monetry Policy,* Englewood Cliffs, N.J., Prentice-Hall, 1963, pp. 60-138.

[156] Eisner, R., "Investments: Facts and Fancy," *American Economic Review,* Vol. 53 (May), 1963, pp. 237-346.

[157] Elliott, J.W., "Theories of Corporate Investment Behaviour Revisited," *American Economic Review,* Vol. 63, 1973, pp. 195-207.

[158] Eltis, W.A., "A Theory of Investment, Distribution, and Employment," *Oxford Economic Papers*, Vol. 17, 1965, pp. 1-23.

[159] Eltis, W.A., *Economic Growth: Analysis and Policy,* London, Hutchinson, 1966.

[160] Eltis, W.A., *Growth and Distribution,* London, Macmillan, 1973.

[161] Eltis, W.A., et al. (eds.), *Induction, Growth and Trade: Essays in Honour of Sir Roy Harrod*, Oxford, U.K., Oxford University Press, 1970.

[162] Engle, R.F., and D.K. Foley, "An Asset Price Model of Aggregate Investment," *International Economic Review,* Vol. 16, 1975, pp. 625-647.

[163] Ethier, W.J., "National and International Returns to Scale in the Modern Theory of International Trade," *American Economic Review,* Vol. 76, pp. 177-190.

[164] Evans, M.K., "A Study of Industry Investment Decisions," *Review of Economic Statistics,* Vol. 49, 1967, pp. 151-164.

[165] Evans, M.K., and E.W. Green, "The Relative Efficiency of Investment Anticipation," *Journal of American Statistical Association,* Vol. 61, 1966, pp. 104-116.

[166] Faurot, D.J., "Interrelated Demand for Capital and Labour in a Globally Optimal Flexible Accelerator Model," *Review of Economic Statistics,* 1978, pp. 25-32.

167

[167] Feige, E.L., and H.W. Watts, "A Investigation of the Consequences of Partial Aggregation of Micro-economic Data," *Econometrica*, Vol. 40, 1972, pp. 343-360.

[168] Feinstein, C. (ed.), *Socialism, Capitalism and Economic Growth*, Cambridge, U.K., Cambridge University Press, 1967.

[169] Feinstein, C.H., "Changes in the Distribution of the National Income in the United Kingdom," in J. Marchal et al. (eds.), *The Distribution of National Income*, London, Macmillan, 1968.

[170] Feldstein, M.S., and J.S. Fleming, "Tax Policy, Corporate Saving and Investment Behavior in Britain," *Review of Economic Studies*, Vol. 38, 1971, pp. 415-434.

[171] Feldstein, M.S., "Domestic Saving and International Capital Movements in the Long-Run and Short-Run," *European Economic Review*, Vol. 21, 1983, pp. 129-151.

[172] Feldstein, M.S., and D.K. Foot, "The Other Half of Gross Investment: Replacement and Modernization Expenditures," *Review of Economic Statistics*, Vol. 53, 1971, pp. 49-58.

[173] Feldstein, M.S., and C. Horioka, "Domestic Saving and International Capital Flows," *Economic Journal*, Vol. 90, 1980, pp. 314-329.

[174] Feldstein, M.S., and M. Rothschild, "Towards an Economic Theory of Replacement Investment," *Econometrica*, Vol. 42, 1974, pp. 393-423.

[175] Fellner, W., et al. (eds.), *Ten Economic Studies in the Tradition of Irving Fisher*, New York, Wiley, 1967.

[176] Ferber, R., *Determinants of Investment Behavior*, NBER Series 18, New York, Columbia University Press, 1967.

[177] Ferguson, C.E., *The Neoclassical Theory of Production and Distribution*, Cambridge, U.K., Cambridge University Press, 1971.

[178] Ferguson, C.E., and R.F. Allen, "Factor Prices, Commodity Prices and the Switches of Technique," *Western Economic Journal*, Vol. 8, 1970, pp. 90-109.

[179] Ferguson, J.M. (ed.), *Public Debt and Future Generations*, Chapel Hill, N.C., North Carolina University Press, 1964.

[180] Findlay, R., "Growth and Development in Trade Models," in [36], pp. 185-236.

[181] Findlay, R., "The Robinsonian Model of Accumulation," *Econometrica*, Vol. 30, 1963, pp. 1-12.

[182] Findlay, R., "A Reply to J. Robinson Findlay's Robinsonian Model of Accumulation: A Comment," *Econometrica*, Vol. 30, 1963, pp. 411-412.

[183] Findlay, R., "Economic Growth and Distributive Shares," *Review of Economic Studies*, Vol. 60, 1959, pp. 167-178.

[184] Fisher, F.M., "Embodied Technical Change and the Existence of an Aggregate Capital Stock," *Review of Economic Studies*, Vol. 32, 1965, pp. 263-288.

[185] Fisher, F.M., "Embodied Technology and the Aggregation of Fixed and Movable Capital Goods," *Review of Economic Studies*, Vol. 35, 1968, pp. 429-442.

[186] Fisher, F.M., "Approximate Aggregation and Leontief Conditions," *Econometrica,* Vol. 37, 1969, pp. 457-469.

[187] Fisher, F.M., "Embodied Technology and the Existence of Labour and Output Aggregates," *Review of Economic Studies,* Vol. 35, 1968, pp. 391-412.

[188] Fisher, F.M., "The Existence of Aggregate Production Functions," *Econometrica,* Vol. 37, 1969, pp. 553-577.

[189] Fisher, F.M., "The Existence of Aggregate Production Functions: Reply," *Econometrica,* Vol. 39, 1971, pp. 553-577.

[190] Fisher, F.M., "Aggregate Production Functions and the Explanation of Wages: A Simulation Experiment," *Review of Economic Studies,* Vol. 53, 1971, pp. 305-326.

[191] Fisher, F.M., et al, "On the Sensitivity of the Level of Output to Savings: Embodiment and Disembodiment: A Clarificatory Note," *Quarterly Journal of Economics,* Vol. 84, 1969, pp. 347-348.

[192] Fisher, F.M., and K. Shell, *The Economic Theory of Price Indices,* New York, Academic Press, 1972.

[193] Fisher, I., *The Theory of Interest,* New York, A.M. Kelley, 1961.

[194] Fisher, W.D., *Clustering and Aggregation in Economics,* Baltimore, Md., John Hopkins University Press, 1969.

[195a] Frankel, M., "The Production Function: Allocation and Growth," *American Economic Review,* Vol. 52, 1962, pp. 995-1022.

[195b] Fraumeni, B.M., and D.W. Jorgenson, "The Role of Capital in U.S. Economic Growth 1948-1976," in [200], pp. 9-250.

[196] Friedman, M., "The Quantity Theory of Money: A Restatement," in M.G. Mueller (ed.), *Readings in Macroeconomics,* New York, Holt, Rinehart and Winston, 1966, pp. 146-160.

[197] Fromm, G. (ed.), *Tax Incentive and Capital Spending,* Washington, D.C., Brookings Institution, 1971.

[198] Fukuoka, M., "Monetary Growth a la Keynes," *Keio Economic Studies,* Vol. 6, 1969, pp. 1-9.

[199] Furstenberg, G.M., *The Government and Capital Formation,* Cambridge, Mass., Ballinger, 1980.

[200] Furstenberg, G.M. (ed.), *Capital Efficiency and Growth,* Cambridge, Mass., Ballinger, 1980.

[201] Furstenberg, G.M., et al., "The Distribution of Investment Between Industries: A Microeconomic Application of the 'q' Ratio," in [200], pp. 395-460.

[202] Gallaway, L.E., "The Theory of Relative Shares," *Quarterly Journal of Economics,* Vol. 78, 1964, pp. 547-591.

[203a] Gareguani, P., "Heterogeneous Capital, the Production Function and the Theory of Distribution," *Review of Economic Studies,* Vol. 37, 1970, pp. 407-436.

[203b] Garegnani, P., "Quantity of Capital," in [135b], pp. 1-78.

[204] Garegnani, P., "On a Change in the Notion of Equilibrium in Recent Work on Value and Distribution," in [58], pp. 25-45.

[205] Garegnani, P. "Notes on Consumption, Investment and Effective Demand I," *Cambridge Journal of Economics,* Vol. 2, 1978, pp. 335-353.

[206] Garegnani, P., "Notes and Consumption, Investment and Effective Demand II," *Cambridge Journal of Economics,* Vol. 3, 1979, pp. 63-82.

[207] Gate, D., "On Optimal Development in a Multi-Sector Economy," *Review of Economic Studies,* Vol. 34, 1967, pp. 1-18.

[208] Georgescu-Roegen, N., *Analytical Economics,* Cambridge, Mass., Harvard University Press, 1967.

[209] Georgescu-Roegen, N., "Some Properties of a Generalized Leontief Model," in [208], pp. 316-337.

[210] Georgescu-Roegen, N., "Limitationality, Limitativeness and Economic Equilibrium," in [208], pp. 339-356.

[211] Glustoff, E., "On the Existence of a Keynesian Equilibrium," *Review of Economic Studies,* Vol. 35, 1968, pp. 327-334.

[212] Goldsmith, R.W., "A Perpetual Inventors of National Wealth," in *Studies in Income and Wealth,* NBER Series, Vol. 14, New York, Columbia University Press, 1951.

[213] Goodwin, R.M., "The Non-Linear Accelerator and Persistence of Business Cycles," *Econometrica,* Vol. 19, 1951, pp. 1-17.

[214] Goodwin, R.M., "Secular and Cylindrical Aspects of the Multiplier and Accelerator," in A. Metzler et al. (eds.), *Income, Employment and Public Policy,* New York, Norton, 1948, pp. 108-132.

[215] Gordon, R.J., "Measurement Bias in Price Indices for Capital Goods," *Review of Income and Wealth,* Vol. 17, 1971, pp. 121-174.

[216] Gordon, R.J., "A New View of Real Investment in Structures, 1919-1960," *Review of Economic Statistics,* Vol. 50, 1968, pp. 417-428.

[217] Gorman, J.A., et al., "Fixed Private Capital in the United States," *Survey of Current Business,* Vol. 65(7), 1985, pp. 36-55.

[218] Gorman, W.M., "Measuring the Quantities of Fixed Factors," in [763], pp. 141-172.

[219] Gould, J.P., "Adjustment Cost in the Theory of Investment of the Firm," *Review of Economic Studies,* Vol. 35, 1968, 47-55.

[220] Gould, J.P., "The Use of Endogeneous Variables in Dynamic Model of Investment," *Quarterly Journal of Economics,* Vol. 83, 1969, pp. 580-599.

[221] Gould, J.P., and R.N. Waud, "The Neoclassical Model of Investment Behavior: Another View," *International Economic Review,* Vol. 83, 1969, pp. 33-48.

[222a] Grandmont, J.M., "Temporary Equilibrium Theory," *Econometrica,* Vol. 45, 1977, pp. 535-572.

[222b] Grandmont, J.M., "The Logic of the Fix-Price," *Scandinavian Journal of Economics,* Vol. 79, 1977, pp. 169-186.

[223] Grandmont, J.M., et al., "On Keynesian Temporary Equilibrium," *Review of Economic Studies,* Vol. 43, 1976, pp. 53-67.

[224] Green, H.A.J., *Aggregation in Economic Analysis,* Princeton, Princeton University Press, 1964.

[225] Greenberg, E., "A Stock Adjustment Investment Model," *Econometrica,* Vol. 32, 1964, pp. 339-357.

[226] Greenberg, E., "Appropriations Data and Investment Decision," *Journal of American Statistical Association,* Vol. 60, 1965, pp. 503-515.

[227] Griffin, T.J., "The Stock of Fixed Assets in the United Kingdom: How to Make the Best Use of the Statistics," *Economic Trends,* No. 276, October 1976 (London, H.M.S.O, 1976), pp. 130-143.

[228] Griliches, Z., "Distributed Lags, A Survey," *Econometrica,* Vol. 35, 1967, pp. 16-49.

[229] Griliches, Z., "Capital Stock in Investment Functions: Some Problems of Concept and Measurement," in *Measurement in Economics: Studies in Mathematical Economics and Econometrics in Memory of Yeh Yehuda,* Grunfeld, Stanford, Calif., Stanford University Press, 1963, pp. 115-137.

[230] Griliches, Z., and N. Wallace, "The Determinants of Investment Revisited," *International Economic Review,* Vol. 6, 1965, pp. 311-329.

[231] Griliches, Z. and Y. Grunfeld, "Is Aggregation Necessarily Bad?," *Review of Economic Statistics,* Vol. 42, 1960, pp. 1-13.

[232a] Grossman, G.M., and E. Helpman, "Endogenous Innovation in the Theory of Growth," *Journal of Economic Perspective,* Vol. 8, 1994, pp. 23-44.

[232b] Grossman, G.M., and E. Helpman, "Trade, Knowledge, Spill-over and Growth," *European Economic Review,* Vol. 35, 1991, pp. 517-526.

[233a] Grossman, S.D., "A Test of Speed of Adjustment in Manufacturing Inventory Investment," *Quarterly Review of Economics and Business,* Vol. 13, 1973, pp. 21-32.

[233b] Grunfeld, Y., "The Determinants of Corporate Investment," in A.C. Harberger (ed.), *Demand for Durable Goods,* Chicago, University of Chicago Press, 1960, pp. 211-266.

[234] Guccione, A., and W.J. Gillen, "A Single Disaggregation of a Neoclassical Investment Function," *Journal of Regional Science,* Vol. 12, 1972, pp. 279-294.

[235] Guesnerie, R., "Production of Public Sector and Taxation in Simple Second Best Model," *Journal of Economic Theory,* Vol. 10, 1975, pp. 127-156.

[236] Haavelmo, T.A., *A Study in the Theory of Investment,* Chicago, University of Chicago Press, 1960.

[237] Hacche, G., *The Theory of Economic Growth,* New York, St. Martin's, 1979.

[238] Hadley, G., and M.C. Kemp, *Variational Methods in Economics,* Amsterdam, North-Holland, 1971.

[239] Hahn, F.H. (ed.), *Readings in the Theory of Growth,* New York, Macmillan, 1972.

[240] Hahn, F.H., *The Share of Wages in the National Income,* London, Weidenfeld and Nicolson, 1972.

[241] Hahn, F.H., "Some Adjustment Processes," *Econometrica,* Vol. 38, 1970, pp. 1-17.

[242] Hahn, F.H., "Keynesian Economics and General Equilibrium Theory:

Reflections on Some Current Debates," in [265], pp. 25-40.

[243] Hahn, F.H., "The Stability of Growth Equilibrium," *Quarterly Journal of Economics,* Vol. 74, 1960, pp. 206-226.

[244] Hahn, F.H., "On Two-Sector Growth Models," *Review of Economic Studies,* Vol. 32, 1965, pp. 339-346.

[245] Hahn, F. H., "Equilibrium Dynamics with Heterogeneous Capital Goods," *Quarterly Journal of Economics,* Vol. 80, 1966, pp. 633-646.

[246] Hahn, F.H., "Exercises in Conjectural Equilibria," *Scandanavian Journal of Economics,* Vol. 79, 1977, pp. 210-226.

[247] Hahn, F.H., *On the Notion of Equilibrium in Economics,* Cambridge, U.K., Cambridge University Press, 1973.

[248] Hahn, F.H., and F.P.R. Brechling (eds.), *The Theory of Interest,* New York, Macmillan, 1965.

[249] Hahn, F.H., and R.C.O. Matthews, "The Theory of Economic Growth: A Survey," *Economic Journal,* Vol. 74, 1964, pp. 779-902.

[250] Haley, C.W., "Taxes, the Cost of Capital and the Firm's Investment Decisions," *The Journal of Finance,* Vol. 26, 1971, pp. 901-917.

[251a] Hall, R.E., "Technical Change and Capital from the Point of View of the Dual," *Review of Economic Studies,* Vol. 35, 1968, pp. 35-46.

[251b] Hall, R.E., "The Macroeconomic Impact of Changes in Income Taxes in Short and Medium Runs," *Journal of Economic Literature,* Vol. 86, 1978, pp. S71-S85.

[252] Hall, R.E., and D.W. Jorgenson, "Application of the Theory of Optimal Capital Accumulation," in [197], pp. 9-60.

[253] Hamada, K., "Optimal Capital Accumulation by an Economy Facing an International Capital Market," *Journal of Political Economy,* Vol. 72, 1964, pp. 379-396.

[254] Hamberg, D., *Models of Economic Growth,* New York, Harper and Row, 1971.

[255] Hansen, B., *Lectures in Economic Theory, Part I: The Theory of Economic Policy and Planning,* Lund, Sweden, Lund, 1967.

[256] Hansen, B., *The Economic Theory of Fiscal Policy,* Cambridge, Mass, Harvard University Press, 1958.

[257] Harcourt, G.C., *Some Cambridge Controversies in the Theory of Capital,* Cambridge, U.K., Cambridge University Press, 1972.

[258] Harcourt, G.C., "A Simple Joan Robinson Model of Accumulation with One Technique: A Comment," *Osaka Economic Papers,* Vol. 11, 1963, pp. 24-28.

[259] Harcourt, G.C., "A Critique of Mr. Kaldor's Model of Income Distribution and Economic Growth," *Australian Economic Papers,* Vol. 2, 1963, pp. 20-36.

[260] Harcourt, G.C., "The Accountant in a Golden Age," *Oxford Economic Papers,* Vol. 17, 1965, pp. 66-80.

[261] Harcourt, G. C., "A Two-Sector Model of the Distribution of Income and the Level of Employment in the Short Run," *Economic Record,* Vol. 41, 1965, pp. 103-117.

[262] Harcourt, G.C., "Review of D. Dewey, Modern Capital Theory," *Economic Journal,* Vol. 77, 1967, pp. 359-361.

[263] Harcourt, G. C., "Investment-Decision Criteria, Investment Incentive and Choice of Technique," *Economic Journal,* Vol. 78, 1968, pp. 77-95.

[264] Harcourt, G.C., "The Cambridge Controversies: Old Ways and New Horizons–or Dead End," *Oxford Economic Papers,* Vol. 28, 1976, pp. 25-65.

[265] Harcourt, G.C. (ed.), *The Microeconomic Foundations of Macroeconomics,* New York, Macmillan, 1977.

[266] Harcourt, G.C., et al. (eds.), *Capital and Growth,* Baltimore, Md, Penguin, 1971.

[267] Harcourt, G.C., and V.G. Massaro, "A Note on Mr. Smifa's Subsystems," *Economic Journal,* Vol. 74, 1964, pp. 715-722.

[268] Harris, D.J., "On Marx's Scheme of Reproduction and Accumulation," *Journal of Political Economy,* Vol. 80, 1972, pp. 505-522.

[269] Harrod, R.F., "An Essay in Dynamic Theory," *Economic Journal,* Vol. 49, 1939, pp. 14-33.

[270] Harrod, R.F., *Towards a Dynamic Economics,* London, Macmillan, 1948.

[271] Harrod, R.F., "Domar and Dynamic Economics," *Economic Journal,* Vol. 69, 1959, pp. 451-464.

[272] Harrod, R.F., "Themes in Dynamic Theory," *Economic Journal,* Vol. 73, 1963, pp. 401-421.

[273] Harrod, R.F., *Economic Dynamics,* London, Macmillan, 1973.

[274] Harrod, R.F., "Review of Joan Robinson's Essay in the Theory of Employment," *Economic Journal,* Vol. 47, 1937, pp. 326-330.

[275] Harrod, R.F., "Domar and Dynamic Economics," *Economic Journal,* Vol. 69, 1959, pp. 451-464.

[276] Harrod, R.F., "Second Essay in Dynamic Theory," *Economic Journal,* Vol. 70, 1960, pp. 277-293.

[277] Hart, A.G., "Capital Appropriations and the Accelerator," *Review of Economic Studies,* Vol. 47, 1965, pp. 123-136.

[278] Hart, A.G., et al. (eds.), *The Quality and Economic Significance of Anticipations Data,* NBER, Princeton, N.J., Princeton University Press, 1960.

[279] Hartman, R., "Adjustment Costs, Price and Wage Uncertainty and Investment," *Review of Economic Studies,* Vol. 40, 1973, pp. 259-268.

[280] Hartman, R., "The Effects of Price and Cost Uncertainty on Investment," *Journal of Economic Theory,* Vol. 5, 1972, pp. 258-266.

[281] Hay, G.A., "Adjustment Costs and Flexible Accelerator," *Quarterly Journal of Economics,* Vol. 84, 1970, pp. 140-143.

[282] Hay, G.A., "Production, Price and Inventory Theory," *American Economic Review,* Vol. 60, 1970, pp. 531-545.

[283] Hayashi, F., "Tobin's Marginal q and Average q: A Neoclassical Interpretation," *Econometrica,* Vol. 50, 1982, pp. 213-224.

[284] Hayashi, F., "Corporate Finance Side of the q Theory of Investment," *Journal of Public Economics,* Vol. 27, 1985, pp. 261-280.

[285] Heal, G.M., *The Theory of Economic Planning,* Amsterdam, North-Holland, 1973.

[286] Heidensohn, K., "Labour's Share in National Income–A Constant?" *Manchester School of Economics, Social Studies* Vol. 37, 1969, pp. 295-321.

[287] Helliwell, J., "Aggregate Investment Equations: A Survey of Issues," Discussion Paper No. 73, Department of Economics, University of British Columbia, 1972.

[288] Helliwell, J., *Public Policies and Private Investment,* Oxford, U.K. Clarendon Press, 1968.

[289] Helliwell, J. and G. Glorieux, "Forward-looking Investment Behavior," *Review of Economic Studies,* Vol. 37, 1970, pp. 499-516.

[290] Helpman, E., and P.R. Krugman, *Market Structure and Foreign Trade,* Cambridge, Mass., MIT Press, 1985.

[291] Hestenes, M.R., "On Variational Theory and Optimal Control Theory," *Journal of Siam Control,* Series A, Vol. 3, 1965, pp. 23-48.

[292] Hestenes, M.R., *Calculus of Variations and Optimal Control Theory,* New York, Wiley, 1966.

[293] Hicks, J.R., "Mr. Harrod's Dynamic Theory," *Economica,* Vol. 16, 1949, pp. 106-121.

[294] Hicks, J.R., "The Measurement of Capital in Relation to the Measurment of Other Economic Aggregates," in [467], pp. 18-31.

[295] Hicks, J.R., "The Mainspring of Economic Theory," *Swedish Journal of Economics,* Vol. 75, 1973, pp. 336-348.

[296] Hicks, J.R., "Capital Controversies: Ancient and Modern," *American Economic Review,* Vol. 64, 1974, pp. 307-316.

[297] Hicks, J.R., "Wages and Interest: The Dynamic Problem," *Economic Journal,* Vol. 45, 1935, pp. 456-468.

[298] Hicks, J.R., *Economic Perspective: Further Essays on Money and Growth,* Oxford, U.K., Oxford University Press, 1977.

[299] Hicks, J.R., *The Theory of Wages,* London, Macmillan, 1963.

[300] Hicks, J.R., *Value and Capital,* Oxford, U.K., Clarendon Press, 1965.

[301] Hicks, J.R., *Capital and Growth,* Oxford, U.K., Clarendon Press, 1965.

[302] Hicks, J.R., *The Crisis in Keynesian Economics,* Oxford, U.K., Blackwell, 1974.

[303] Hicks, J.R., *Capital and Time,* Oxford, U.K., Clarendon Press, 1973.

[304] Hicks, J.R., *Methods of Dynamic Economics,* New York, Oxford University Press, 1985.

[305] Hicks, J.R., "Thoughts on the Theory of Capital–The Corfu Conference," *Oxford Economic Papers,* Vol. 12, 1960, pp. 123-132.

[306] Hines, A.G., *On the Reappraisal of Keynesian Economics,* London, Martin Robertson, 1971.

[307] Hirshleifer, J., *Investment, Interest and Capital,* Englewood Cliffs, N.J., Prentice-Hall, 1970.

[308] Hotelling, H., "A General Mathematical Theory of Depreciation," *Journal of American Statistical Association,* Vol. 20, 1925, pp. 340-353.

[309] Hulten, C.R., and F.G. Wykoff, "The Estimation of Economic Depreciation Using Vintage Asset Prices," *Journal of Econometrics,* Vol. 15, 1981, pp. 367-396.

[310] Hulten, C.R., "Growth Accounting with Intermediate Inputs," *Review of Economic Studies,* Vol. 45, 1978, pp. 511-518.

[311] Hunt, E.K., and J.G. Schwartz (eds.), *A Critique of Economic Theory,* Baltimore, Md., Penguin, 1972.

[312] Hymer, S., "Capital Theory and Investment Behavior," *American Economic Review,* Vol. 53, 1963, pp. 247-259.

[313] Ijiri, Y., "Fundamental Queries in Aggregation Theory," *Journal of American Statistical Association,* Vol. 66, 1971, pp. 766-782.

[314] Inada, K., "Investment in Fixed Capital and the Stability of Growth Equilibrium," *Review of Economic Studies,* Vol. 33, 1966, pp. 19-30.

[315] Inada, K., "On the Stability of Two-Sector Growth Models," *Review of Economic Studies,* Vol. 31, 1964, pp. 127-142.

[316a] Inada, K., "Some Structural Characteristics of the Turnpike Theorem," *Review of Economic Studies,* Vol. 31, 1964, pp. 43-58.

[316b] Inada, K., "On the Existence of a Keynesian Equilibrium," *Review of Economic Studies,* Vol. 35, 1968, pp. 327-334.

[317a] International Monetary Fund, *Financial Statistics,* Various Issues, Washington, D.C., 1974-1998.

[317b] Johansen, L., "Substitution versus Fixed Production Coefficient in the Theory of Economic Growth: A Synthesis," *Econometrica,* Vol. 27, 1959, pp. 157-176.

[318] Johansen, L., *Production Functions,* Amsterdam, North-Holland, 1972.

[319] Johnson, H.G., "The Neoclassical One-Sector Growth Model: A Geometrical Exposition and Extension to Monetary Economy," *Economica,* Vol. 33, 1966, pp. 265-287.

[320] Johnson, H.G., *The Two-Sector Model of General Equilibrium,* London, Allen and Unwin, 1971.

[321] Johnson, H.G., *The Theory of Income Distribution,* London, Gray-Mills, 1973.

[322] Johnson, H.G., "A Simple Joan Robinson Model of Accumulation with One Technique," *Osaka Economic Papers,* Vol. 10, 1962, pp. 28-33.

[323] Jones, H.G., *An Introduction to Modern Theories of Economic Growth,* New York, McGraw-Hill, 1975.

[324] Jones, R.W., and P.B. Kenen (eds.), *Handbook of International Economics,* Vol. 1, Amsterdam, North-Holland, 1984.

[325] Jorgenson, D.W., "Capital Theory and Investment Behavior," *American Economic Review,* Supplement, Vol. 53 (May), 1963, pp. 247-259.

[326] Jorgenson, D.W., "Anticipations and Investment Behavior," in *Brookings Quarterly Econometric Model of the United States,* J.S. Duesenberry et al. (eds.), Chicago, Rand McNally, 1965, pp. 35-94.

[327] Jorgenson, D.W., "Econometric Studies of Investment Behavior: A Survey," *Journal of Economic Literature,* Vol. 9, 1971, pp. 1111-1147.

[328] Jorgenson, D.W., "Investment Behavior and Production Function," *Bell*

Journal of Economics and Management Science, Vol. 3, 1972, pp. 220-251.

[329] Jorgenson, D.W., "The Theory of Investment Behavior," in *Determinants of Investment Behavior,* R. Ferber (ed.), National Bureau of Economic Research, New York, Columbia University Press, 1967, pp. 129-155; also in S. Mittra (ed.), *Dimensions of Macroeconomics,* New York, Random House, 1971, pp. 129-155.

[330] Jorgenson, D.W., "Investment and Production: A Review," in *Frontiers of Quantitative Economics,* Vol. II, Intriligator M.D. et al. (eds.), New York, North-Holland, 1974, pp. 341-375.

[331] Jorgenson, D.W., "The Economic Theory of Replacement," in *Essays in Honour of Jan Tinberger,* W. Sellykaerts (ed.), White Plains, N.Y., IASP, 1974, pp. 189-221.

[332] Jorgenson, D.W., et al., *Optimal Replacement Policy,* Amsterdam, North-Holland, 1967.

[333] Jorgenson, D.W., et al., "A Comparison of Alternative Econometric Models of Corporate Investment Behavior," *Econometrica,* Vol. 38, No. 2, 1970, pp. 187-212.

[334] Jorgenson, D.W., et al., "The Predictive Performance of Econometric Models of Quarterly Investment Behavior," *Econometrica,* Vol. 38, (March), 1970, pp. 213-224.

[335] Jorgenson, D.W., and C.D. Siebert, "A Comparison of Alternative Theories of Corporate Investment Behavior," *American Economic Review,* Vol. 58, 1968, pp. 681-712.

[336] Jorgenson, D.W., and C.D. Siebert, "Optimal Capital Accumulation and Corporate Investment Behavior," *Journal of Political Economy,* Vol. 76, 1968, pp. 1123-1151.

[337] Jorgenson, D.W., and J.A. Stephenson, "Anticipations and Investment Behavior in U.S. Manufacturing 1947-1965," *Journal of Americal Statistical Association,* Vol. 64, March, 1969, pp. 67-87.

[338] Jorgenson, D.W., and J. Stephenson, "Investment Behavior in U.S. Manufacturing 1947-60," *Econometrica,* Vol. 35, 1967, pp. 169-220.

[339] Jorgenson, D.W., and J.A. Stephenson, "Issues in the Development of the Neoclassical Theory of Investment Behavior," *Review of Economic Statistics,* Vol. 51, 1969, pp. 346-353.

[340] Jorgenson, D.W., et al. (eds.), *Technology and Capital Formation,* Cambridge, Mass., MIT Press, 1989.

[341] Junanker, P.N., *Investment: Theories and Evidence,* London, Macmillan, 1972.

[342] Kahn, R.F., "Exercise in the Analysis of Growth," *Oxford Economic Papers,* Vol. 11, 1956, pp. 143-156.

[343] Kahn, R.F., "Malinvand on Keynes," *Cambridge Journal of Economic,* Vol. 1, 1977, pp. 375-388.

[344] Kahn, R.F., "The Relation of Home Investment to Unemployment," *Economic Journal,* Vol. 41, 1931, pp. 173-198.

[345] Kahn, R.F., *Selected Essays on Employment and Growth,* Cambridge,

U.K., Cambridge University Press, 1972.

[346] Kaldor, N., "Alternative Theories of Distribution," *Review of Economic Studies,* Vol. 23, 1955, pp. 83-100.

[347] Kaldor, N., "Capital Accumulation and Economic Growth," in [467], pp. 177-222.

[348] Kaldor, N., "A Model of Economic Growth," *Economic Journal* Vol. 67, 1957, pp. 391-624.

[349] Kaldor, N., "Marginal Productivity and the Macro-Economic Theories of Distribution," *Review of Economic Studies,* Vol. 33, 1966, pp. 309-319.

[350] Kaldor, N., "Some Fallacies in the Interpretation of Kaldor," *Review of Economic Studies,* Vol. 37, 1970, pp. 1-7.

[351] Kaldor, N., "The Irrelevance of Equilibrium Economics," *Economic Journal,* Vol. 82, 1972, pp. 1237-1235.

[352] Kaldor, N., and J.A. Mirrlees, "New Model of Economic Growth," *Review of Economic Studies,* Vol. 29, 1961-1962, pp. 174-192.

[353] Kaldor, N., *Essays on Value and Distribution,* New York, Holmes and Meier, 1980.

[354] Kaldor, N., *Essays on Economic Stability and Growth,* New York, Holmes and Meier, 1980.

[355] Kaldor, N., *Further Essays on Economic Theory,* New York, Holmes and Meier, 1978.

[356] Kaldor, N., *Causes of the Slow Rate of Growth of the United Kingdom, Inaugural Lecture,* Cambridge, U.K., Cambridge University Press, 1966.

[357] Kalecki, M., *Theory of Economic Dynamics,* New York, Modern Reader, 1968.

[358] Kalecki, M., *Essays on the Dynamics of the Capitalist Economy,* Cambridge, U.K. Cambridge University Press, 1971.

[359] Kalecki, M., *Essays on the Theory of Economic Fluctuations,* Cambridge, Cambridge University Press, 1939.

[360] Kalecki, M., *Selected Essays on the Economic Growth of the Socialist and Mixed Economy,* Cambridge, U.K., Cambridge University Press, 1972.

[361] Kalecki, M., "The Determinants of Profits," *Economic Journal,* Vol. 52, 1942, pp. 258-267.

[362] Kalman, R., "The Theory of Optimal Control and the Calculus of Variations," in R. Bellman (ed.), *Mathematical Optimization Techniques,* Berkeley, Calif., University of California Press, 1963, pp. 309-331.

[363] Kantorovich, L.M., *Essays in Optimal Planning,* New York, Inter-Arts and Science Press, 1976.

[364] Katz, M., "The Cost of Borrowing, the Terms of Trade and the Determination of External Debt," *Oxford Economic Papers,* Vol. 34, 1982, pp. 332-345.

[365] Kemmeny, J.G., et al., "A Generalization of the von Neumann Model of an Expanding Economy," *Econometrica,* Vol. 24, 1956, pp. 115-135.

[366] Kemp, M.C., and P.C. Thanh, "On a Class of Growth Models," *Econometrica,* Vol. 32, 1966, pp. 257-282.

[367] Kendrick, J.W. (ed.), *International Comparison of Productivity and the*

Causes of the Slowdown, Cambridge, Mass., Ballinger, 1984.

[368] Kendrick, J.W., *The Formation and Stock of Total Capital,* New York, National Bureau of Economic Research, 1976.

[369] Kennedy, C., "Induced Bias in Innovation an the Theory of Distribution," *Economic Journal,* Vol. 74, 1964, pp. 541-547.

[370] Kennedy, C., and A.P. Thirlwall, "Technical Progress–A Survey," *Economic Journal,* Vol. 82, 1972, pp. 11-72.

[371] Kennedy, C., "Harrod on Neutrality," *Economic Journal,* Vol. 72, 1962, pp. 249-250.

[372] Keynes, J.M., "The General Theory of Employment," *Quarterly Journal of Economics,* Vol. 52, 1937, pp. 209-223.

[373] Keynes, J.M., "Relative Movements of Real Wages and Output," *Economic Journal,* Vol. 49, 1939, pp. 34-51.

[374] Keynes, J.M., *The General Theory of Employment, Interest and Money,* New York, Harcourt, Brace Jovanovich, 1964.

[375] Keynes, J.M., *A Treatise on Money,* London, Macmillan, 1930.

[376] Keynes, J.M., *The Collected Writings of J.M. Keynes,* Vols. 13 and 14, New York, Macmillan, 1973.

[377] King, M.A., "Taxation and Investment Incentive in a Vintage Investment Model," *Journal of Public Economics,* Vol. 1, 1972, pp. 121-148.

[378] King, M.A., "Taxation and the Cost of Capital," *Revew of Economic Studies,* Vol. 41, 1974, pp. 21-36.

[379] King, M.A., *Public Policy and the Corporation,* London, Chapman and Hall, 1977.

[380] Kirzner, I.M., *An Essay on Capital,* New York, Augustus M. Kelly, 1966.

[381] Kisselgoff, A., and F. Modigliani, "Private Investment in Electric Power and the Acceleration Principle," *Review of Economic Statistics,* Vol. 39, 1957, pp. 363-379.

[382] Klein, L.R., "Issues in Econometric Studies of Investment Behaviour," *Journal of Economic Literature,* Vol. 12, 1974, pp. 43-49.

[383] Klein, L.R., "Some Theoretical Issues in the Measurement of Capacity," *Econometrica,* Vol. 28, 1960, pp. 272-286.

[384] Klein, L.R., *The Keynesian Revolution,* New York, Macmillan, 1950.

[385] Klein, L.R., "Macroeconomics and the Theory of Rational Behavior," *Econometrica,* Vol. 14, 1946, pp. 93-108.

[386] Klein, L.R., "Remarks on the Theory of Aggregation," *Econometrica,* Vol. 14, 1946, pp. 303-312.

[387] Klein, L.R., "Studies in Investment Behavior," in *Conference on Business Cycles,* University National Bureau Conference, NBER, Series No. 2, New York, Columbia University Press 1951, pp. 233-318.

[388] Klein, L.R., and R.S. Preston, "Some New Results in the Measurement of Capacity Utilization," *American Economic Review,* Vol. 57, 1967, pp. 34-58.

[389] Klein, L.R., and R.F. Kosobund, "Some Econometrics of Growth: Great Ratios of Economics," *Quarterly Journal of Economics,* Vol. 75, 1961, pp. 173-198.

[390] Klein, L.R., and V. Long, "Capacity Utilization: Concept, Measurement and Recent Estimates," *Brookings Papers on Economic Activity,* Vol. 3, 1973, pp. 743-756.

[391] Klotz, B.P., *Productivity Analysis in Manufacturing Plants,* BLB Staff Paper 3, U.S. Department of Labor, Washington, D.C., 1970.

[392] Knight, F.H., *Risks, Uncertainty and Profit,* Boston, Mass., Houghton Mifflin, 1921.

[393] Know, A.D., "The Acceleration Principle and the Theory of Investment: A Survey," *Economica,* Vol. 19, 1952, pp. 269-297.

[394] Koopmans, T.C., "Measurement without Theory," *Review of Economic Statistics,* Vol. 29, 1947, pp. 161-172.

[395] Koopmans, T.C., "Economic Growth at a Maximal Rate," *Quarterly Journal of Economic,* Vol. 78, 1964, pp. 355-394.

[396] Koopmans, T.C., "On the Concept of Optimal Growth," in *The Econometric Approach to Development Planning,* Rome, Pontificiae Academae Scientiarum Scripta Varia, 1965, pp. 225-300.

[397] Koopmans, T.C., "Intertemporal Distribution and 'Optimal' Economic Growth," in [175], pp. 95-126.

[398] Koopmans, T.C., "Objectives, Constraints and Outcomes in Optimal Growth Models," *Econometrica,* Vol. 35, 1967, pp. 1-15.

[399] Koopmans, T.C., "Models Involving a Continuous Time Variable," in [400], pp. 384-932.

[400] Koopmans, T.C. (ed.), *Statistical Inference in Dynamic Economic Models,* New York, Wiley, 1950.

[401] Koopmans, T.C., *Three Essays on the State of Economic Science,* New York, McGraw-Hill, 1957.

[402] Koopmans, T.C. (ed.), *Activity Analysis of Production and Allocation: Proceedings of a Conference,* Cowles Foundation Monograph No. 13, New York, Wiley, 1951.

[403] Korliras, P.G., and R.S. Thorn (eds.), *Modern Macroeconomics,* New York, Harper and Row, 1979.

[404] Kornai, J., "Autonomous Control of the Economic System," *Econometrica,* Vol. 41, 1973, pp. 509-528.

[405] Kornai, J., *Mathematical Planning of Structural Decisions,* New York, North-Holland, 1975.

[406] Kornai, J., *Economics of Shortage,* Vols. 1 and 2, Amsterdam, North-Holland, 1980.

[407] Koshimura, S., *Theory of Capital Reproduction and Accumulation,* Kitchener, Ontario, DPG, 1975.

[408] Koyck, L.M., *Distributed Lags and Investment Analysis,* Amsterdam, North-Holland, 1954.

[409] Koyck, L.M., et al., "Economic Growth, Marginal Productivity of Capital and the Rate of Interest," in [248], pp. 242-266.

[410] Kravis, I.B., "Relative Income Shares in Fact and Theory," *American Economic Review,* Vol. 49, 1959, pp. 917-949.

[411] Kregel, J., *The Reconstruction of Political Economy: An Introduction to*

Post-Keynesian Analysis, London, Macmillan, 1973.

[412] Kregel, J.A., *Rate of Profit, Distribution and Growth: Two Views,* London, Macmillan, 1971.

[413] Kregel, J.A., *The Theory of Economic Growth,* London, Macmillan, 1972.

[414] Krugman, P., "A Model of Innovation, Technology Transfer and the World Distribution of Income," *Journal of Political Economy,* Vol. 87, 1978, pp. 253-266.

[415] Kubota, K., "A Re-Examination of the Existence and Stability Propositions in Kaldor's Growth Models," *Review of Economic Studies,* Vol. 35, 1968, pp. 353-360.

[416] Kuh, E., *Capital Stock Growth: A Micro-Economic Approach,* Amsterdam, North-Holland, 1963.

[417] Kuh, E., "An Essay on Aggregation Theory and Practice," in W. Sellekaerts (ed.), *Econometrics and Economic Theory: Essays in Honour of Jan Tinbergen,* New York, International Arts and Science Press, 1974, pp. 57-99.

[418] Kurz, M., "A Two-Sector Extension of Swan's Model of Economic Growth: The Case of No Technical Change," *International Economic Review,* Vol. 7, 1965, pp. 68-79.

[419] Kurz, M., "Optimal Paths of Accumulation under the Minimum Time Objective," *Econometrica,* Vol. 33, 1965, pp. 42-66.

[420] Kurz, M., "Substitution vs Fixed Production Coefficients: A Comment," *Econometrica,* Vol. 31, 1963, pp. 209-217.

[421] Kurz, M., "Optimal Economic Growth and Wealth Effects," *International Economic Review,* Vol. 9, 1968, pp. 348-357.

[422] Kurz, M., "The General Instability of a Class of Competitive Growth Processes," *Review of Economic Studies,* Vol. 35, 1968, pp. 155-174.

[423] Kurz, M., "Tightness and Substitution in the Theory of Capital," *Journal of Economic Theory,* Vol. 1, 1969, pp. 244-272.

[424] Kuznets, S., *Capital in the American Economy,* Princeton, N.J., Princeton University Press, 1961.

[425] Kuznets, S., "Modern Economic Growth: Findings and Reflections," *Americal Economic Review,* Vol. 63, 1973, pp. 247-258.

[426] Kuznets, S., *Six Lectures on Economic Growth,* Glencoe, Ill., Free Press, 1959.

[427] Lachmann, L.M., "Complementarity and Substitution in Theory of Capital," *Economica,* Vol. 14, 1947, pp. 108-119.

[428] Lachmann, L.M., *Capital Expectations and the Market Process,* Kansas City, Kansas, Sheed Andrews and McMeel, 1977.

[429] Lachmann, L.M., *Capital and Its Structure,* London, Bell, 1956.

[430] Laing, N.F., "Two Notes on Pasinetti's Theorem," *Economic Records,* Vol. 45, 1969, pp. 373-385.

[431] Lancaster, K., "Mrs. Robinson's Dynamics," *Economica,* Vol. 27, 1960, pp. 63-70.

[432] Landes, D.S., *The Unbounded Prometheus,* Cambridge, U.K., Cambridge University Press, 1969.

[433] Lange, O., "The Place of Interest in the Theory of Production," *Review of Economic Studies,* Vol. 3, 1936, pp. 159-192.

[434] Lau, L.J., "A Characterization of the Normalized Restricted Profit Function," *Journal of Economic Theory,* Vol. 12, 1976, pp. 131-163.

[435] Leijonhufvud, A. (ed.), *On Keynesian Economics and Economics of Keynes,* New York, Oxford University Press, 1968.

[436] Leijonhufvud, A. (ed.), *Information and Coordination: Essays in Macroeconomic Theory,* Oxford, Oxford University Press, 1981.

[437] Leontief, W., "The Fundamental Assumptions of Mr. Keynes," in [438], pp. 87-92.

[438] Leontief, W., *Essays in Economics,* Oxford, Oxford University Press, 1966.

[439] Leontief, W., "Theoretical Assumptions and Nonobserved Facts," *American Economic Review,* Vol. 61, 1971 (May), pp. 1-7.

[440] Leontief, W.W., "Composite Commodities and the Problem of Index Numbers," *Econometrica,* Vol. 4, 1936, pp. 39-59.

[441] Leontief, W.W., "Implicit Theorizing: A Methodological Criticism of the Neo-Cambridge School," *Quarterly Journal of Economics,* Vol. 51, 1936, pp. 337-351.

[442] Leontief, W.W., "A Note on the Interrelation of Subsets of Independent Variables of a Continuous Function with Continuous First Derivatives," *Bulletin of the American Mathematical Society,* Vol. 53, 1947, pp. 343-350.

[443] Leontief, W.W., "Introduction to a Theory of the Internal Structure of Functional Relationship," *Econometrica,* Vol. 15, 1947, pp. 361-373.

[444] Leontief, W.W., *The Structure of the American Economy, 1919-1939,* New York, Oxford University Press, 1951.

[445] Lerner, A.P., *The Economics of Control,* New York, MacMillan, 1944.

[446a] Lerner, A.P., "On the Marginal Product of Capital and Marginal Efficiency of Investment," *Journal of Political Economy,* Vol. 61, 1953, pp. 1-14.

[446b] Lerner, A.P., "On Some Recent Development in Capital Theory," *American Economic Review,* Vol. 55, 1965, pp. 284-295.

[447] Levhari, D., "A Nonsubstitution Theorem and Switching of Techniques," *Quarterly Journal of Economics,* Vol. 79, 1965, pp. 98-105.

[448] Levhari, D. and P.A. Samuelson, "The Non-Switching Theorem Is False," *Quarterly Journal of Economics,* Vol. 80, 1966, pp. 518-519.

[449] Levhari, D., "On the Sensitivity of the Level of Output to Savings: Embodiment and Disembodiment," *Quarterly Journal of Economics,* Vol. 81, 1967, pp. 524-528.

[450] Lewis, A., *The Theory of Economic Growth,* London, Allen and Unwin, 1955.

[451] Lindahl, E., *Studies in Theory of Money and Capital,* London, Allen and Unwin, 1939.

[452] Lindsay, R. (ed.), *The Nation's Capital Needs: Three Studies,* New York, Committee for Economic Development, 1979.

[453] Lipsey, L., et al., *Measurement of Saving, Investment and Wealth*, Chicago, University of Chicago Press, 1989.

[454] Liviatan, O., "A Macro-Absorption Approach for Estimating the Foreign Debt Burden," *Economic Development and Cultural Change*, Vol. 32, 1984, pp. 901-913.

[455] Liviatan, N., "A Diagrammatic Exposition of Optimal Growth," *American Economic Review*, Vol. 60, 1970, pp. 302-309.

[456] Lovell, M.C., "Manufacture's Inventories, Sales Expectations and the Acceleration Principle," *Econometrica*, Vol. 29, 1961, pp. 267-296.

[457] Lovell, M.C., "Buffer Stocks, Sales Expectations and the Acceleration Principle," *Econometrica*, Vol. 30, 1962, pp. 267-296.

[458] Lovell, M.C., "Determinants of Inventory Investment," in *Models of Income Distribution*, NBER Studies in Income and Wealth, Princeton, N.J., Princeton University Press, 1964, pp. 193-195.

[459] Lowe, A., *The Path of Economic Growth*, New York, Cambridge University Press, 1976.

[460] Lowe, A., "The Classical Theory of Economic Growth," *Social Research*, Vol. 221, 1954, pp. 127-158.

[461] Lucas, R., "Adjustment Costs and the Theory of Supply," *Journal of Political Economy*, Vol. 75, 1967, pp. 321-334.

[462a] Lucas, R., "Optimal Investment Policy and the Flexible Accelerator," *International Economic Review*, Vol. 8, 1967, pp. 78-85.

[462b] Lucas, R.E., "On the Mechanics of Economic Development," *Journal of Monetary Economics*, Vol. 22, 1988, pp. 3-42.

[463] Lund, P.J., *Investment: The Study of Economic Aggregate*, San Francisco, Calif., Oliver and Boyd, 1971.

[464] Lund, P.J., and K. Holden, "An Econometric Study of Private Sector Gross Fixed Capital Formation in the United Kingdom, 1923-1938," *Oxford Economic Papers*, Vol. 20, 1968, pp. 56-76.

[465] Lundberg, E., *Instability and Economic Growth*, New Haven, Conn., Yale University Press, 1968.

[466] Lundberg, E., *Studies in the Theory of Economic Expansion*, New York, Kelley, 1954.

[467] Lutz, F.A., and D.C. Hague (eds.), *The Theory of Capital (A Conference Held by the International Economic Association.)* New York, St. Martin's, 1961.

[468] Lutz, F.A., *The Theory of Interest*, Chicago, Aldine, 1968.

[469] Luxemburg, R., *The Acculmulation of Capital*, Routledge and Kegan Paul, 1951.

[470a] Lydall, H., "A Theory of Distribution and Growth with Economies of Scale," *Economic Journal*, Vol. 81, 1971, pp. 91-112.

[470b] Lydall, H., "On Measuring Technical Progress," *Australian Economic Papers*, Vol. 8, 1969, pp. 1-12.

[471] Macbean, A.I., *Export Instability and Economic Development*, Cambridge, Mass., Harvard University Press, 1966.

[472] Maccini, L.J., " Delivery Lags and Demand for Investment," *Review of*

Economic Studies, Vol. 40, 1973, pp. 269-281.

[473] Magill, M.J.P., *On General Economic Theory of Motion,* New York, Springer-Verlag, 1970.

[474] Mainwaring, L., *Value and Distribution in Capitalist Economies,* New York, Cambridge University Press, 1984.

[475] Makarov, V.L., *Mathematical Theory of Economic Dynamics and Equilibria,* New York, Springer-Verlag, 1977.

[476] Malinvaud, E., "Capital Acculmulation and Efficient Allocation of Resources," *Econometrica,* Vol. 21, 1952, pp. 233-268.

[477] Malinvaud, E., "The Analogy between Atemporal and Intertemporal Theories of Resources Allocation," *Review of Economic Studies,* Vol. 28, 1961, pp. 143-160.

[478] Malinvaud, E., *Profitability and Unemployment,* New York, Cambridge University Press, 1980.

[479] Malinvaud, E., *The Theory of Unemployment Reconsidered,* Oxford, Blackwell, 1977.

[480] Malinvaud, E., and M.O.L. Bacharach (eds.) *Activity Analysis in the Theory of Growth and Planning,* London, Macmillan, 1967.

[481] Manescu, M., *Economic Cybernetics,* Kent, Tennessee, Abacus Press, 1980.

[482] Mangasarian, O.L., "Sufficient Conditions for Optimal Control of Non-Linear Systems," *Journal SIAM Control,* Vol. 4, 1966, pp. 139-152.

[483] Manne, A.D., "Capital Expansion and Probabilistic Growth," *Econometrica,* Vol. 29, 1961, pp. 632-649.

[484] Marglin, S., "Investment and Interest: A Reformulation and Extension of Keynesian Theory," *Economic Journal,* Vol. 80, 1970, pp. 910-931.

[485] Marglin, S., "The Social Rate of Discount and the Optimal Rate of Investment," *Quarterly Journal of Economics,* Vol. 77, 1963, pp. 95-111.

[486] Marglin, S.A., *Approaches to Dynamic Investment Planning,* Amsterdam, North-Holland, 1963.

[487] Marshall, A., *Principles of Economics,* 8th ed., London, Macmillan, 1920.

[488] Marshall, N. (ed.), *Keynes: Updated or Out-dated,* Lexington, Mass., Health, 1970.

[489] Martirena-Martel, A.M., "Optimal Inventory and Capital Policy Under Uncertainty," *Journal of Economic Theory,* Vol. 3, 1971, pp. 241-253.

[490] Marx, K., *Capital,* London, Allen and Unwin, 1928.

[491] Masse, P., *Optimal Investment Decisions,* Englewood Cliffs, New Jersey, Prentice-Hall, 1962.

[492] Matthews, R.C.O., "The New View of Investment," Comment, *Quarterly Journal of Economics,* Vol. 90, 1964, pp. 164-176.

[493] May, K.O., "The Aggregation Problem for a One-Industry Model," *Econometrica,* Vol. 14, 1946, pp. 285-298.

[494] May, K.O., "Technological Change and Aggregation," *Econometrica,* Vol. 15, 1947, pp. 51-63.

[495] McCallum, B.T., "The Instability of Kaldorian Models," *Oxford Economic Papers,* Vol. 21, 1969, pp. 56-65.

[496] Meade, J.E., *A Neo-Classical Theory of Economic Growth,* London, Allen and Unwin, 1962.

[497] Meade, J.E., *The Growing Economy,* London, Allen and Unwin, 1968.

[498] Meade, J.E., *The Stationary Economy,* London, Allen and Unwin, 1965.

[499] Meade, J.E., "The Rate of Profit in a Growing Economy," *Economic Journal,* Vol. 73, 1963, pp. 665-674.

[500] Meade, J.E., "Life-Cycle Savings, Inheritance and Economic Growth," *Review of Economic Studies,* Vol. 33, 1966, pp. 61-78.

[501] Meade, J.E., "The Outcome of the Pasinetti Process: A Note,*" Economic Journal,* Vol. 76, 1966, pp. 161-165.

[502] Meade, J.E., and F.H. Hahn, "The Rate of Profit in a Growing Economy," *Economic Journal,* Vol. 75, 1965, pp. 445-448.

[503] Mehta, G., *The Structure of the Keynesian Revolution,* New York, St. Martin's, 1978.

[504] Meyer, J., and R. Glauber, *Investment Decisions, Economic Forecasting, and Public Policy,* Boston, Mass., Harvard University Press, 1957.

[505] Meyer, J., and E. Kuh, *The Investment Decision,* Cambridge, Massachusetts, Harvard University Press, 1957.

[506] Mikesell, R.F., *The Economics of Foreign Aid,* Chicago, Aldine Pub., 1968.

[507] Milgate, M., "Keynes on the Classical Theory of Interest," Cambridge *Economic Journal, Vol.* 3, 1977, pp. 307-315.

[508] Milgate, M., *Capital and Employment,* New York, Academic Press, 1982.

[509] Miller, N.C., "A General Equilibrium Theory of International Capital Flows," *Economic Journal,* Vol. 78, 1968, pp. 312-320.

[510] Mills, E.S., "The Theory of Inventory Decisions," *Econometrica,* Vol. 25, 1957, pp. 222-238.

[511] Mills, E.S., *Price, Output and Inventory Policy,* New York, Wiley, 1962.

[512] Milne, F., "The Adjustment Cost Problem with Jumps in the State Variable," in [578], pp. 107-125.

[513] Minasian, J., "Research and Development Production Functions, and Rates of Return," *American Economic Review,* Vol. 59, 1969, pp. 80-86.

[514] Mirrlees, J.A., "The Dynamic Nonsubstitution Theorem," *Review of Economic Studies,* Vol. 36, 1969, pp. 67-76.

[515] Mirrlees, J.A., "Optimal Growth When Technology Is Changing," *Review of Economic Studies,* Vol. 34, 1967, pp. 95-124.

[516] Mirrlees, J.A., and N. Stern (eds.), *Models of Economic Growth* (Proceeding-International Economic Association), London, Macmillan, 1973.

[517] Mishan, E.J., *The Cost of Economic Growth,* London, Staples Press, 1967.

[518] Modigliani, F., "Business Reasons for Holding Inventories and their Macro-economic Implications," in *Problems of Capital Formation: Concepts, Measurement and Factors,* NBER Studies in Income and Wealth, Princeton, N.J., Princeton University Press, 1957.

[519] Modigliani, F., "Long-run Implications of Alternative Fiscal Policies and

Burden of the National Debt," *Economic Journal,* Vol. 71, 1961, pp. 730-755.

[520] Modigliani, F., and M.H. Miller, "The Cost of Capital, Corporate Finance and the Theory of Investment," *American Economic Review,* Vol. 48, 1958, pp. 261-297.

[521] Moriguchi, C., "Aggregation over Time in Macroeconomic Relations," *International Economic Review,* Vol. 2, 1970, pp. 427-440.

[522] Morishima, M., *Marx's Economics: A Dual Theory of Value and Growth,* New York, Cambridge University Press, 1973.

[523] Morishima, M., and G. Catephores, *Value, Exploitation and Growth,* New York, McGraw-Hill, 1978.

[524] Morishima, M., *Equilibrium, Stability and Growth,* New York, Oxford University Press, 1964.

[525] Morishima, M., "A Historical Note on Professor Sono's Theory of Separability," *International Economic Review,* Vol. 2, 1961, pp. 272-275.

[526] Morishima, M., *Theory of Economic Growth,* Oxford, Clarendon Press, 1969.

[527] Morishima, M., "Refutation on the Nonswitching Theorem," *Quarterly Journal of Economics,* Vol. 80, 1966, pp. 520-525.

[528a] Morrison, T.K., "Manufactured Exports and Protection in Developing Countries: A Cross-Country Analysis," *Economic Development and Cultural Change,* Vol. 25, 1976, pp. 151-158.

[528b] Mortenson, D.T., "Generalized Costs of Adjustment and Dynamic Factor Demand Theory," *Econometrica,* Vol. 41, 1973, pp. 657-667.

[529] Musgrave, J.C., "Fixed Reproducible Tangible Wealth in the United States: Revised Estimates," *Survey of Current Business*, Vol. 66 (No. 1), 1986, pp. 51-75.

[530] Nadiri, M.I., "An Alternative Model of Business Investment Spending," *Brookings Papers on Economic Activity,* Vol. 3, 1972, pp. 547-578.

[531] Nadiri, M.I., "Some Approaches to the Theory and Measurement of Total Factor Productivity: A Survey," *Journal of Economic Literature,* Vol. 8, 1970, pp. 1137-1177.

[532] Negishi, T., *Microeconomic Foundations of Keynesian Macroeconomics,* New York, North-Holland, 1979.

[533] Nell, E.J., "Theories of Growth and Theories of Value," *Economic Development and Cultural Change,* Vol. 16, 1967, pp. 15-26.

[534] Nell, E.J., "A Note on Cambridge Controversies in Capital Theory," *Journal of Economic Literature,* Vol. 8, 1970, pp. 41-44.

[535] Nelson, R.R., and E.S. Phelps, "Investment in Humans, Technological Diffusion, and Economic Growth," *American Economic Review,* Vol. 56, 1966, pp. 69-75.

[536] Nelson, R.R., and S.G. Winter, "Neoclassical vs Evolutionary Theories of Economic Growth: Critique and Prospectus," *Economic Journal,* Vol. 84, 1974, pp. 886-905.

[537] Nerlove, M., "Lags in Economic Behaviour," *Econometrica,* Vol. 40, 1972, pp. 221-252.

[538] Neumann, J.V., "A Model of General Economic Equilibrium," *Review of Economic Studies,* Vol. 13, 1945-1946, pp. 1-9.

[539] Newbery, D.M.G., and A.B. Alkinson, "Investment, Savings and Employment in the Long-Run," *International Economic Review,* Vol. 13, 1972, pp. 460-475.

[540] Ng, Y.K., "Optimal Savings, Individual Decisions and the Diminishing Marginal Productivity of Capital," *Economic Journal,* Vol. 80, 1970, pp. 749-752.

[541] Nickell, S.J., *The Investment Decisions of Firms,* New York, Cambridge University Press, 1978.

[542] Nickell, S.J., "A Closer Look at Replacement Investment," *Journal of Economic Theory,* Vol. 10, 1975, pp. 54-88.

[543] Nickell, S.J., "On the Role of Expectations in the Pure Theory of Investment," *Review of Economic Theory,* Vol. 41, 1974, pp. 1-20.

[544] Nickell, S.J., "Uncertainty and Lags in the Investment Decisions of Firms," *Review of Economic Studies,* Vol. 44, 1977, pp. 249-263.

[545] Nordhaus, W.D., "The Falling Share of Profit," *Brookings Papers on Economic Activity,* Vol. 1, 1974, pp. 169-208.

[546] Nti, K.O., and K.K. Dompere, "Technological Progress and Optimal Factor Demand," *International Journal of Production Economics,* Vol. 49, 1997, pp. 117-130.

[547] Nuti, D.M., "The Degree of Monopoly in the Kaldor-Mirrlees Growth Model," *Review of Economic Studies,* Vol. 36, 1969, pp. 257-260.

[548] Nuti, D.M., "Vulgar Economy in the Theory of Income Distribution," *De Economist,* Vol. 4, 1970, pp. 363-369.

[549] Nuti, D.M., "Capitalism, Socialism, and Steady Growth," *Economic Journal,* Vol. 80, 1970, pp. 32-57.

[550] Ohlin, B., "Some Notes on the Stockholm Theory of Savings and Investments: Part I and II," *Economic Journal,* Vol. 47, 1937, pp. 221-240.

[551] Okamoto, T., and K. Inada, "A Note on the Theory of Economic Growth," *Quarterly Journal of Economics,* Vol. 76, 1962, pp. 503-507.

[552] Paige, D., "Economic Growth: The Last Hundred Years," *National Institute of Economic Review,* Vol. 16, 1961, pp. 24-49.

[553] Pasinetti, L., "Switches of Technique and the Rate of Return in Capital Theory," *Economic Journal,* Vol. 79, 1969, pp. 508-531.

[554] Pasinetti, L., "Rate of Profit and Income Distribution in Relations to the Rate of Economic Growth," *Review of Economic Studies,* Vol. 29, 1961-1962, pp. 267-279.

[555] Pasinetti, L., "New Results in an Old Framework: Comment on Samuelson and Modigliani," *Review of Economic Studies,* Vol. 33, 1966, pp. 303-306.

[556] Pasinetti, L.L., "A Comment on Professor Meade's Rate of Profit in a Growing Economy," *Economic Journal,* Vol. 74, 1964, pp. 488-489.

[557] Pasinetti, L.L., "The Rate of Profit in a Growing Economy: A Reply," *Economic Journal,* Vol. 76, 1966, pp. 158-160.

[558] Pasinetti, L.L., "Changes in the Rate of Profit and Switches of Tech-

niques," *Quarterly Journal of Economics,* Vol. 80, 1966, pp. 503-517.

[559] Pasinetti, L.L., "Again on Capital Theory and Solow's Rate of Return," *Economic Journal,* Vol. 80, 1970, pp. 428-431.

[560] Pasinetti, L.L., "A New Theoretical Approach to the Problems of Economic Growth," in *The Econometric Approach to Development Planning,* Pontificiae Academiae Scientiaruvm, Scripta Varia, Amsterdam, North-Holland, 1965, pp. 571-696.

[561] Pasinetti, L.L., *Growth and Income Distribution: Essays in Economic Theory,* Cambridge, U.K., Cambridge University Press, 1974.

[562] Pasinetti, L.L., *Structural Change and Economic Growth,* Cambridge, U.K., Cambridge University Press, 1981.

[563] Patinkin, D., et al. (eds.), *Keynes, Cambridge, and the General Theory,* New York, Macmillan, 1977.

[564] Patterson, K.D., and K. Schott (eds.), *The Measurement of Capital: Theory and Practice,* London, Macmillan, 1978.

[565] Pearce, I.F., "The End of the Golden Age in Solovia: A Further Fable of Growth Men Hoping to Be 'One Up' on Oiko," *American Economic Review,* Vol. 52, 1962, pp. 1088-1097.

[566] Phelps, B.E.H. and P.E. Hart, "The Share of Wages in National Income," *Economic Journal,* Vol. 62, 1952, pp. 253-277.

[567] Phelps, B.E.H., and B. Weber, "Accumulation, Productivity, and Distribution in the British Economy, 1870-1938," *Economic Journal,* Vol. 63, 1953, pp. 263-288.

[568] Phelps, E.S., "The Golden Rule of Accumulation: A Fable for Growthmen," *American Economic Review,* Vol. 51, 1961, pp. 638-643.

[569] Phelps, E.S., "Substitution, Fixed Proportions Growth and Distribution," *International Economic Review,* Vol. 4, 1963, pp. 265-288.

[570] Phelps, E.S., "Models of Technical Progress and the Golden Rule of Research," *Review of Economic Studies,* Vol. 33, 1966, pp. 133-145.

[571] Phelps, E.S., *Golden Rules of Economic Growth,* New York, Norton, 1966.

[572] Phelps, E.S., "A New View of Investment: A Neoclassical Analysis," *Quarterly Journal of Economics,* Vol. 68, 1962, pp. 548-567.

[573] Phelps, E., and K. Shell, "Public Debt, Taxation and Capital Intensiveness," *Journal of Economic Theory,* Vol. 1, 1969, pp. 330-346.

[574] Phelps, E.S., et al., *Microeconomic Foundations of Employment and Inflation Theory,* New York, Norton, 1970.

[575] Pigou, A.C., "Mr. J.M. Keynes' General Theory of Employment, Interest and Money," *Economica,* Vol. 3, 1936, pp. 63-72.

[576] Pigou, A.C., *The Theory of Unemployment,* London, Macmillan, 1933.

[577] Pigou, A.C., *Industrial Fluctuations,* London, Macmillan, 1927.

[578] Pitchford, J.D., et al. (eds.), *Application of Central Theory to Economic Analysis,* New York, North-Holland, 1977.

[579] Pontryagin, L.S., et al., *The Mathematical Theory of Optimal Process,* New York, Wiley Interscience, 1977.

[580] Radner, R., "Paths of Economic Growth That Are Optimal with Regard

Only to Final States," *Review of Economic Studies,* Vol. 28, 1961, pp. 98-104.

[581] Radner, R., "Dynamic Programming of Economic Growth," in [480], pp. 111-141.

[582] Ramsey, F.P., "A Mathematical Theory of Savings," *Economic Journal,* Vol. 38, 1928, pp. 543-559.

[583] Reder, M.W., "Alternative Theories of Labour's Share," in M. Abramovitz et al. (eds.), *The Allocation of Economic Resource,* Stanford, California, Stanford University Press, 1959, pp. 68-80.

[584] Redfern, P., "Net Investment in Fixed Assets in United Kingdom, 1938-1953," *Journal of Royal Statistical Society,* Series A, Vol. 118, 1955, pp. 141-182.

[585] Riach, P.A., "A Framework for Macro-Distribution Analysis," *Kyklos,* Vol. 22, 1959, pp. 542-565.

[586] Ricardo, D., "On the Principles of Political Economy and Taxation," in P. Sraffa (ed.), *The Works and Correspondence of David Ricardo,* Vol. I, Cambridge, Cambridge University Press, 1951.

[587] Richmond, J., "Aggregation and Identification," *International Economic Review,* Vol. 17, 1976, pp. 47-56.

[588a] Rishel, R.W., "An Extended Pontryagin Principle for Control Systems Whose Control Laws Contain Measures," *Journal of Society for Industrial and Applied Mathematics,* Vol. 3, 1965, pp. 191-205.

[588b] Rivera-Batiz, F.L., et al., *International Finance and Open Economy Macroeconomics,* New York, Macmillan, 1985.

[589] Robinson, J., "A Model of Accumulation," in [693], pp. 346-386.

[590] Robinson, J., *The Accumulation of Capital,* London, Macmillan, 1965.

[591] Robinson, J., *Collected Economic Papers,* Vols. 2 and 3, Oxford, Blackwell, 1964.

[592] Robinson, J., "The Existence of Aggregate Production Functions: Comment," *Econometrica,* Vol. 39, 1971, p. 405.

[593] Robinson, J., *The Rate of Interest and Other Essays,* New York, Macmillan, 1952.

[594] Robinson, J., "The Production Function and the Theory of Capital," *Review of Economic Studies,* Vol. 21, 1953-54, pp. 81-106.

[595] Robinson, J., *Essays in the Theory of Economic Growth,* New York, St. Martin's Press, 1962.

[596] Robinson, J., "Model of Accumulation," in [653a], pp. 115-140.

[597] Robinson, J., "Prelude to a Critique of Economic Theory," in [311], pp. 197-204.

[598] Robinson, J., *Collected Economic Papers,* Vol. 1, Oxford, Blackwell, 1963.

[599] Robinson, J., *Contributions to Modern Economics,* Oxford, Blackwell, 1978.

[600] Robinson, J.V., "Findlay's Robinsonian Model of Accumulation: A Comment," Econometrica, Vol. 30, 1963, pp. 408-412.

[601a] Robinson, J., "Pre-Keynesian Theory after Keynes," *Australian Economic*

Papers, Vol. 3, 1965, pp. 25-35.

[601b] Robinson, J., "The Classification of Inventions," *Review of Economic Studies,* Vol. 5, 1938, pp. 139-142.

[602] Robinson, J., "The Unimportance of Reswitching," *Quarterly Journal of Economics,* Vol. 89, 1975, pp. 32-39.

[603] Robinson, J., "What Are the Questions?," *Journal of Economic Literature,* Vol. 15, 1977, pp. 1318-1339.

[604] Robinson, J., "Michael Kalecki on the Economics of Capitalism," *Oxford Bulletin of Economic Statistics,* Vol. 39, 1977, pp. 7-17.

[605] Robinson, J., "Equilibrium Growth Models," *American Economic Review,* Vol. 51, 1961 pp. 360-369.

[606] Robinson, J., "A Neo-Classical Theorem," *Review of Economic Studies,* Vol. 29, 1962, pp. 219-226.

[607] Robinson, J., "Accumulation and the Production Function," *Economic Journal,* Vol. 69, 1959, pp. 433-442.

[608] Robinson, J., "The Theory of Value Reconsidered," *Australian Economic Papers,* Vol. 8, 1969, pp. 13-19.

[609] Robinson, J., "Capital Theory Up to Date," *Canadian Journal of Economics,* Vol. 3, 1970, pp. 309-317.

[610] Robinson, J., "Prelude to a Critique of Economic Theory," *Oxford Economic Papers,* Vol. 8, 1961, pp. 53-58.

[611] Robinson, J., "Harrod after Twenty-One Years," *Economic Journal,* Vol. 80, 1970, pp. 731-737.

[612] Robinson, J., "Economic Growth and Capital Accumulation–A Comment," *Economic Records,* Vol. 33, 1957, pp. 103-108.

[613a] Robinson, J., "Solow on the Rate of Return," *Economic Journal,* Vol. 74, 1964, pp. 410-417.

[613b] Robinson, J., "Comment on Samuelson and Modigliani," *Review of Economic Studies,* Vol. 33, 1966, pp. 307-308.

[614] Robinson, J., and K.A. Naqui, "The Badly Behaved Production Function," *Quarterly Journal of Economics,* Vol. 81, 1967 pp. 579-591.

[615a] Romer, P.M., "The Origins of Endogeneous Growth," *Journal of Economic Perspectives,* Vol. 8, 1994, pp. 3-24.

[615b] Romer, P.M., "Increasing Returns and Long-run Growth," *Journal of Political Economy,* Vol. 94, 1986, pp. 1002-1037.

[615c] Romer, P.M., "Endogeneous Technological Change," *Journal of Political Economy,* Vol. 98, Part II, pp. S71-S102.

[616a] Rose, H., "The Possibility of Warranted Growth," *Economic Journal,* Vol. 69, 1959, pp. 313-332.

[616b] Rose, H., "Effective Demand in the Long Run," in [515], pp. 25-52.

[617] Rostow, W.W., *Theorists of Economic Growth from David Hume to the Present,* New York, Oxford University Press, 1990.

[618] Rothschild, K.W., "The Limitations of Economic Growth Models," *Kyklos,* Vol. 22, 1959, pp. 567-586.

[619] Rothschild, K.W., "Some Recent Contributions to a Macro-Economic Theory of Income Distribution," *Scottish Journal of Political Economics,*

Vol. 8, 1961, pp. 173-199.

[620] Rowley, J.C.R., "Investment and Neoclassical Production Functions," *Canadian Journal of Economics,* Vol. 5, 1972, pp. 430-435.

[621] Rowley, J.C.R., and P.K. Trivedi, *Econometrics of Investment,* New York, Wiley, 1975.

[622] Rowthorn, R.E., "What Remains of Kaldor's Law?" *Economic Journal,* Vol. 85, 1975, pp. 10-19.

[623] Rowthorn, R.E., "A Reply to Lord Kaldor's Comment," *Economic Journal,* Vol. 85, pp. 897-901.

[624] Rymes, T.K., *On the Concept of Capital and Technical Change,* Cambridge, U.K., Cambridge University Press, 1971.

[625] Salter, W.E.G., "The Production Function and the Durability of Capital," *Economic Records,* Vol. 35, 1959, pp. 47-66.

[626] Salter, W.E.G., "Productivity Growth and Accumulation as Historical Process," in E.A.G. Robinson (ed.), *Problems in Economic Development,* London, Macmillan, 1987, pp. 266-291.

[627] Salter, W.E.G., *Productivity and Technical Change,* London, Cambridge University Press, 1960.

[628] Samuelson, P.A., "A Modern Treatment of the Ricardian Economy: Capital and Interest Aspects of the Pricing Process," *Quarterly Journal of Economics,* Vol. 73, 1959, pp. 217-231.

[629] Samuelson, P.A., "Parable and Realism in Capital Theory: The Surrogate Production Functions," *Review of Economic Studies,* Vol. 29, 1962, pp. 193-206.

[630] Samuelson, P.A., "A Summing-up," *Quarterly Journal of Economics,* Vol. 80, 1966, pp. 568-583.

[631] Samuelson, P.A., "Abstract of a Theorem Concerning Substitutability in Open Leontief Models," in [402], pp. 142-146.

[632] Samuelson, P.A., "Efficient Path of Capital Accumulation in Terms of the Calculus of Variations," in K.J. Arrow et al. (eds.), *Mathematical Methods in Social Science,* Stanford, Calif., Stanford University Press, 1959, pp. 77-88.

[633] Samuelson, P.A., "The Evaluation of Social Income: Capital Formation and Wealth," in [467], pp. 32-57.

[634] Samuelson, P.A., "A Brief Survey of Post-Keynesian Developments," in R.L. Lekachman (ed.), *Keynes' General Theory, Reports of Three Decades,* London, Macmillan, 1963, pp. 331-347.

[635a] Samuelson, P.A., "Interactions between the Multiplier Analysis and the Principle of Acceleration," *Review of Economic Statistics,* Vol. 21, 1939, pp. 75-78.

[635b] Samuelson, P.A., "Paul Douglas' Measurement of Production Functions and Marginal Productivities," *Journal of Political Economy,* Vol. 87, 1979, pp. 566-593.

[636] Samuelson, P.A., "Two Generalizations of the Elasticity of Substitution," in [763], pp. 467-480.

[637] Samuelson, P.A., "A Theory of Induced Innovation along KennedyWeiz-

sacker Lines," *Review of Economic Statistics,* Vol. 47, 1965, pp. 343-356.

[638] Samuelson, P.A., and F. Modigliani, "The Pasinetti Paradox in Neo-classical and More General Models," *Review of Economic Studies,* Vol. 33, 1966, pp. 269-302.

[639] Samuelson, P.A., and F. Modigliani, "Reply to Pasinetti and Robinson," *Review of Economic Studies,* Vol. 33, 1966, pp. 321-330.

[640] Sargent, J.R., "Recent Growth Experience in the Economy of United Kingdom," *Economic Journal,* Vol. 78, 1968, pp. 19-42.

[641] Sargent, J.R., "Economic Growth: Theory and Policy Formation," in [160], pp. 120-139.

[642] Sato, K., "On the Adjustment Time in Neoclassical Growth Models," *Review of Economic Studies,* Vol. 33, 1966, pp. 263-268.

[643] Sato, K., "Fiscal Policy in a Neoclassical Growth Model: An Analysis of the Time Required for Equilibrating Adjustment," *Review of Economic Studies,* Vol. 30, 1963, pp. 86-98.

[644] Sato, K., "The Harrod-Domar Model vs. the Neoclassical Growth Model," *Economic Journal,* Vol. 74, 1964, pp. 380-387.

[645] Sato, K., "The Neo-classical Theorem and Distribution of Income and Wealth," *Review of Economic Studies,* Vol. 33, 1966, pp. 331-335.

[646] Sato, K., *Production Function and Aggregation,* Amsterdam, North-Holland, 1975.

[647] Schmookler, J., *Invention and Economic Growth,* Cambridge, Mass., Harvard University Press, 1966.

[648] Schneider, E., "Income and Income-Distribution in Macro-Economic Theory," *International Economic Papers,* Vol. 8, 1958, pp. 111-121.

[649] Schramm, R., "The Influence of Relative Prices, Production Conditions and Adjustment Cost on Investment Behavior," *Review of Economic Studies,* Vol. 37, 1970, pp. 361-376.

[650] Schumpeter, J.A., "Theoretical Problems of Economic Growth," *Journal of Economic History* (Suppl.), Vol. 8, 1947, pp. 1-9.

[651a] Schumpeter, J.A., "The Analysis of Economic Change," *Review of Economic Statistics,* Vol. 17, 1935, pp. 2-10.

[651b] Schumpeter, J.A., *The Theory of Economic Development,* New York, Oxford University Press, 1980.

[652a] Scott, M.F.G., "Investment and Growth," *Oxford Economic Papers,* Vol. 28, 1976, pp. 317-363.

[652b] Segerstrom, P.S., "Innovation, Imitation and Economic Growth," *Journal of Political Economy,* Vol. 49, 1991, pp. 807-827.

[653a] Sen, A. (ed.), *Growth Economics,* Baltimore, Md., Penguin, 1974.

[653b] Sen, A., *The Choice of Techniques,* Oxford, Blackwell, 1962.

[654a] Sen, A., "Neo-Classical and Neo-Keynesian Theories of Distribution," *Economic Record,* Vol. 39, 1963, pp. 53-64.

[654b] Sen, A., On Optimizing the Rate of Saving," *Economic Journal,* Vol. 71, 1961, pp. 479-496.

[655] Sen, A., "The Money Rate of Interest in the Pure Theory of Growth," in [248], pp. 267-280.

[656] Shackle, G.L.S., *Epistemics and Economics: A Critique of Economic Doctrines,* Cambridge, U.K., Cambridge University Press, 1972.

[657] Shackle, G.L.S., *Keynesian Kaleidics,* Edinburgh, Edinburgh University Press, 1974.

[658] Shell, K., "A Model of Inventive Activity and Capital Accumulation," in [659], pp. 67-85.

[659] Shell, K. (ed.), *Essays on the Theory of Optimal Economic Growth,* Cambridge, Mass., MIT Press, 1967.

[660] Shell, K., and J.E. Stiglitz, "The Allocation of Investment in a Dynamic Economy," *Quarterly Journal of Economics,* Vol. 81, 1967, pp. 592-609.

[661] Shinkai, Y., "On Equilibrium Growth of Capital and Labor," *International Economic Review,* Vol. 1, 1960, pp. 107-111.

[662] Shtern, Iu, "Production Functions and the Possibility of Using Them in Economic Calculations," *Problems of Economics,* Vol. 16, 1973, pp. 59-83.

[663] Sidrauski, M., "Rational Choice and Pattern of Growth in a Monetary Economy," *American Economic Review,* Vol. 57, 1967, pp. 534-544.

[664] Simon, H.A., and A. Ando, "Aggregation of Variables in Dynamic Systems," *Econometrica,* Vol. 29, 1961, pp. 111-138.

[665] Smith, V.L., *Investment and Production,* Cambridge, Mass., Harvard University Press, 1966.

[666] Solow, R.M., "A Contribution to the Theory of Economic Growth," *Quarterly Journal of Economics,* Vol. 70, 1956, pp. 65-95.

[667a] Solow, R.M., "Investment and Technical Progress," in K. Arrow et al. (eds.), *Mathematical Methods in Social Sciences,* Stanford, Calif., Stanford University Press, 1959, pp. 89-104.

[667b] Solow, R.M., "Perspectives on Growth Theory," *Journal of Economic Perspectives,* Vol. 8, 1994, pp. 45-54.

[668] Solow, R.M., "Technical Change and the Aggregate Production Function," *Review of Economic Statistics,* Vol. 39, 1957 pp. 312-320.

[669] Solow, R.M., "On the Rate of Return: A Reply to Pasinetti," *Economic Journal,* Vol. 80, 1970, pp. 423-428.

[670] Solow, R.M., "Distribution in the Long and Short Run," in J. Marchal et al. (eds.), *The Distribution of National Income,* London, Macmillan, 1968, pp. 449-475.

[671] Solow, R.M., "Note on Uzawa's Two Sector Model of Economic Growth," *Review of Economic Studies,* Vol. 29, 1961, pp. 48-50.

[672] Solow, R.M., "Substitution and Fixed Proportion in the Theory of Capital," *Review of Economic Studies,* Vol. 29, 1962, pp.207-218.

[673] Solow, R.M., *Capital Theory and Rate of Return,* Amsterdam, North-Holland, 1963.

[674] Solow, R.M., *Growth Theory: An Exposition,* Oxford, Oxford University Press, 1970.

[675] Solow, R.M., "The Production Function and the Theory of Capital," *Review of Economic Studies,* Vol. 23, 1955-1956, pp. 101-108.

[676] Solow, R.M., "Technical Progress, Capital Formation, and Economic

Growth," *American Economic Review,* Vol. 52, 1962, pp. 76-86.

[677] Solow, R.M., et al., "Neoclassical Growth with Fixed Factor Proportions," *Review of Economic Studies,* Vol. 33, 1966, pp. 79-116.

[678] Sono, M., "The Effect of Price Changes on the Demand and Supply of Separable Goods," *International Economic Review,* Vol. 2, 1961, pp. 239-271.

[679a] Spaventa, L., "Rate of Profit, Rate of Growth, and Capital Intensity in a Simple Production Model," *Oxford Economic Papers,* Vol. 22, 1970, pp. 129-147.

[679b] Spaventa, L., "Notes on Problems of Transition between Techniques," in [516], pp. 168-192.

[680] Sraffa, P., "The Laws of Returns under Competitive Conditions," *Economic Journal,* Vol. 36, 1926, pp. 535-550.

[681] Sraffa, P., *Production of Commodities by Means of Commodities: Prelude to a Critique of Economic Theory,* Cambridge, U.K., Cambridge University Press, 1960.

[682] Srinivasan, T.N., "Optimal Savings in a Two-Sector Model of Growth," *Econometrica,* Vol. 32, 1964, pp. 358-373.

[683] Starrett, D.A., "Switching and Reswitching in a General Production Model," *Quarterly Journal of Economics,* Vol. 79, 1969, pp. 673-687.

[684] Stein, J., *Money and Capacity Growth,* New York, Columbia University Press, 1971.

[685] Stein, J.L., "Money and Capacity Growth," *Journal of Political Economy,* Vol. 74, 1966, pp. 451-465.

[686] Stein, J.L., "Neoclassical and Keynes-Wicksell Monetary Growth Models," *Journal of Money Credit and Banking,* Vol. 1, 1969, pp. 153-171.

[687] Stigler, G.L., *Production and Distribution Theories: The Formative Period,* New York, Macmillan, 1941.

[688] Stiglitz, J.E., "The Cambridge-Cambridge Controversy in the Theory of Capital: A View from New Haven: A Review Article," *Journal of Political Economy,* Vol. 82, 1974, pp. 893-903.

[689] Stiglitz, J.E., "A Two Sector–Two Class Model of Economic Growth," *Review of Economic Studies,* Vol. 34, 1967, pp. 227-238.

[690] Stiglitz, J.E., "Allocation of Heterogeneous Capital in a Two-Sector Model of Economic Growth," *International Economic Review,* Vol. 10, 1969, 373-390.

[691] Stiglitz, J.E., "Non-Substitution Theorems with Durable Capital Goods," *Review of Economic Studies,* Vol. 37, 1970, pp. 543-553.

[692] Stiglitz, J.E., "Recurrence of Techniques in a Dynamic Economy," in [516], pp. 138-161.

[693] Stiglitz, J.E., and H. Uzawa (eds.), *Readings in the Modern Theory of Economic Growth,* Cambridge, Mass., MIT Press, 1969.

[694] Summers, L.H., "Taxation and Corporate Investment: A q-Theory Approach," *Brookings Papers on Economic Activity,* Vol. 1, 1981, pp. 67-140.

[695] Swan, T.W., "Growth Models of Golden Ages and Production Func-

tions," in K.E. Berrill (ed.), *Economic Development with Special Reference to East Asia,* London, Macmillan, 1963.

[696] Swan, T., "Economic Growth and Capital Accumulation," *Economic Record,* Vol. 32, 1956, pp. 334-361.

[697] Symposium, "Symposium on Paradoxes in Capital Theory," *Quarterly Journal of Economics,* Vol. 80, 1966.

[698] Takayama, A., "On a Two-Sector Model of Economic Growth: A Comparative Statics Analysis," *Review of Economic Studies,* Vol. 30, 1963, pp. 95-104.

[699] Takayama, A., "On a Two-Sector Model of Economic Growth with Technological Progress," *Review of Economic Studies,* Vol. 32, 1965, pp. 251-262.

[700] Takayama, A., *Mathematical Economics,* Hinsdale, Ill., Dryden Press, 1974.

[701] Takayama, A., *International Trade,* New York, Holt, Rinehart and Winston, 1972.

[702] Taubman, P. and M. Wilkinson, "User Cost, Capital Utilization and Investment Theory," *International Economic Review,* Vol. 11, 1970, pp. 209-215.

[703] Taubman, P.J., and T.J. Wales, "The Impact of Investment Subsides in a Neoclassical Theory of Investment Behavior," *Review of Economic Statistics,* Vol. 51, 1969, pp. 287-298.

[704] Terborgh, G., *Dynamic Equipment Policy,* New York, McGraw-Hill, 1949.

[705] Thalberg, B., "The Market for Investment Goods: An Analysis Where Time of Delivery Enters Explicitly," *Review of Economic Studies,* Vol. 27, 1960, pp. 99-108.

[706] The Econometrics of Price Determination Conference, Washington, D.C., Board of Governors, Federal Reserve System and Social Science Research Council, 1970.

[707] Theil, H., "The Aggregation Implications of Identifiable Structural Macro-relations," *Econometrica,* Vol. 27, 1959, pp. 14-29.

[708] Theil, H., *Linear Aggregation of Economic Relation,* Amsterdam, North-Holland, 1954.

[709] Thompson, R.G., and D.G. Malvin, "Optimal Operations and Investments of the Firm," *Management Science,* Vol. 15, 1968, pp. 49-56.

[710] Thurow, L., "Disequilibrium Neoclassical Investment Function," *Review of Economic Statistics,* Vol. 51, 1969, pp. 431-435.

[711] Tinbergen, J., "Statistical Evidence on the Acceleration Principle," *Economica,* Vol. 5, 1938, pp. 164-176.

[712] Tinbergen, J., "Optimum Savings and Utility Maximization over Time," *Econometrica,* Vol. 30, 1959, pp. 481-490.

[713] Tinbergen, J., "Annual Survey of Significant Developments in General Economic Theory," *Econometrica,* Vol. 2, 1934, pp. 13-36.

[714] Tinbergen, J., "An International Economic Policy," *Indian Journal of Economics,* Vol. 38, 1957, pp. 11-16.

[715] Tinbergen, J., *Economic Policy: Principles and Design,* Amsterdam, North-Holland, 1956.

[716] Tinbergen, J., and H. Bos, *Mathematical Models of Economic Growth,* New York, McGraw-Hill, 1962.

[717] Tinsley, P.A., "On Optimal Dynamic Adjustment of Quasi-fixed Factors," Washington, D.C., Federal Reserve Board Special Study No. 9, 1969.

[718] Tinsley, P.A., "On Ramps, Turnpikes and Distributed Lag Approximations of Optimal Intertemporal Adjustment," Western Economic Journal, Vol. 8, 1970, pp. 397-411.

[719] Tobin, J., "Money, Capital and Other Stores of Value," *American Economic Review,* Vol. 51, 1961, pp. 21-37.

[720] Tobin, J., "Towards a General Kaldorian Theory of Distribution," *Review of Economic Studies,* Vol. 27, 1959-1960, pp. 119-120.

[721] Tobin, J., "Money and Economic Growth," *Econometrica,* Vol. 33, 1965, pp. 671-684.

[722] Tobin, J.,"Life-Cycle Saving and Balanced Growth," in [175], pp. 127-146

[723] Tobin, J., "A Dynamic Aggregative Model," *Journal of Political Economy,* Vol. 63, 1955, pp. 103-115.

[724] Tobin, J., "Asset Markets and Cost of Capital," in [25], pp. 235-262.

[725] Tobin, J., *Essays in Economics,* Vol. 1: *Macroeconomics,* New York, North-Holland, 1971.

[726] Tobin, J., *Asset Accumulation and Economic Activity: Reflections on Contemporary Economic Theory,* Oxford, Blackwell, 1980.

[727] Tomovic, R., and M. Vukobratovic, *General Sensitivity Theory,* New York, Elsevier, 1972.

[728] Treadway, A.B., "Adjustment Cost and Variable Inputs in the Theory of Competitive Firm," *Journal of Economic Theory,* Vol. 2, 1970, pp. 329-347.

[729] Treadway, A.B., "On Rational Entrepreneurial Behavior and the Demand for Investment," *Review of Economic Studies,* Vol. 36, 1969, pp. 227-239.

[730] Treadway, A.B., "The Globally Optimal Flexible Accelerator," *Journal of Economic Theory,* Vol. 7, 1974, pp. 7-39.

[731] Treadway, A.B., "The Rational Multivariate Flexible Accelerator," *Econometrica,* Vol. 39, 1971, pp. 845-856.

[732] Trivedi, P. K., "Inventory Behaviour in U.K. Manufacturing, 1956-1967," *Review of Economic Studies,* Vol. 37, 1970, pp. 517-536.

[733] Tuchscherer, T., "Keynes' Model and the Keynesians," *Journal of Post-Keynesian Economics,* Vol. 1 1979, pp. 96-108.

[734] Uzawa, H., "Time Preference and the Penrose Effect in a Two-Class Model of Economic Growth," *Journal of Political Economy,* Vol. 77, 1969, pp. 628-652.

[735] Uzawa, H., "On a Two-Sector Model of Economic Growth: I," *Review of Economic Studies,* Vol. 29, 1961, pp. 40-47.

[736] Uzawa, H., "On a Two-Sector Model of Economic Growth: II," *Review*

of Economic Studies, Vol. 30, 1963, pp. 105-118.

[737] Uzawa, H., "Neutral Inventions and the Stability of Growth Equilibrium," *Review of Economic Studies,* Vol. 28, 1961, pp. 117-124.

[738] Uzawa, H., "An Optimum Fiscal Policy in an Aggregate Model of Economic Growth," in I. Adelman and E. Thorbecke (eds.), *Theory and Design of Economic Development,* Baltimore, Md., Johns Hopkins University Press, 1960.

[739] Uzawa, H., "Optimal Growth in a Two-Sector Model of Capital Accumulation," *Review of Economic Studies,* Vol. 31, 1964, pp. 1-24.

[740] Uzawa, H., "The Penrose Effect and Optimum Growth," *Economic Studies Quarterly,* Vol. 19, 1968, pp. 1-14.

[741] Vanek, J., *Maximal Economic Growth,* Ithaca, N.Y., Cornell University Press, 1968.

[742] Van Long, N. and N., Vousden, "Optimal Control Theorems," in [578], pp. 11-34.

[743] Vind, K., "Control Systems with Jumps in the State Variables," *Econometrica,* Vol. 35, 1967, pp. 273-277.

[744] Wakas, L., *Elements of Pure Economics,* Homewood, Ill., Irwin, 1954.

[745] Walters, A.A., "Production and Cost Functions: An Econometric Survey," *Econometrica,* Vol. 31, 1963, pp. 1-66.

[746] Wan, H.Y., *Economic Growth,* New York, Harcourt Brace, Jovanovich, 1971.

[747] Wan, H.Y., "Optimal Saving Programs under Intertemporally Dependent Preferences," *International Economic Review,* Vol. 11, 1970, pp. 521-547.

[748] Ward, M., *The Measurement of Capital: The Methodology of Capital Stock Estimates,* in O.E.C.D., 1976.

[749] Warga, J., "Variational Problems with Unbounded Controls," *Journal of Society of Industrial and Applied Mathematics on Control,* Vol. 3, 1966, pp. 424-438.

[750] Weintraub, E.R., *Microfoundations: The Compatibility of Microeconomics, and Macroeconomics,* Cambridge, U.K., Cambridge University Press, 1979.

[751] Weitzman, M., "Shiftable Versus Non-shiftable Capital: A Synthesis," *Econometrica,* Vol. 39, 1971, pp. 511-529.

[752] Weizsacker, C.C. Von, *Steady State Capital Theory: Lecture Notes in Operation Research and Mathematical Systems,* New York, Springer-Verlag, 1971.

[753] Weizsacker, C.C. Von, "Existence of Optimal Programs of Accumulation for an Infinite Time Horizon," *Review of Economic Studies,* Vol. 32, 1965, pp. 85-104.

[754a] Weizsacker, C.C. Von, "Lemmas for a Theory of Approximate Optimal Growth," *Review of Economic Studies,* Vol. 34, 1967, pp. 143-151.

[754b] Weizsacker, C.C. Von, "Notes on Endogenous Growth of Productivity," in [516], pp. 101-137.

[755] Whitaker, J K., "Vintage Capital Models and Econometric Production

Functions," *Review of Economic Studies,* Vol. 33, 1966, pp. 1-18.

[756] Wicketeed, P.H., *Coordination of the Laws of Production and Distribution,* London, Macmillan, 1894.

[757] Wicksell, K., *Lectures on Political Economy,* Vol. 1, New York, Kelley, 1967.

[758] Wicksell, K., *Lectures on Political Economy,* Vol. 2, London, Routledge and Kegan, 1935.

[759] Wicksell, K., *Value, Capital and Rent,* London, Allen and Urwin, 1954.

[760] Wicksell, K., *Interest and Prices,* London, Macmillan, 1936.

[761] Winston, G.C., "The Theory of Capacity Utilization and Idleness," *Journal of Economic Literature,* Vol. 12, 1974, pp. 1301-1320.

[762] Witte, J.G., "The Microfoundations of the Social Investment Functions," *Journal of Economic Literature,* Vol. 71, 1963, pp. 441-456.

[763] Wolfe, J.N. (ed.), *Value, Capital and Growth,* Edinburgh, Edinburgh University Press, 1968.

[764] Wood, A., *A Theory of Profits,* Cambridge, U.K., Cambridge University Press, 1975.

[765] Worswick, G.D.N., "Mrs. Robinson on Simple Accumulation: A Comment with Algebra," *Oxford Economic Papers,* Vol. 11, 1959, pp. 125-141.

[766] Yaari, M., "On the Existence of an Optimal Plan in a Continuous-Time Allocation Process," *Econometrica,* Vol. 32, 1964, pp. 576-590.

[767] Yance, J.V., "A Model of Price Flexibility," *American Economic Review,* Vol. 50, 1960, pp. 401-418.

[768] Youngson, A.J., "The Disaggregation of Investment in the Study of Economic Growth," *Economic Journal,* Vol. 66, 1956, pp. 236-243.

[769] Zarembka, P., "Marketable Surplus and Growth in the Low Income Economy," *Journal of Economic Theory,* Vol. 2, 1970, pp. 107-121.

[770] Zarnowitz, V., *Orders, Production and Investment: A Cylindrical and Structural Analysis,* NBER, New York, Columbia University Press, 1973.

[771] Zauberman, A., *Mathematical Theory in Soviet Planning,* New York, Oxford University Press, 1976.

[772] Zellner, A., "On the Aggregate Problem: A New Approach to a Troublesome Problem," in K.A. Fox et al. (eds.) *Economic Models, Estimation and Risk Programming: Essay in Honor of Gerhard Tintner,* New York, Springer-Verlag, 1969.

Index

About the Author

KOFI KISSI DOMPERE is Associate Professor of Economics at Howard University. He is coauthor of *Epistemics of Development Economics* (Greenwood, 1995) and author of a companion to the present volume, *The Theory of Aggregate Investment in Open Economic Systems* (Greenwood, 1999). Additionally, Dompere has published a number of researched essays on the effects of technological progress on factor demand, inventory accumulation and prices. He has also authored a number of complementary essays on the theory of fuzzy decisions and cost-benefit analysis.

ISBN 0-313-30796-2

EAN

9 780313 307966

HARDCOVER BAR CODE

DATE DUE

APR 2 0 2001

HIGHSMITH #45230